PLACES IN KNOTS

PLACES IN KNOTS

Remoteness and Connectivity
in the Himalayas and Beyond

Martin Saxer

CORNELL UNIVERSITY PRESS   ITHACA AND LONDON

Thanks to generous funding from the European Research Council, Starting Grant HIGHLAND CONNECTIONS (637764), the e-book editions of this book are available as open access volumes through the Cornell Open initiative.

Library of Congress Cataloging-in-Publication Data

Names: Saxer, Martin, 1971– author.
Title: Places in knots : remoteness and connectivity in the Himalayas and beyond / Martin Saxer.
Description: Ithaca [New York] : Cornell University Press, [2022] | Includes bibliographical references and index.
Identifiers: LCCN 2022023038 (print) | LCCN 2022023039 (ebook) | ISBN 9781501766862 (hardcover) | ISBN 9781501766893 (paperback) | ISBN 9781501766879 (pdf) | ISBN 9781501766886 (epub)
Subjects: LCSH: Communities—Nepal. | Nepali people—Social networks. | Transnationalism. | Nepali people—Social conditions. | Human geography—Nepal. | Social change—Nepal. | Nepal—Social conditions.
Classification: LCC HN670.9 .S28 2022 (print) | LCC HN670.9 (ebook) | DDC 307.095496—dc23/eng/20220607
LC record available at https://lccn.loc.gov/2022023038
LC ebook record available at https://lccn.loc.gov/2022023039

Contents

Acknowledgments

The Himalayas had come to me long before I set foot in them. I had seen photographs and films, and I had read stories about the adventures and spiritual wonders in these mountains. When I was eighteen, I would sit on the doorstep of an old farmhouse in eastern Switzerland and dwell in this remote dreamscape. The more time I actually spent in the highlands, the more the valleys and villages that I had imagined as isolated revealed themselves as open and fundamentally oriented toward the outside world. The cosmopolitanism I encountered in seemingly out-of-the-way places made me ponder the ways in which remoteness and connectivity are entwined. How do we understand Himalayan experiences of global history? And what can we learn from it regarding the global imaginaries of remoteness that undergird public understandings of how the world today is structured?

This book traces my efforts to find answers to these questions. I seldom found myself alone on this journey, and the people I met along the way are too numerous to count. A few, however, became friends and traveling companions—both on foot and in mind. Without them, this book would not have been possible.

My interest in the Walung area of eastern Nepal was sparked by Tamla Ukyab. Over several days he told me his life's story in his house in Kathmandu. Meeting Tamla made me think about the lasting importance of pathways in the Himalayas and the role of place in a community of itinerant traders. Tenzing Ukyab, a relative of Tamla's, introduced me to the Walung Community of North America. I am deeply grateful for their support and openness. In Humla, the district in western Nepal bordering the Kailash area of Tibet, Tshewang Lama was my compass. With his knowledge and experience as a lawyer, historian, anthropologist, entrepreneur, and politician, Tshewang guided my research more than anybody else. His influence as teacher and friend since 2007 cannot be overstated.

While Tamla, Tenzing, and Tshewang were my mentors, it was their sons and daughters with whom I spent weeks hiking and talking. Rinzin Lama, Nyima Dorjee Bhotia, and Sagar Lama were my main collaborators. Their efforts at translation were the turf from which this book emerged. I am deeply grateful for their friendship. Their relatives hosted us in Walung and Upper Humla. Rinzin's uncle and aunt accompanied us on my first trip to the Limi Valley. On another trip, it was Sagar's uncle who hiked back to his village to fetch a horse when I fell on my knee and couldn't walk anymore. I thank them for the energy and spirit with which they took care of me.

In Kathmandu, I often stayed with Jürg Merz and Bandana Prajapati. Returning to their house and family after long weeks in the mountains always felt like coming home. Their inside knowledge about the world of nongovernmental organizations (NGOs) and development agencies helped me tremendously. My family and I also stayed with Marion Wettstein and Alban von Stockhausen. I thank them for their friendship and hospitality (and their daughter Anaïs for sharing her toys with my daughter).

I would like to thank the International Centre for Integrated Mountain Development (ICIMOD), especially Eklabya Sharma and Rajan Kotru, for hosting me as a research fellow and providing me with excellent support. My gratitude also goes to my colleagues at ICIMOD for all the discussions over lunch and many cups of sweet Nepali tea. Abhimanyu Panday, Swapnil Chaudhari, Corinna Wallrapp, and many others liberally shared their insights with me.

This book emerged from two generously funded research projects. Between 2011 and 2015, I was working on the question of what China's rise means for those living directly along its borders. The *Neighboring China* project was supported by a Swiss National Science Foundation Grant, a postdoctoral fellowship at the Asia Research Institute (ARI), National University of Singapore, and a Marie Curie Fellowship (298595) by the European Union. Between 2015 and 2020, I had the privilege to lead the Highland Asia research group at the Ludwig-Maximilians Universität Munich (LMU). The project *Remoteness & Connectivity: Highland Asia in the World* was funded by a European Research Council Starting Grant (637764). At ARI in Singapore, Prasenjit Duara's reading group on inter-Asian connections shaped my thinking in deep and lasting ways. At LMU, Alessandro Rippa, Carolin Maertens, Aditi Saraf, Marlen Elders, Galen Murton, Philipp Schorch, and all the members of our Contemporary Anthropology Reading Group made for an exceptionally warm-hearted and stimulating environment.

I wrote an initial draft of this book while teaching a course on *Highland Asia in the World* at LMU Munich. I am grateful to the participating students for their comments and for bearing with me during this experiment.

Nadine Plachta, Lisa Rail, Travis Klingberg, and Galen Murton read drafts of my manuscript at various stages. I thank them for their insights, guidance, and friendship. I would also like to thank the two anonymous reviewers for deep engagement with my book, their insightful comments, and their encouragement.

Parts of three published articles found entry into this book. The idea of pathways (chapter 4) and some of the Walung stories are taken from "Pathways.

A Concept, Field Site and Methodological Approach to Study Remoteness and Connectivity" (Saxer 2016b); the first part of chapter 5 is based on "New Roads, Old Trades" (Saxer 2017); and materials published in "Between China and Nepal: Trans-Himalayan Trade and the Second Life of Development in Upper Humla" (Saxer 2013b) were reworked into sections of chapter 3.

Abbreviations

ADB	Asian Development Bank
ANCA	Api Nampa Conservation Area
ARIES	Artificial Intelligence for Ecosystem Services
CBD	Convention on Biological Diversity
CIA	Central Intelligence Agency
CITES	Convention on International Trade in Endangered Species of Wild Fauna and Flora
CNY	Chinese yuan renminbi
DRSP	District Roads Support Programme
GBPIHE	G. B. Pant Institute of Himalayan Environment and Development
GDP	gross domestic product
GIS	geographic information system
GIZ	Deutsche Gesellschaft für Internationale Zusammenarbeit; German Society for International Cooperation
GLOF	glacial lake outburst flood
ICIMOD	International Centre for Integrated Mountain Development
ISO	International Organization for Standardization
IUCN	International Union for Conservation of Nature
KCA	Kanchenjunga Conservation Area
KSL	Kailash Sacred Landscape
KSLCDI	Kailash Sacred Landscape Conservation and Development Initiative
KSLIS	Kailash Sacred Landscape Information System
LMU	Ludwig Maximilians University Munich
LSY	Landscape *Yatra*
MEA	Millennium Ecosystem Assessment
NPR	Nepalese rupee
PLA	People's Liberation Army
PRC	People's Republic of China
SDC	Swiss Agency for Development and Cooperation
TAAAS	Tibet Academy of Agricultural and Animal Husbandry Sciences
TAR	Tibet Autonomous Region
TCM	traditional Chinese medicine

TCV	Tibetan Children's Village
UNESCO	United Nations Educational, Scientific, and Cultural Organization
VDC	Village Development Committee
WFP	World Food Programme

A Note on Names

The names of places and people in the Himalayan borderlands are often rendered in a variety of ways. Nepali, Indian, Tibetan, and Chinese systems of transliteration conflict with each other and lead to vastly different spellings. The town of Purang in the Kailash area of western Tibet, for example, often appears as Bulan in Chinese texts translated to English, while Burang would be the official Chinese transcription. In Tibetan transliteration (Wylie), the town's name would be *spu hreng*.

Further complicating the matter is the fact that in some cases, the original meaning of the Tibetan name is not clear. Waltse in the Limi Valley (often referred to as Halji) is a case in point. In Tibetan, Waltse could be *dbal tse* and mean a sharp, pointed mountain peak; the syllable *wa* could also mean a fox or even a wolf. I was told all of these versions.

Choosing one system of transliteration over others for the sake of consistency would thus not do justice to the situation. For places, I therefore use a common written form that is phonetically close to the local names rather than any "official" spelling. For instance, the village of Walung in the Kanchenjunga region is officially called Olangchung Gola in Nepal. I use Walung throughout this book. Unless specifically marked, I also use phonetic transcription rather than transliteration for terms in local Tibetan dialects.

The names of people in this manuscript are mostly pseudonyms, unless they are public figures. However, some of the main protagonists—particularly the ones who read English—chose to appear with their real names.

PLACES IN KNOTS

Life insurance seminar, Queens, New York City. *Source*: Martin Saxer, 2016.

Prologue

JUGGLING WORLDS

Sunday morning in Jackson Heights, a neighborhood in the borough of Queens, New York City. Standing in front of the subway station, I can listen to the chatter of the commuters passing by—a mixture of Spanish, Nepali, Hindi, and Bengali. A delivery truck decorated with "Free Tibet" stickers drives up next to me. I move a few steps away to remain in sight. I have a meeting with Tenzing Ukyab. He promised to pick me up by car and told me to wait outside the station. I hope he will recognize me.

A few minutes later, Tenzing arrives and waves at me. I hop on the passenger seat to start a ride through the many worlds Tenzing and his friends keep juggling here. Tenzing is in his mid-fifties and originally from a place called Walung, a little village in eastern Nepal close to the Tibetan border. I am here to learn about the Walung community in New York. Tenzing, the former president of the Walung Community of North America is my guide. He promised to introduce me. This is not an easy task, he admits. "People are very, very busy here," he says. They work hard and often have several jobs. And the weekends are even busier with all the community events.

Today, the weekly Tibetan class is taking place in the basement flat that the Walung Community of North America rents to hold events. A dozen people, mostly women, have gathered to improve their Tibetan language skills. Their native language is a Tibetan dialect, but most of them grew up in Nepal and only a few of them have learned to read and write Tibetan. The class includes reading a religious text. The teacher is a lama whose wife is from Walung. I sit and listen to the rhythmic chanting, waiting for the lesson to wind down.

1

Tenzing quickly lines up a couple of interviews for me. I explain my interest in the old trading village of Walung and the cosmopolitan biographies of its people. I ask a few simple questions to start the conversation. Soon, however, I realize that the language students are in a hurry to catch another event taking place at the Sherpa Association. The topic is life insurance, which seems to strike a chord with many here. I give up on my interviews and join the crowd.

We head to the posh new Sherpa Association house a few blocks away. More than a hundred people are already waiting for the event to begin. The banner on the stage reads "insurance terror"—in a mix of English and Nepali. A Nepali TV host leads the event. Four insurance experts present their takes on the topic and answer questions.

The most engaged of them is a Chinese woman in her late thirties. Her name is Wei Wei—like the popular instant noodle soup everybody knows in Nepal. Wei Wei works as an independent insurance agent. While she doesn't speak Nepali, she is clearly familiar with the needs and fears of immigrant communities. "You have come to America to make money and have a better life. You work hard, and you don't mind working hard. But how to protect your hard-earned money, how to protect your family?" she asks rhetorically. "We have all come here for education, for work, and regardless of whether we speak good English or not— we are not stupid! Don't let yourselves be fooled!" she continues. Then, she explains the differences between term and whole life insurance and the pitfalls of the latter.

The event quickly becomes emotional. Many are here to vent their frustration with life insurance companies. One young man has signed four insurance contracts for him and his family. He is currently paying a monthly premium of US$1,450. He feels cheated.

After more than three hours, the Nepali TV host tries to bring the session to an end. There is unrest and disappointment in the audience because so many issues still remain unclear. Wei Wei takes side with the audience, saying that she will stay until all questions are answered. "And if you get hungry, I will buy you food."

During the event, Tenzing's phone keeps buzzing. There are yet more worlds to juggle. Currently, the Asia Week is taking place in New York, with exhibitions and auctions of Asian art at Sotheby's and elsewhere. Tenzing tours the many events to expand his network of customers and see what is currently in demand. He trades in everything Tibetan, from furniture and antiques to jewelry, carpets, and Buddha statues.

A week later, Tenzing shows me his impressive outlet on the ground floor of ABC Carpet & Home, a fancy emporium at a prime and auspicious address in the heart of Manhattan: 888 Broadway. Tenzing's store brings a breath of Himalayan style into the vast assemblage of contemporary interior design and indigenous treasures from around the world. ABC Carpet & Home was featured in Vogue and Vanity Fair; the Obamas were said to come here for shopping. ABC Carpet & Home advertises itself as a "portal into collective creativity," presenting "commerce as a vehicle for insight and for action in the aid of creating a better world."

From 888 Broadway we walk up to Union Square. It is a warm spring day in Manhattan. We buy a coffee and find a bench to sit and talk. It is Saturday, Greenmarket day at Union Square. In their early days in New York, Tenzing and his wife worked here at the farmers market. At one point, he says, almost all the vendors were Nepali or Tibetan.

As many ambitious young men from Himalayan villages, Tenzing tried his luck in various businesses and careers. At one time, he ran a shop in Kathmandu, then he worked as a language and culture instructor for the Peace Corps. He managed to obtain a visa to Japan and planned to build a life there. He didn't like it and came back to Nepal. He also worked as a research assistant for an American PhD student. When she invited him to visit her in the United States, he packed two big suitcases full of merchandise—"we always do business, you know"—and flew to Seattle. He stayed at her house for a couple months, trying not to be a burden and figure out what to do next. He finally came to New York and worked his way up, paying taxes, bringing his family to the United States, starting his own business, and finally becoming a US citizen.

While we talk, Tenzing receives two phone calls from a detention center at the US–Mexico border. A fellow Walungnga needs help—a bond, an address, a place to stay. People are still arriving. Many follow the arduous route through South and Central America.

Tenzing is a role model for many new arrivals—not just for his success in business but also for his social engagement. He got involved in various efforts to help the Walung community both in the United States and in Nepal. Presently, his mission is to build a road from the Tibetan border to Walung. He shows me a letter to the local government of the neighboring county in the Tibet Autonomous Region of the People's Republic of China, asking for assistance. He wrote it in Nepali and his daughter translated it into English. Tenzing laughs while remembering how his US-born daughter, who grew up amid the Tibetan exile community and their critical stance toward China, was slightly irritated by the conciliatory tone of the letter. But the stakes are high, and Tenzing fears that without a road and help from China, Walung will not have a future.

In the afternoon, Tenzing and I visit a Tibetan art gallery nearby. Then I head back to my Airbnb in Queens. Overwhelmed by all these stories, all the ventures and worlds Tenzing and his friends are engaging in—from religious Tibetan classes to "insurance terror," from posh design at 888 Broadway and contemporary Tibetan art to detention centers and plans for a Himalayan road—I switch on the TV. It is March 2016. Donald Trump is on all channels. His campaign is gaining steam. My Airbnb host, a Latina immigrant herself, has put a copy of "Make America Great Again" on my desk. What an irony! While the xenophobic rhetoric of the president-to-come blames immigrants for America's decline, the American dream cannot be more alive than among the people I just met.

Pondering over this irony, another thought crosses my mind. I realize that seeing the Walungnga in New York as an immigrant community aspiring to the American dream—one of several hundred in Queens alone—may only capture half the story here. What if the American dream pursued by these Himalayan immigrants is rather a continuation of an old *Himalayan* dream? If so, what would this mean for seemingly remote mountain villages and their global connections? What would it imply for notions like remoteness, migration, and diaspora?

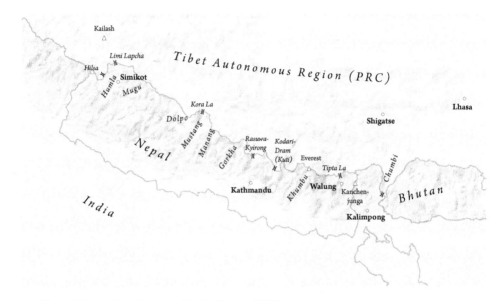

Map of the region. *Source*: Martin Saxer, 2019.

INTRODUCTION

In 2011, five years before Tenzing introduced me to the world of Himalayan communities in Queens, New York, I was looking for a guide and research assistant to accompany me to Walung. I had just started a new project on the question of what China's rapid economic development meant for the people living directly along its borders. The Walung area of northeastern Nepal had caught my attention. During my previous work on the creation of a Tibetan medicine industry, I had learned that many of the medicinal herbs traditionally imported from Nepal were not shipped through the main road between Kathmandu and Lhasa. Instead, they were traded along the old and, I assumed at the time, largely defunct trade routes across Himalayan passes along the border. Walung, I had heard, was one of the places this cross-border business was taking off.

Sitting in a coffee shop in Kathmandu, I stumbled on the Facebook page of the Walung Community of North America. I wrote a message explaining that I was an anthropologist working on trade and exchange in the Himalayan borderlands, that I had read about the importance of Walung as an old trading hub, and that I was interested in the recent revival of trans-Himalayan trade. Fifteen minutes later, I received a phone call on my Nepali number from a relative of the president of the Walung Community of North America. Within days, I met with several Walungnga in Kathmandu.

At that time, I did not make much of the fact that my entry into Walung circles was mediated by a member of the community on the other side of the globe. I took the circuitous route of communication as an example of how uneven the much-heralded space-time compression of our era was. While reaching Himalayan villages at the border with China still required long bus rides, mountain flights, and days of hiking, news and rumors were no longer dependent on messengers treading the trails. Over the years, I came to understand that my initial contact with Walung was more than serendipity helped by social media. The relations of Himalayan communities between a mountain village, Kathmandu, and a neighborhood in New York City are not just a matter of remittances from the diaspora and dreams of a better life back home. These relations are part of everyday life in ways much wider and deeper than I presumed.

In this book, I focus on two mountain regions in Nepal close to the Tibetan border: the Walung area and Upper Humla in the northeastern and northwestern corners of the country, respectively. Both Walung and Upper Humla are home to Tibetan-speaking populations that thrived on the once vibrant trans-Himalayan trade between the Tibetan Plateau and the plains of South Asia. In both places, like in the majority of villages across the region, agriculture and pastoralism have never been able to guarantee subsistence. Following the demarcation of the border between Nepal and China in the early 1960s, both places found themselves at the very margins of nation-states and needing to expand their business ventures into new territories in Nepal and abroad. Historically as well as today, it is not uncommon for people from Walung and Upper Humla to spend most of their lives outside their village of origin—on business trips and foraging expeditions, as transhumant herders, monks, and students. Yet there is a strong sense of place and belonging in Himalayan communities. This sense of place and belonging is neither based on a sedentary life in one locality, nor does it stem from a nostalgic imaginary of a homeland fostered in a global diaspora; it is rather derived from the shared experience of repeated movement between a limited number of localities. These localities are so tightly enlaced that I came to think of them as places in knots.

My concern with these two Tibetan borderlands in northern Nepal is fundamentally translocal. What happens outside profoundly shapes lives and dreams in these mountain valleys. And the other way around, being part of a community named after a Himalayan village or valley is crucial for the ambitions and endeavors of those spending most of their time outside. The story I seek to tell, then, is not so much about out-migration and the ties between home and diaspora, but rather about the evolving configurations of these places in knots that continue to shape translocal Himalayan lives.

Before the 1960s, such place-knots included trading districts in cities like Shigatse or Kolkata, a village close to the Nepal–Tibet border, and perhaps a seasonal trade mart along the way. The entanglements between these places through investment, marriage, and ritual friendship were crucial to facilitate business. Some places in these knots have since lost their relevance, while others—the neighborhoods of Boudha in Kathmandu and Jackson Heights in New York City—are being tied in. The basic challenge of making community in a translocal setting, however, has remained.

Remoteness

If Himalayan communities evolve in knots of places rather than individual localities, this process is also shaped by global agendas regarding development, migration, heritage, and conservation. These agendas are based on particular imaginaries about the role and position of Himalayan villages in the wider world. One dominant figure of thought that undergirds these imaginaries is *remoteness* and its assumed antidote, *connectivity*.

Even the base camp of Mount Everest has Wi-Fi now. In early 2017, the Nepal Telecommunications Authority announced their plans with some fanfare (Giri 2017) and later that year, Everest Link, a small Sherpa-owned company, set up a hot spot. The global media responded promptly. "If you can get Wi-Fi on Mount Everest, then you can probably get it anywhere on Earth," VentureBeat heralded (Takahashi 2017). National Geographic followed up with a story on Everest Link CEO Tsering Gyaltsen Sherpa, the "super-charged Nepali entrepreneur" who led "his native Khumbu Valley into the 21st century" (Wilkinson 2019).

More puzzling than live Instagram stories from one of the world's more crowded campsites is perhaps the fact that Wi-Fi in the Himalayas makes headlines. The reason, I believe, lies in a deep-rooted assumption about the spatial and temporal logic that structures global difference. On one end of the spectrum is the contemporary global space—connected, vibrant, polluted, diverse, and mostly urban; a space in which Himalayan migrant communities in New York live next to Wall Street and the United Nations. On the other end of the spectrum are the last pockets of remoteness—timeless, wild, authentic, mostly poor, sometimes dangerous, and always already on the verge of being steamrolled by the forces of modernity.

Mountain villages in Nepal find themselves imagined squarely at the latter end of this spectrum. In descriptions of the Himalayas, the trope of remoteness is pervasive. Coffee-table books and travel agencies use it to advertise the last realms of untouched Buddhist culture; nongovernmental organizations (NGOs) in their reports emphasize remoteness to undergird the urgency of their projects; and Tsering Gyaltsen Sherpa, the CEO of Everest Link, writes in a blog post for the company that provides his weatherproof equipment that the Nepal he calls home is "entirely remote" (Sherpa 2017).

Remoteness is seldom just a descriptive device. As a figure of thought, it defines challenges and missions. It comes packaged with expectations of its imminent unmaking through more and better connectivity. And, almost always, it serves as an analytical starting point: remote communities, in the highlands of Asia and elsewhere, are seen as backward, authentic, or unruly *because*—for better or worse—they are isolated and far away from developed, urban centers.

When the trope of remoteness underpins analysis, several things get lost.

First, the trope of remoteness assumes a degree of isolation. Looking at a place from the outside, remote areas may indeed seem out-of-the-way and isolated; but, as Edwin Ardener (2012, 523) notes with respect to supposedly remote areas in Cameroon and Scotland, "from the inside outwards, there was an almost exaggerated contrary sense of the absence of any barrier to the world."[1]

This observation reminds me of my experiences in the highlands of Nepal. The lives of the families I met during the research for this book are not just revolving around a remote mountain village but, quite the contrary, around a veritable obsession with the outside world, a high degree of mobility, and a sense of community that is clearly not local. Many leave their native valleys for education (Childs and Choedup 2019; Childs et al. 2014) or their transnational business ventures (Fisher 1986; Ratanapruck 2007). Their ambitions and endeavors reach far beyond the Himalayas. What I see is thus not isolation but cosmopolitanism.

This cosmopolitan orientation is not a recent phenomenon. As a contact zone (Pratt 1991) between China and South Asia, the arid Tibetan Plateau and the monsoon-fed hills and plains in Nepal and India, the Himalayas have long been home to populations serving as avid brokers between economic, political, and cultural spheres.

Second, in public discourse, remoteness often goes together with marginality. In the case at hand, this is only partially true. There is no denying that Himalayan villages and valleys remain severely underrepresented in the political arenas in which their future is debated. From the 1854 Muluki Ain (Höfer 1979), Nepal's Hindu civil code that put the Tibetan-speaking mountain people in the lowest category of "enslavable alcohol drinkers," to corvée obligations (Holmberg, March, and Tamang 1999) and questions of citizenship (Shneiderman 2013, 2015), Himalayan populations have faced outright discrimination and marginalization. At the same time, however, the largely Tibetan-speaking populations straddling the borders between the People's Republic of China and its southern neighbors attract much attention. They do so internationally through the networks offered by global Buddhism, the "Tibet question," tourism, or debates on the "third pole" and climate change. They also feature prominently in national conversations on security, migration, federalism, and development. Close to the sensitive skin of the "geo-bodies" (Thongchai 1994; Billé 2018) of China, Nepal, and India, the Himalayas often play an outsize role in national imaginaries. In other words, there is no shortage of attention on the Himalayas and its populations. This combination of inhabiting niches in a contact zone at the edge of nation-states and overwhelming media attention often translates into global connections and opportunities that truly marginalized communities elsewhere can only dream of.[2]

Third, remoteness carries strong connotations of subsistence-oriented lifestyles and poverty. While the Himalayan districts of Nepal and the Tibet Autonomous Region across the border are listed at the bottom of national development statistics, Himalayan populations are far from universally poor. Business and trade are of paramount importance in this context, especially since most of the higher Himalayan villages and valleys do not guarantee agricultural or agropastoral subsistence. In the old days, trade in salt from Tibet and grain from Nepal, combined with all kinds of goods in demand in Tibet and India, was not just crucial for survival, it was also widely seen as the main avenue to prosperity. The CEO of Everest Link, for example, may use remoteness to explain his ambition, yet he is also a member of a prolific trading community in the Himalayas—the same one that built the impressive community center in Queens where I attended an "insurance terror" seminar. Rather than being a "super-charged" exception from an otherwise rural and agropastoral community, the CEO of Everest Link follows in many ways the footsteps of his forefathers who did business between Tibet, Nepal, and India.

The trope of remoteness glosses over such long-standing entanglements. It leaves little room for stories that do not conform to the narrative of the "big transformation" that allegedly sweeps across the globe, eventually finding its way to the most hidden corners and bringing them into the fold of a globally connected world.

To be clear: My aim is not to claim that "*they* have never been truly remote" just as "*we* have never been modern" (Latour 1993). Such a claim would simply invert and thereby reiterate anthropology's obsession with the other. Remoteness may not have much *analytical* value, yet it is more than just a ghost blurring the gaze of outside observers. The fantasy of the remote as the "most other of others" (Gupta and Ferguson 1992, 6, liberally quoting Hannerz 1986, 363) not just lingers on in the West or the global North. It is put to work by all parties involved—as a figure of thought and as a potentially useful positionality on the global stage. While in the spatial and temporal imaginaries of globalization, remoteness appears as connectivity's alter ego—one a reflection of the other—from the perspective of seemingly remote highlands, the self-proclaimed centers of globalization rather feel akin to some kind of cousin: a probably rich, often a bit boisterous, and sometimes overbearing one who is nonetheless family and whose company can be inspiring and useful.

As argued elsewhere (Saxer 2019), remoteness is fundamentally a relational condition—a perspective bred in places that consider themselves to be the opposite of remote (see Tsing 1994, 2005; Ferguson 1999; Ardener 2012; Harms et al. 2014). Once an area surfaces on the radars of states, development agencies, or mining companies as "remote," it does so with certain ambitions that already carry the seed of a future relation involving the selective unmaking of remoteness for a specific purpose. As these ambitions are embedded in larger political and economic agendas, remoteness is seldom the kind of prehistoric leftover as it is sometimes cast. Remoteness, rather, is actively made and unmade, and thus tends to return at particular historical junctures (Saxer and Andersson 2019).[3]

In the Himalayas, the current incarnation of remoteness was triggered by twentieth-century geopolitics: the demarcation of borders in the 1960s, the history of Tibet under Chinese rule, and the decline of erstwhile forms of trade. This arrival of remoteness altered long-standing relations with Tibet. At the same time, it fostered new ties to development agencies with their prestige and money, to the international tourism and mountaineering industry, and recently to China, with its new business opportunities. In this context, remoteness is a useful asset. The claim to authentic cultural heritage in hidden Buddhist valleys attracts tourism; the notion of remote wilderness resonates with conservation agendas; and the sketchy presence of the Nepali state combined with China's hunger for natural resources drives trade in medicinal plants and wildlife products.

Seen this way, connectivity is not stamped on the other side of the coin of remoteness, leaving us with an either-or. Neither do remoteness and connectivity define the two ends of a gamut between marginality and integration. They rather stand for diffuse yet omnipresent figures of thought folding into each other in particular ways. Their various entanglements, I seek to show, profoundly affect Himalayan experiences of global history.

A generation after the end of the Cold War, remoteness is not on the way out; neither is universal connectivity on the horizon. The Himalayas are crisscrossed by sensitive borders, rich in biodiversity and natural resources, and imbued with fantasies of future infrastructure. A multitude of stakes are attached to these frontiers. Quests for border security and resource extraction clash with ideas of development and conservation. Amid the rumblings of these discordant visions, those targeted frequently find themselves wedged between conflicting agendas, which can both afford new opportunities and lead to further marginalization. In this sense, the Himalayas are not only a contact zone between ecological and economic spheres but also between analytic stakes and ambitious interventions that come along with them.

The notion of places in knots is my starting point to tackle these lines of friction and, hopefully, allow for a new perspective on seemingly remote areas in the world at large.

Long before I started thinking about places in knots, I found myself tied into one. First, it was the Walungnga of New York who put me in touch with members of the community in Kathmandu. Then, the Walungnga residing in Kathmandu set me up to travel to Walung. Nyima, a fellow anthropologist who grew up in the village, agreed to accompany me. We flew to Biratnagar and found a share jeep to Taplejung, the district headquarters.

A general strike had been announced and our driver tried to circumvent the road blockages that were being set up everywhere. In 2012, six years after the end of a decade-long civil war, tensions remained high. A few months before, the constitutional assembly tasked with writing a new constitution was dissolved; new elections were announced and then postponed. A major bone of contention remained the federal restructuring of the former Kingdom of Nepal. Taplejung, our destination, was the center of the Limbu movement that campaigned for a federal state of its own.

Once we arrived in Taplejung and descended into the Tamur Valley, the world of fraught Nepal politics quickly faded away. Walking up the valley through lush green forests harboring black cardamom plantations, we crossed path with dozens of Walungnga. *Phutuk*, the yearly monastery festival, had just ended, triggering an exodus of Walungnga intending to spend the winter in Taplejung, Hile, or Kathmandu. All Walung families, I learned, had at least one other place where some if not all family members would spend much of the year.

We entered the Kanchenjunga Conservation Area (KCA), Nepal's first fully community-managed conservation project. We duly registered at the checkpoint and set out to climb the path that follows the Tamur River. From my previous research on trade in medicinal plants (Saxer 2011; 2013a, 104), I knew that the area was one of the main sources for *Swertia chirayita*, known as *chiraito* in Nepal and *tigta* in Tibet. The Mountain Institute, a US-based conservation NGO, was running a project to cultivate *chiraito* in the buffer zone of the KCA.[4] This, they hoped, would reduce unmanaged collection within the conservation area. On the way to Walung, we saw huge quantities of the herb, bundled and ready to be sold to Tibet. However, we learned that most of it was still collected in the conservation area rather than cultivated in the buffer zone.

On the third day, a few hours before reaching Walung, we met a couple of civil engineers surveying the prospective road that was supposed to connect Taplejung with Walung and the Tibetan border. According to the plan, the engineers

Crossing a river on the way to Walung. *Source*: Martin Saxer, 2012.

Members of the Limi Youth Society in Kathmandu. *Source*: Martin Saxer, 2011.

said, the road was to be completed by 2014. Accustomed to promises followed by years of suspension, nobody believed that this would be the case. In fact, nothing happened after the initial survey until Tenzing pushed the matter with his letter asking local Tibetan authorities in China for assistance.

Reading my field notes from this first visit to Walung, I see now that the three big strands of this book were already present. First is the theme of community and place. The Walungnga were clearly not the kind of "local community" that would fight (as the Limbu did) for territorial sovereignty amid Nepal's constitutional turmoil. A second theme is the importance of old pathways and the quest for new roads. And third is the story of the efforts of NGOs and development agencies to improve the health of mountains and people by setting up community-managed conservation areas or teaching people how to grow herbs they used to collect.

These three themes structure the three parts of this book. Each of them holds a conceptual proposition, which I will now sketch out in broad strokes.

Locality and Community

The first part of this book—*Locality and Community*—is concerned with the making and maintaining of communities between Himalayan villages and neighborhoods in Kathmandu and New York City. Exploring locality and community in a context in which mobility has always been at the core of livelihood strategies challenges the notion of the "local community," which continues to shape the global rhetoric of development and conservation. The communities of Walung and Upper Humla are less concerned with a single village than with a small number of places intertwined in deep and lasting ways. Village rules mandating presence, monastic obligations, and norms of marriage become enmeshed in the vagaries of border business, opportunities for paid labor in Tibet, the activities of welfare societies in Kathmandu and New York, and the ritual needs to cater for local deities.

These communities are clearly different from the closed corporate peasant villages Eric Wolf described in Mexico and Java (Wolf 1955, 1957, 1986). Although Wolf never meant his observations to become a grand theory of nonurban regions applicable around the world, anthropologists have since ferociously criticized the "sedentarist metaphysics" (Malkki 1992) such isomorphism of place and culture implies (Gupta and Ferguson 1992). Arjun Appadurai, for example, notes that the very term "native" so intrinsically relevant to the discipline of anthropology not only denotes origin from a certain place but people somehow incarcerated in those places (Appadurai 1988, 36–37). As a counter image, he suggests the notion of global ethnoscapes (Appadurai 1996) to make sense of a world in which communities are no longer bound to a particular territory. Deterritorialization and complex diasporas affect social relations, loyalties, cultural production, and the politics of home and belonging, he argues.

While I agree with Appadurai that the "loosening of the holds between people, wealth, and territory" raises questions about the "nature of locality as a lived experience" (Appadurai 1996, 49, 52), I see different processes at work in the Himalayas. Wealth and territory were never quite as tight a link in mobile trading societies; the work of joining places into knots tells a different story than disjuncture; the diagnosis of deterritorialization is difficult to reconcile with the realities of Himalayan terrain; and "diaspora" is both too vague and too full a term to describe the challenge of making a translocal community between places in a knot.

Moreover, the public imaginary of remoteness as a supposedly defining condition in the Himalayas has served as a strong repellent against the insights of Appadurai, Gupta, Ferguson, Malkki, and the many others arguing along similar lines. In global urban space, we speak of the LGTBQ community or the scientific community. The term community is no longer tied to questions of origin or a single locality. In areas considered remote, however, the rural peasant community remains the guiding figure of thought and the "local" seems to stick with "community." Discussions about benefit sharing in relation to the Convention on Biological Diversity and its Nagoya Protocol, for example, implicitly take the local (and often remote) community as their point of reference. Similarly, development and conservation projects focus on "local communities."

This double vision—isolated and closed communities in remote areas, open and cosmopolitan ones everywhere else—continues to haunt global debates on development, mobility, and identity. It results in a pronounced disconnection between the discussions led in the offices of state planners and development organizations and the experiences and ambitions of those they target—a gap I have witnessed on a daily basis during my tenure as a research fellow at the International Centre for Integrated Mountain Development (ICIMOD) in Kathmandu.

It is against this background that I started thinking about places in knots. The three chapters comprising the first part of the book develop and test the notion of place-knots from different angles.

In chapter 1—*Tying Places into Knots*—I meet Tenzing and half a dozen of his fellow New Yorkers again in the village of Walung. Building on these encounters, I explore the intimate ties and the conflicts that arise in the process of tying and retying places into a knot.

Chapter 2—*Moving In, Moving Up, Moving Out*—gives more historical background on Walung and its mobile population. I tell the story of the changing figurations of remoteness and connectivity since the 1950s and argue that moving out is better understood as an expansion of a given community rather than simply as out-migration. Tracing the mobile biographies of elderly Walungnga who witnessed these transformations, I show the ways in which social mobility remains linked to physical mobility.

While Walung entirely lacks agriculture, the economy of most Tibetan-speaking Himalayan villages along the border is based on a mixture of trade, agriculture, and pastoralism. Leaving Walung for Upper Humla, chapter 3—*Binding Rules*—looks into a context in which agropastoralism is an integral part of livelihoods. Most people here also spend most of the time outside their villages. In Upper Humla, however, strict village rules, the norm of polyandry, and monastic obligations play a crucial role, particularly in the Limi Valley bordering Tibet. The story of a mother anxious about her son's uncertain ambitions provides the entry point into a discussion of the work and trouble of tying places into knots. The son hangs out in the town of Purang across the border in Tibet, where most people from Limi work on Chinese construction sites over the summer. He seems less than keen to marry and take up his responsibilities in his household and village. He is not alone in this dilemma. As resistance to strict rules is growing, the monks arrange a meeting to set new fines for breaking the rules—an attempt to adjust and retie a place-knot in a rapidly changing socioeconomic environment.

The notion of place-knots affords a perspective on mobility and community that gives narratives of migration and diaspora a new twist. Global Himalayan ventures, I argue, are a means of expanding a community and, unlike simple rural-urban migration and moving out, do not necessarily sever community bonds.

Pathways

Doreen Massey suggests that we understand place as a collection of "stories-so-far" (Massey 2005, 130). Pondering this idea while walking Himalayan trails, I noted that the stories I kept hearing on the way were typically stories of journeys—journeys actually made between the places in a knot. Following up on this observation, the second conceptual proposition, and the second part of the book, examines these journeys and the routes they take place.

Against this background, I trace the transformations of western Himalayan trade, local efforts at building new roads, the cycles of boom and bust in the business of wildlife and medicinal plants, and the ebbs and tides of the Nepal–China border regimes associated with them.

In the Himalayas, exchange, movement, and ambition usually congregate along certain lines defined by the geographical features of terrain, such as valleys cutting through the main Himalayan range or passes known to be free of snow for much of the year. In chapter 4—*The Business of Wayfaring*—I suggest calling these lines of repeated movements *pathways*. A pathway, I argue, is more than just another term for a venerable trade route but rather a site along which life unfolds. Very often, proximity to a pathway is more important than the distance to an urban center. Pathways are thus as much a social as a topographical configuration. They frequently stand in competition to each other, and their importance is linked to infrastructure as well as shifting border regimes and market demands.

A source of inspiration in this endeavor to understand Himalayan pathways is Tim Ingold's distinction between wayfaring and transport (Ingold 2008). As a mode of movement, wayfaring gives attention to the land that opens along the path and the myriad of interactions that take place. Transport, on the other hand, is concerned with the logistics of moving goods and people from place to place. This neat distinction, however, gets more complicated in the Himalayas. Here, wayfaring was always in the service of transport, and the "business of wayfaring" is directly dependent on infrastructure.

In chapter 5—*A Quest for Roads*—I discuss the role of roads for the business of wayfaring. After a decade of road construction frenzy on the Tibetan Plateau, many valleys in northern Nepal are now easily accessible from the north while they still lack road access from within Nepal. This has led to a quest for new roads down from the Chinese border into the valleys of northern Nepal. Both in Humla and in Walung, such road projects were privately initiated. This chapter tells the story of these road construction projects, the revival of the old Himalayan institution of the seasonal trade mart, and the complex interactions with the state.

It examines a brief period of a boom followed by a tightening of border regimes and shows how the construction of roads in the name of connectivity is related to the emergence of new forms of remoteness and marginalization. Tracing the transformations in the business of wayfaring from sheep and goat caravans to mules and trucks, I discuss how they relate to investment in education, a shortage of agropastoral labor, and ambitions to profit from the new China trade.

Closely related to the quest for roads and their effects on old pathways is the question of distribution. After one of the roads described in chapter 5 was opened as a rough dirt track, I spent a couple of weeks with one of its initiators. He tried his luck as a government contractor, shipping subsidized rice to Humla in the context of a looming food crisis. Navigating the bureaucratic jungle of crossing borders and trying to find pack animals while a gold rush for one particular medicinal herb was raging through Humla, he encountered conflict between his role as a contractor and the frustrations of many households in Humla over the system of rice subsidies. Chapter 6—*The Labor of Distribution*—analyzes these issues. Distribution is at once a logistic problem and a matter of distributive justice. Both are intrinsically tied to the Himalayan business of wayfaring. I show how subsidies for rice and salt have altered the balance between the two dimensions of distribution. The subsidies have affected the role and position of Himalayan brokers and altered Himalayan trade as well as the relations between places in a knot. Engaging with James Ferguson's book *Give a Man a Fish* (2015), I argue that global development not only has a sedentarist bias but also emphasizes production over distribution.

Curation at Large

The third and last part of the book looks into the development industry and its initiatives in the Himalayas. They shape the wider sociopolitical context in which the work of maintaining translocal community and the business of wayfaring take place.

With a plethora of development agencies and NGOs seeking to address Nepal's most urgent problems, and a developmental state across the border in China rapidly reconstructing Tibet, the Himalayas find themselves enmeshed in a variety of external interventions. Unlike earlier "schemes to improve the human condition" imbued with high-modernist hubris (Scott 1998), the current mainstream of development discourse focuses on green and participatory approaches. This calls for a different analytic perspective. I propose the idea of *curation at large* in order to analyze contemporary interventions in the name of development and conservation. Curation is thereby not understood in the museum sense of the term but rather in its original meaning of *curare*—to heal or to cure. The fragile mountain ecosystem, people suffering from underdevelopment, and cultural heritage are the primary targets of curation. The curational interventions to this end often ignore what I describe as place-knots and pathways. However, they also channel subsidies, open career paths, and provide temporary niches for lucrative business endeavors. The efforts of curating seemingly out-of-the-way places, then, facilitates certain kinds of connections while reinforcing remoteness for the sake of preservation.

Chapter 7—*Curation at Large*—and the preceding vignette describe a two-day planning workshop for the Kailash Sacred Landscape Conservation and Development Initiative (KSLCDI), one of ICIMOD's signature projects. While Upper Humla lies right at the center of the initiative's project map, no local expert was among the 150 participants from China, India, and Nepal. During the two days I spent in a fancy hotel in Kathmandu, and especially in the coffee breaks between a tightly scheduled stream of presentations, frictions between the Chinese delegation and their Indian and Nepali counterparts came to light. While the delegations engaged in a shared universe of development rhetoric, the underlying curational ambitions differed substantially.

ICIMOD's transboundary landscape initiatives are inspired by the "landscape approach." In Chapter 8—*Landscapes, Dreamscapes*—I explore how such global approaches to development and conservation inform ICIMOD's programs and the practices of my colleagues. I argue that, for all their benefits, such ideas also obscure and partially erase the livelihood strategies, dreams, and ambitions of those they seek to help. A comparison of ICIMOD's approaches with the current efforts of the People's Republic to cure Tibet reveals a shared language yet a different emphasis. The Himalayan valleys along the northern border of Nepal find themselves wedged between these overlapping curational ambitions, which both have direct implications on the ground.

Chapter 9—*Mapping Mountains*—explores in more detail ICIMOD's tools and methods to research the ground realities they seek to understand. Mapping and geographic information system (GIS) technology are of utmost importance in this respect. A few weeks after the planning session I attended a workshop to assess the value of the "cultural ecosystem services" in the Kailash Sacred Landscape with the help of artificial intelligence. While the endeavor failed, it clearly revealed that mapping is more than just an effort to gain a graphical representation of reality. It serves as an ontogenetic strategy with the purpose of curating the reality it pretends to describe (Kitchin and Dodge 2007).

Weaving together the work of tying place-knots, the effort to tarmac and regulate old pathways, the business of wayfaring, the labor of distribution, and the curational ambitions of interventions in the name of development and conservation, the tenth and final chapter—*Translating Ambitions*—addresses the question of collaboration. It tells the story of four young Humli and Walungnga I met over the past decade. While they helped me understand their cosmopolitan Himalayan lives, I helped them translate their experiences into the language of global development and academia. The chapter revisits the triangle of conceptual propositions regarding remote places and the cosmopolitan ambitions of those who call them—in one way or another—home.

The epilogue—*Navidad*—leads back to Queens, New York, where a young man tells me the story of his journey from Nepal to the United States of America—a wayfaring odyssey following the pathways of migrants and drugs through South and Central America. His is a journey that goes against the grain of curational ambitions at large and, instead, relies on the assistance of the translocal Walung community.

In a nutshell, the three parts of book present three intertwined themes: the notion of *place-knots* reveals the ways in which community is made translocally and sets the stage; the idea of *pathways* follows the storied threads woven into these place-knots and reconsiders the relationships between evolving socio-spatial configurations; and the concept of *curation at large* helps reflect on the context of global development and conservation efforts in the Himalayas.

While these three conceptual propositions are grounded in Himalayan particularities, they raise fundamental questions relevant for seemingly remote yet cosmopolitan communities around the globe. They suggest an approach to study globalization not from above or from below but from the edge.

Part 1

LOCALITY AND COMMUNITY

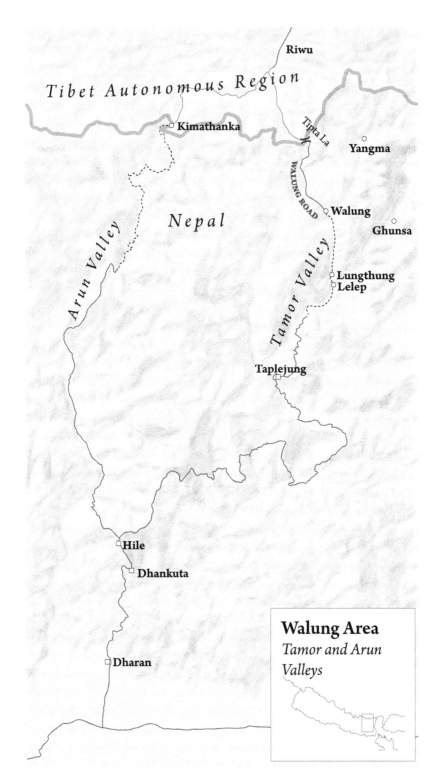

Map of the Walung area (Tamor and Arun Valleys). *Source*: Martin Saxer, 2019.

TYING PLACES INTO KNOTS

In late November 2016, nine months after my stay in Queens, I meet Tenzing again in Walung. He arrives with a delegation of five fellow New York residents by helicopter to attend *phutuk*, the yearly monastery festival. Next to the improvised helipad below the monastery, a welcome gate greets the honored guests. Tenzing and his peers are the main sponsors of this year's festival.

The village is bustling during the days of phutuk. Members of the Walung community from all over Nepal and abroad gather for the three-day event. Most Walung families own houses or rent flats in Taplejung, Hile, Kathmandu, or Darjeeling, where most family members stay for most of the year. While there is still a small government-run primary school in Walung, the majority of children leave the village for education. Those pursuing business equally spend considerable amounts of time outside the village. Over the winter, few people stay in Walung. After the festival, many will move to the lower hills or Kathmandu.

During phutuk, however, the Walung houses are brimful. Next to the monastery, a little tent city has emerged. This is the time to catch up with old friends and family, spend long nights telling stories, singing, and drinking *tongba*—the hot millet wine served in bamboo vessels and sipped through long bamboo straws.

The festival includes masked dances (*cham*) and a series of rituals purifying the village and catering to local deities. The rituals consist of chanting ritual texts that take three days to complete and offerings to appease the deities and harness their power and protection. Renewing the bonds between community and the gods of the land (*yul lha*) is crucial to ensure the continuing fortune of Walung and its people. The rituals are powerful and resonate beyond the village. When phutuk is performed, "even the nomads in Tibet feel it," Tenzing remarks. An important lama based in Sikkim has been invited to lead this year's rituals. The lama, a *ngagpa*, is originally from Walung. He lived in Taiwan for many years, studying in the monastery of a great master.[1]

While the rituals slowly progress, there is ample time to chat. One of the guests from New York tells me about his life as an Uber driver and the football team for which he passionately plays. One of my traveling companions, a Kyrgyz anthropologist, finds common ground with another Walungnga who lived in Odessa. They speak Russian together. Another of my companions, a Chinese anthropologist, is impressed by the Sikkim lama's fluent Mandarin.[2] The event has a cosmopolitan vibe. It reminds me of Nepali anthropologist Dor Bahadur Bista's observation during his visit in 1958:

> Many successful and rich traders are in residence here. [They] travel extensively in Tibet as far as Lhasa and in India to Delhi, Bombay and Calcutta. They are well-informed about the outside world. . . . Possession of transistor radios, with which they tune in to music and daily news broadcasts, is not at all uncommon. (Bista 1967, 174)

Walung's cosmopolitan vibes clearly predate the gradual arrival of telecommunication in the Himalayas. Right from the beginning, Walung had ties with the outside world. According to the story told in Walung, once upon a time, seven families came from Tibet and established the settlement. There are no records of when these families arrived. Most probably, the village was founded amid the larger wave of Tibetan populations settling along the southern flanks of the central and eastern Himalayas that started with the expansion of the Qing empire and the establishment of a unified Tibet under the control of the Gelug school of Tibetan Buddhism in the mid-seventeenth century. The village is mentioned in the Sikkim Chronicles as marking the frontier of Greater Sikkim during Chogyal Phuntsog Namgyal's seventeenth-century rule (Sprigg 1995, 91; Subba 2008, 160). However, the Chronicles were written long after the fact, and it remains unclear whether Walung was already a village at that time. Dor Bahadur Bista writes that Walung "is said to be about two hundred years old" (Bista 1967, 175). When I asked people in Walung about the age of the village, their estimates ranged from 150 to 400 years.[3]

What seems certain, however, is that Walung was not chosen as a place to grow barley or buckwheat. Built on the loose soil of a glacial moraine above the Tamur River, the village is clearly not designed for agricultural subsistence. There are a few kitchen gardens but no fields and no irrigation. The village consists of about sixty wooden houses, most of them impressively large two-story build-

The village of Walung as seen from the monastery. *Source*: Martin Saxer, 2012. From "The Other Image," www.theotherimage.com/series/walung/.

ings covered with wooden shingles. The houses feature cobblestone foreyards to unload the yak caravans coming from Tibet, storerooms in the basements, and living quarters on the top floors. Each of the houses flies prayer flags on two tall poles at both ends. The flags already caught the attention of British botanist Joseph Dalton Hooker in 1848. He describes Walung as a "populous village of large and good painted wooden houses, ornamented with hundreds of long poles and vertical flags, looking like the fleet of some foreign port" (Hooker 1854, 199).

Hooker's maritime association is an apt metaphor. Walung's fortunes always depended on trade. Situated at one of the most direct routes between Shigatse in Tibet and the plains of northern India, a day south of the Tipta Pass usually open for most of the year, Walung was a commercial center, a mountainous harbor for goods exchanged between the Tibetan Plateau and South Asia. The two-story houses with their extensive storerooms on the ground floor were designed to stock large amounts of Nepali grain and Tibetan salt—the staples of trans-Himalayan trade. At 3,200 meters above sea level, Walung is the lowest and most southern point that yak caravans from Tibet can comfortably reach, and thus it is an ideal location for a trading hub.

Apart from salt and grain, trade in a number of other products, including musk, horses, dyes, or wristwatches, promised substantial profits. Throughout Nepal, Walung traders still have a reputation of being wealthy. However, prosperity was neither universal nor stable. Chapter 2 will trace the recent history of Walung along the biographies of its people. Here, it suffices to note that Walung has never been an isolated, self-sufficient mountain village. While not everybody was a trader, almost all families in Walung were in one way or another linked to the business of trade, be it rearing yaks, portering, or running teahouses along the trails. Dependent on trade, the fortunes of Walung remain tied to the vagaries of markets, geopolitics, and borders.

Through this history of trade, the people of Walung look back at generations of experience venturing out into the world. Their ambitions resonate with those found among other Tibetan-speaking communities in the Himalayas traditionally based on trade—from Ladakh to Humla, Mustang, Manang, and Solu-Khumbu.

Wim van Spengen (2000) and Prista Ratanapruck (2007), for example, tell a very similar story about the transnational ventures of Manangi traders. Equipped with international trading privileges and passports already in the 1960s, Manangi traders did not so much *migrate* but rather *expand* their trading ventures as far as Hong Kong and Bangkok, establishing themselves through capital investment and marriage along the way while firmly remaining part of the Manangi trading community. Beyond the Himalayas, similar strategies of expansion can be found among Afghan traders, as Magnus Marsden (2016) shows, or among Uygur traders in Central Asia, as Rune Steenberg (2014) convincingly argues.

In the case of Walung, trading privileges go back to a so-called *lal mohor*, a red-sealed letter by the king of Nepal. It granted the *goba*, the hereditary headman, broad legal and economic autonomy in exchange for taxes paid annually to the court. Joseph Dalton Hooker reports that the goba of Walung was said to pay 6,000 rupees, the equivalent of 600 pounds, to the king of Nepal—a considerable sum, given that the value of a yak was between two and three pounds at that time (Hooker 1854, 204, 220). Although he admits that the revenue derived from trade must be considerable, he discredits this figure as "no doubt a great exaggeration." He writes: "They [the Walungnga] levy a small tax on all imports, and trade a little on their own account, but are generally poor and very indolent" (Hooker 1854, 205).

Rich or poor? Indolent or ambitious? Hooker clearly wasn't sure what to make of what he saw and learned. He simply could not reconcile the image of wealth in a remote Himalayan village with its "indolent" residents and the absence of agriculture. In a way, as I will argue in the course of this book, Hooker's mid-nineteenth-century confusion still haunts many of the basic assumption about the Himalayas. Although Walung may be a special case with its almost exclusive dependence on trade, the long-standing reliance on nonagricultural income is a widespread phenomenon throughout the region, and prosperity is often associated with business rather than agriculture.

The long history of Himalayan trade and mobility raises the issue of community and locality and the conflation of the two in the trope of the "local community." Historically, the disciplines of anthropology and geography have undeniably played an important role in putting the "local community" on the agenda, often in response to older and less benevolent perspectives on non-Western people: When European settlers encountered people in uncharted territories, they were usually conceived of a "local tribes"—as people without history, as Eric Wolf (1982) famously put it; similarly, Chinese imperial officials saw themselves confronted with the task of civilizing local "barbarians" in the borderlands of the empire (Fiskesjö 1999; Shin 2006; Brindley 2003), and those disciplined by British colonial forces in the frontiers were regularly depicted as members of "unruly chieftains" and "local clans" (Hopkins 2008, 18–21).

Especially in its remote and ethnic incarnation, the "local community" stands for the archetypal other: It is a priori *community* rather than *society* and *local* rather than *global* and thus, by implication, *traditional* rather than *modern*, *ethnic* rather than *diverse*, *backward* rather than *developed*, *clean* rather than *polluted*, and *subsistence oriented* rather than *capitalist and industrial*. As a trope, the notion of the "local community" conceptually binds people to place.

Since the late 1980s, social theorists in anthropology, geography, sociology, and related disciplines have voiced strong concerns against such conflations of people and place. Arjun Appadurai (1988, 37) portrays the endeavor of anthropologists to ascribe native status to local people as a form of implicit confinement, a spatial incarceration that ties identity to a particular ecosystem to which they are supposed to be ideally adapted. The task of ethnography, he argues, is thus the "unraveling of a conundrum: what is the nature of locality as a lived experience in a globalized, de-territorialized world?" (Appadurai 1996, 52). He addresses this conundrum with term "global ethnoscapes" (Appadurai 1991) as a means to describe the realities of diasporas and migrant communities.

James Clifford (1997, 1988), writing against dominant territorialized connotations of culture, critically notes that social science has preferred studying roots rather than routes. In a similar vein, Akhil Gupta and James Ferguson challenged the implicit isomorphism of space, place, and culture in public debate. They argue that taking a preexisting local (or localized) community as a starting point glosses over the "construction of space as place or locality in the first instance," and discussing the !Kung in the Kalahari Desert—who, like Himalayan communities, have been described as isolated and surviving in a harsh environment—they further argue that "instead of assuming the autonomy of the primeval community, we need to examine how it was formed as a community out of the interconnected space that always already existed" (Gupta and Ferguson 1992, 8). Along the same lines, Liisa Malkki shows that sedentarism is taken for granted even when talking about refugees—their "uprooting" and "displace-ment" is what underpins the analysis of all kinds of problems arising in the di-aspora; in public debate, there is a veritable "sedentarist metaphysics" at work (Malkki 1992, 31).

Doreen Massey identifies this persistent identification of place with commu-nity as the source of a basic and continuing misunderstanding about how people relate to place. Places are not made by looking inward but rather by seeing them in relation to other places. Massey thus suggests an outward-looking rather than self-enclosing sense of place (Massey 1994, 146–56). Resonating with this debate, John Urry, Mimi Sheller, and Jonas Larson proposed mobility as a new paradigm, and Ulf Hannerz's work firmly established the notion of transnationalism in the analyses of long-distance flows and cross-boundary connections (Hannerz 1996; Urry 2000, 2007; Sheller and Urry 2006; Larsen, Urry, and Axhausen 2006).

In the effort to unmake dominant narratives, Katharyne Mitchell (1997) notes that terms like transnationalism, mobility, flows, and deterritorialization have, at times, almost become fetishized. Amid calls for a more "grounded transna-tionalism" (Brickell and Datta 2011, 3), the notion of the translocal has recently gained currency, focusing again on the continuing importance of place and the codependent fate of localities (Freitag and Oppen 2010; Greiner and Sakdapol-rak 2013; Munkelt et al. 2013). Around the globe, emerging "modes of living" are distinctly translocal (Porst and Sakdapolrak 2017, 111) and the field of every-day practices transcends scales (Brickell and Datta 2011). Following Doreen Massey's observation (1994, 169) that the identity of a place does not stem from its internal history but its interactions with other places, Tim Oakes and Louisa Schein (2006) analyze such practices in their volume *Translocal China*. They show that in China, the system of household registrations (*hukou*) continues to tie identities and fortunes to specific places (Oakes and Schein 2006, 5, 15). At the same time, the country has witnessed the largest labor migration in the history of humankind with scores of rural residents seeking employment in the factories that produce the world's consumer goods.

As much as these debates helped disentangle the conflation of community and locality, the "local community" has remained a powerful trope. It contin-ues to frame imaginaries of remote and rural places around the globe. Consider, for example, the global development and aid industry that takes the "local com-munity" as its primary target. After numerous failures with top-down modern-ist development agendas in the 1960s and 1970s, the call for participatory approaches has come to be seen as a condition sine qua non for sustainable and effective development. Without reference to the participation of a local commu-nity, development projects hardly find funding today. While in the 1980s and 1990s, local communities were frequently blamed for environmentally damaging practices such as shifting cultivation or extensive overgrazing (Hathaway 2013), they are now increasingly acknowledged for their role as stewards of fragile environments, and their local knowledge is recognized as an important asset for conservation. The Convention on Biological Diversity (CBD), signed in Rio de Janeiro in 1992, first adopted this perspective in an international agreement; the Nagoya Protocol, signed in 2010 and entered into force in 2014, takes this a step further and mandates access and the fair sharing of benefits derived from indigenous knowledge and local resources. All these legal frameworks directly depend on the idea of local communities.[4]

The "local community" has also emerged as the guardian of *cultural* diversity, which is again both underpinning the call for protection but also opening avenues for local income generation. The safeguarding of cultural heritage ties in with the needs of the tourism industry. Local community, local customs, and local cuisines are seen as important assets to develop places into destinations. They guarantee a marketable difference in a world that is increasingly experienced as uniform. Ethnicity and remoteness amplify such imaginaries and add value to a local community's tourism potential.[5]

This is not just a Western phenomenon. The local community as resource of cultural diversity and thus worthy of preservation is important around the globe. China, for example, has seen a massive surge of domestic tourism looking for glimpses into different and preferably "remote" and "ethnic" worlds (Oakes 1998; Schein 1997, 1999; Anagnost 1997), and heritage making has become a veritable industry throughout the country (Saxer 2014, 2012). In a certain way, such contemporary notions of the local community in tourism and development are a mirror image of older imperial perspectives: there, the unruly tribe as an obstacle to civilization and progress; here, the descendants of the antipodes offering an antidote to the ills of modernity.

Within this larger political and economic context, membership in a "local community" is more than just a question of origin and cultural belonging. If anything, "the importance of being local" (Armbrecht Forbes 1999)—to make claims and be heard on the global stage and to gain access to subsidies, quotas for minority students in state universities, jobs with nongovernmental organizations (NGOs), or parliament seats—has only increased over the past decades. Similarly, "being local" is important beyond the nation-state. Fair trade labels, for example, explicitly certify the existence of a particular *local* community or cooperative in contrast to *transnational* agribusinesses, and organizations like the international peasants' movement La Via Campesina aim at providing *local* smallholder communities with a voice in the *global* arena.

The idea of the local community also tacitly provides the backdrop and baseline in the current debate about out-migration and labor shortage in empty mountain villages. In the highlands of Asia, from the Pamirs to the Himalayas, out-migration and depopulation are a reality. In many villages, including Walung, the vast majority of teenagers and young adults are absent, be it for education, business, or work. Where there is agriculture, fields increasingly lay fallow because of limited labor resources. A study by Geoff Childs, Sienna Craig, Cynthia Beall, and Buddha Basnyat (2014) on two districts in northern Nepal paints a stark picture in this respect: Both in Mustang and in Nubri/Tsum, around three-quarters of the population between ten and nineteen years of age live away from home. In the villages of Nubri, the number of people living elsewhere has risen by 180 percent between 1997 and 2012. In their 2019 book *From a Trickle to a Torrent*, Geoff Childs and Namgyal Choedup trace in great detail the costs and benefits of sending children to schools outside the valleys. "While education opens opportunities for the younger generation, it leaves the older generation with a debilitated labor force, new challenges to household succession, and vulnerabilities in old age," the authors show (Childs and Choedup 2019, 69). The problem of out-migration, be it for education or labor, has prominently surfaced on the agendas of NGOs and development organizations. An increasing number of projects are trying to counter the trend with local training and the promotion of community-based tourism as a potential source of income that would keep people in the villages and prevent the disintegration of "local communities" (ICIMOD 2017a).

In brief, the "local community" is still a dominant figure of thought. It undergirds designs of progressive political movements as much as state interventions and NGO projects in the name of development, cultural heritage, and conservation. The "local community" thus remains an important topic to study. However, glossing over translocal realities, it may not be an ideal *analytical* starting point.

The case of Walung with its mobile population traditionally spending much time outside the village is clearly difficult to reconcile with the idea of the local community. Neither is Walung home to a *local* community, nor is the Walung community limited to a single locality. The conceptual efforts at putting mobility, translocal practices, and migration center stage are better used to describe the mobile lives of Himalayan trading communities. However, most of the conceptual work of deconstructing the conflation of locality and community is derived from studies of urban migrant communities. What I see in Walung and other Himalayan villages along the Tibetan border is something more specific than concepts such as ethnoscapes or translocal networks would suggest. My ambition is not to replace such conceptual propositions with a radically new theoretical perspective. My stakes are humbler: I am concerned with the question of how the places in which the lives of these Himalayan communities unfold are woven—or tied—into each other and how a specific kind of mobility and ambition actively fosters such knots.

The odysseys starting in Himalayan villages and ending in Queens, New York, cannot be aptly described in well-known categories such as labor migration or rural-urban migration. The ambitions of the people I got to know are quite different from those of many young adults throughout rural Asia seeking employment in Malaysia or the Gulf States. They are not looking for "off-farm income" to sustain a family at home through remittances, as the lingo of NGOs tends to put it.[6] The model, especially for young men, is rather to venture out and "make it" somewhere by establishing a business—even if this involves phases of working in salaried jobs for a while, like Tenzing and his peers at the farmers market in New York. These dreams and ambitions are not just a result of the necessities and opportunities of our current era of globalization; the old legacies of Himalayan trade and mobility clearly resonate in them.

Take, as a comparison, the dreams and ambitions of dairy farmers in the village in eastern Switzerland where I grew up. Income from dairy farming does not guarantee a living, and there is ample evidence to suggest that this has been the case at least since the nineteenth century (Dawson 1986). While the majority of my former neighbors have to seek employment outside agriculture to make ends meet, none of them would dream about venturing out and starting a business in Zurich or New York. On the contrary, business professionals and traders are looked on with much disdain. They are seen as profiteers, trying to get rich without doing any actual work. Social status, here, is tied to land and the number of cattle one owns. Capital accumulation with the intention to move out is not something anybody would seriously consider.

The mobile lives of the people of Walung and other places in the Himalayas are also quite different from those of highly skilled Indian or Chinese professionals establishing themselves in the United States and, for that matter, from my own experiences as an academic moving from job to job around the globe. A question that keeps coming up in conversations with young business-minded friends from the highlands of Asia is why I do not make better use of my privilege to travel, meet people, and do research. Why not start a business with all this knowledge? My reluctance in this respect is often seen as slightly weird and certainly not very clever—especially given the meager salary an academic earns.

In Himalayan communities, where prosperity and social status is based on trade and exchange rather than sedentarist agriculture, identity and livelihood strategies evolve around *relations*—both between people and between places—and, accordingly, an active investment in making and maintaining these relations. Against this background, moving out and establishing oneself somewhere new may be better understood as a form of expanding community than as mere out-migration in search of labor.

Here is a simple observation: The places that play a role in the translocal community of Walung are not countless. Family endeavors usually circle around three, four, or maybe five specific locations. For richer trading families in the early 1950s, these locations included Shigatse, Walung, Taplejung, and Kolkata; for poorer families, the trade mart in Sar across the border in Tibet, Walung, and the winter settlement of Tawa further down the valley. With the decline of the Tibet trade, Darjeeling and Hile replaced Sar and Shigatse, and for many Walung families today, life takes place between Walung, the neighborhood of Boudha in Kathmandu, and the borough of Queens in New York City. Endeavors and ambitions revolve around a limited number of localities (often neighborhoods rather than cities) tightly woven together. What I witness is a limited form of translocality rather than a worldwide diaspora. What I see are places, more than two but less than many, tied into a knot. These place-knots are created through the expansion of community rather than out-migration. In other words, it is the pull that ties the knot.

This observation points to a set of issues regarding locality and community that tend to be overlooked both by the trope of the "local community" and concepts such as global ethnoscapes and transnational diasporas. How are these knots tied? And what are the tensions that come with tying? Let me discuss these questions in turn.

The Work of Tying

The first step toward understanding locality and community is the simple acknowledgment that most places—except prisons, army camps, or the like—are not experienced as areas with boundaries around them. Taking a lead from Doreen Massey, places are rather "articulated moments in networks of social relations and understandings, but where a large proportion of those relations, experiences and understandings are constructed on a far larger scale," which in turn, "allows a sense of place which is extroverted" and "integrates in a positive way the global and the local" (Massey 1994, 5, 154–5). Places, then, are an effect of the "folding of spaces, times and materials," as Kevin Hetherington notes (1997, 197). Rather than bounded spaces, places in themselves are already knots—knots that do not *contain* life but are rather formed of the very lines along which life is lived. As Tim Ingold (2007, 100) notes, "Lines are bound together *in* the knot, but they are not bound *by* it."

If a place in itself is a knot, how to understand a knot made of places as far apart as Walung, Kathmandu, and Queens, each with a particular positionality and embedded in their own larger contexts? As the ties between places are not necessarily a function of proximity—especially in the present era of telecommunications and uneven "space-time-compression" (Harvey 1989)—conventional maps with dots representing places, and lines or arrows showing the connections between them, do not adequately capture the entanglements that I am concerned with. The places in a place-knot feel much closer than such graphical representations would suggest. The Cartesian projection of Himalayan experiences of mobility and place onto Euclidean abstractions of the world tells us little about locality and community.

As an alternative and non-Euclidean approach to think about relations between places, Eric Sheppard suggests the notion of "wormhole geographies" (2002, 323). The term wormhole, derived from relativity theory, describes instantaneous passages between localities in a warped space-time continuum. The notion of wormholes, he argues, allows us to shift our spatial imaginations from topography to topology and offers a better way to describe close ties between distant places. "The positionality of two places," he writes, "should be measured [. . .] not by the physical distance separating them, but the intensity of their interconnectedness" (Sheppard 2002, 324).

We may not need to resort to bended time and space and cosmological metaphors to describe what is at stake, however. Place-knotting is something quite ordinary. As Tim Ingold argues, knotting is the fundamental principle of coherence in a world where things are continually coming into being through movement and growth. Human existence is not fundamentally place-bound, he argues, but "place-binding" (Ingold 2008, 33). Places, then, are not so much experienced as locations in space; they rather emerge as "topics, joined in stories of journeys actually made." As a gathering of things, "every place [. . .] is a knot of stories" (Ingold 2007, 41). It is no coincidence that the English word "topic" is cognate with the Greek term *topos*—place.

The phutuk festival in Walung is place-binding in precisely this sense. The annual rituals performed at this event to appease the local protector deities and harness their power rekindle the bonds between people and place. Ignoring the importance of a local deity would put the fortunes of the entire translocal community at risk. Phutuk reinforces the positionality of Walung within the wider sacred landscape of the Himalayas.[7] This place-making effort, however, is only possible in correspondence with the Walung community living outside—with the lama from Sikkim and Tenzing and his peers as sponsors from abroad.

Becoming a patron, a *jindak*, is a well-established mode of engagement in Tibetan societies. The institution of the jindak links outwardly oriented business endeavors with the needs and obligations of a local monastic institution. Sponsoring rituals was, and in many places still is, an obligation rotating between the richer households of a village. Today, sponsoring often takes place at the intersection of transnational business and religious networks. It ties religion to commercial success—giving ABC Carpet & Home's slogan of "commerce as a vehicle for insight and for action in the aid of creating a better world" a Himalayan twist. Being a jindak provides an avenue for successful businesspeople to gain merit in exchange for financial support of a monastic institution. Regardless of scale, sponsoring provides a means to renew the ties between places in a knot.[8]

Entangling business with religion goes beyond monastic events like phutuk. Take, for example, the Walung Uplifting Society in Kathmandu, one of the many Walung welfare organizations across the globe. Housed together with a monastery and the Savings and Credit Association in a new building in Boudha, its purpose is not just providing a space for religious events in the capital. It is one of the places where the extent and the coherence of the Walung community are continuously negotiated. Membership in the Walung Uplifting Society is not automatic for those with Walung roots, and neither are Walung origins a precondition. To become a member, one has to buy oneself in. This makes the Uplifting Society open to others, including Tibetan refugees with ties to Walung or people from the surrounding villages. The Savings and Credit Association that is associated with the Uplifting Society pools savings with the purpose of granting credit to individual entrepreneurs for a reasonable interest rate. The monastery situated in the same building is a house of worship but also an integral part of the Walung presence in Kathmandu. Just like the phutuk festival, it requires donations and sponsors to operate. All three—the Walung Uplifting Society, the Savings and Credit Association, and the monastery—help tie the different locations in which Walung live into a knot. The knot, in turn, serves as a resource for the cosmopolitan endeavors the Walungnga are engaged in.

In Walung, the rituals are slowly progressing. Each stage is carefully captured by at least a dozen cameras and smartphones. Some may argue that in our age of spectacle (Debord 1970), visual representation has become more important than ritual itself, that filming and taking pictures turn participants into consumers, and that religion becomes colorful heritage in the process. This, however, would not do justice to what is at stake. Filming and taking pictures have become an active way of participation, and the cameras and smartphones are an integral part of the ritual's equipment. Once back in an area with mobile reception, the festival-goers from afar will share their images and clips on social media, and the stories of their journeys will reiterate the bonds of the Walung

Masked dance during phutuk in Walung. *Source*: Martin Saxer, 2016.

community and the importance of the village as a place in the knot. Filming, thus, is part of the labor of tying. Through this labor, the place-knot emerges rather as a topic than as a set of locations with flows of money and merit between them. That those who long ago moved out of Walung and seldom come back actively participate in this endeavor only adds to the relevance of the event.

Just as a place is always already a knot of stories, it is through stories of journeys—those made and remembered but also those planned or dreamed of—that the three, four, or five places in what I call a place-knot are bound together. In other words, the same movements and stories that let a locality emerge as a place are what ties a place-knot.

As the rituals proceed, we take time to inspect progress on the road from Walung to Tibet, for which Tenzing requested permission to hire an excavator from China in the letter he wrote to the authorities of Riwu, the county across the border. Since my stay in New York, the required ecological assessment has been carried out and all the paperwork is done. The first two kilometers from Walung, following the river, have just been completed. Seventy people from Walung, at least one per family, worked for two weeks to manually open the track. The effort may have been modest, but it is symbolically important, and it attracted some media attention. Tenzing hopes that this will help the project.

Two members of parliament from Taplejung District have pledged $40,000 each (in US dollars), and $45,000 was earmarked for the road in the budget of the Village Development Committee (VDC).[9] However, private initiative is still required to get the project off the ground, Tenzing is convinced. Privately, he contributed $50,000, and while in Kathmandu, he approached the rich Walung families in the hope of raising another $30,000. Tenzing in convinced that the road is crucial for Walung's future. Trade through Walung is competing with other border crossings to Tibet. Without a road, chances are slim to rekindle the kind of ties with Tibet that are necessary to trigger a revival of Walung as entrepôt.

While roads feature prominently on the agendas of both Nepal and the People's Republic of China, state planners tend to envision them as corridors facilitating the flow of global trade. The global, however, does not flow—"it hops instead, efficiently connecting the enclaved points in the network while excluding (with equal efficiency) the spaces that lie between the points" (Ferguson 2006, 47). To prevent this requires circumspection, money, and work. As I will discuss in more detail in chapter 5, the construction of roads is of utmost importance for the role and position of seemingly remote villages in the "spaces between," and road construction has become the prime arena in which between private initiatives, local politics, and state planning clash and converge.

Knots That Block

Making roads to foster old trading connections, performing rituals to rekindle the bonds of people and local gods, or engaging in the complex of welfare, credit, and religion are all part and parcel of the work of tying the localities where Walung life takes place into a knot. The work of tying, however, is not necessarily harmonious, and the resulting knot can be experienced as unjust or even suffocating. While the knot is a metaphor of cohesion and purposeful emplacement, it also stands for blockages, for entanglements too tight and in need of untangling.

Sarah Green, in a special issue on Anthropological Knots in the journal *HAU*, highlights these more troublesome implications of the knot as metaphor—namely, the "double binds that come together and get caught up with each other" (Green 2014, 6). Departing from Tim Ingold's concern with knots as the fundamental principle of coherence, Green suggests that past episodes of knot-tying always leave traces that are worth following up in order to explore the "tensions, paradoxes, double binds, and sheer material and political inequalities that are exercised when differences become entangled with one another" (Green 2014, 7).

During the last day of phutuk, such tensions and double binds come to light. The rituals are completed, and a round of speeches to honor the special guests and jindaks conclude the event. The Buddhist festival quickly acquires an altogether different atmosphere, which anybody familiar with public events in South Asia knows all too well. The volume of the Chinese sound system used for the recitations of Buddhist texts over the past three days has been turned up considerably for the lengthy speeches. Amid this procedure, an elderly woman gets up and starts shouting. People first try to ignore her and then to calm her down. But she has no intention to be silenced. The elderly woman, one of the few permanent Walung residents, is the helper of the single monk who stays in the village throughout the year. Informally, she has taken over much of the day-to-day chores of looking after the monastery. "All these speeches for those coming from far away!" she shouts. "And here is the man who actually takes care of the monastery, this man here, he is not even mentioned!" She points to the elderly monk who is performing his duty, putting white Tibetan scarves around the necks of the guests of honor. She is furious, and the festival-goers do not know how to deal with her. Finally, still shouting, she is led away.

For her, the labor of tying performed with money and religious authority from abroad means that her own investment and the investment of her friend, the single resident monk, are being eclipsed. She feels both left out and strangled by all the tying.

The notion of place-knots, like ethnoscapes or wormholes, is a metaphorical device. It is meant to shed light on a particular set of practices and experiences of place-making in mobile communities. The basic task of maintaining community between places far apart is, of course, not an exclusively Himalayan challenge. However, fostering social relations within a community at large is so much at the heart of the type of mobilities I am concerned with; in fact, the "world multiple" (Omura et al. 2019) of Himalayan place-knots makes for a fertile ground to take on these questions.

The sudden outbreak of latent tensions during phutuk is a stark reminder of the geometries of status, power, and influence at work. In Walung, the pulls that tie the knot I seek to describe have been anything but symmetrical. These asymmetries and hierarchical relations of power are an outcome of the particular history of Walung and its changing fortunes, to which I will turn in chapter 2.

MOVING IN, MOVING UP, MOVING OUT

Trans-Himalayan trade has long been at the core of Nepal's relations with Tibet. Several wars were fought over trade; many agreements were signed and many
broken again. The history and politics of trans-Himalayan trade define the context in which the story of Walung unfolded. Some brief historical background
is necessary to situate Walung in the larger context of Himalayan politics and
to understand how it became tied in a knot.

In the sixteenth century, the Malla kings acquired minting rights for the currency used in Tibet. In the eighteenth century, the last Malla rulers started
adulterating the coins they minted in order to finance their war against the ri-
valing Gorkha Kingdom. The Tibetans, of course, felt cheated. When Prithvi Narayan Sha, the Gorkha ruler, defeated the Mallas in 1768 and unified Nepal, he
inherited the currency problem. In 1775, an agreement was reached, giving Tibet an equal right to determine the composition of the coins minted in Nepal.
In return, Tibet promised to close the eastern trade route through Sikkim and
the Chumbi Valley. The British East India Company had developed an interest
in direct trade with Tibet along this route, much to the dislike of the Gorkha
rulers. Bhutan had briefly held the Chumbi Valley but was driven out again with
the help of the Tibetans. To keep the monopoly on trade with Tibet, the Gorkhas attacked Sikkim and captured Darjeeling. This military intervention and the
1775 agreement with Tibet prevented direct trade between Lhasa and Kolkata
and protected business on the two main trade routes from Tibet to Kathmandu
through Kyirong and Kuti.[1]

However, the question of the old Malla currency, which was still widely in circulation, was not addressed in the 1775 agreement. This led to further tension. Bahadur Sha, Prithvi Narayan's second son and acting regent from 1785 to 1794, went twice to war with Tibet over the unresolved issue. The first campaign, in which Nepal had the upper hand, ended in a treaty signed in Kyirong in 1789. This treaty set the exchange rate for old Malla coins at two to one. Nepal agreed to withdraw its troops but obtained the right to have a representative in Lhasa and jurisdiction over its subjects in Tibet. Nepali traders in Lhasa could thus not be tried by a Tibetan court. In addition, the agreement stipulated once more that all trade was to go through Nepal and the routes through Sikkim and Bhutan were to remain closed (Uprety 1998, 36).

This one-sided treaty benefiting Nepal never really found acceptance in Tibet. The Nepali side complained that the Tibetans were not honoring the agreement. As a result, Nepali troops once more marched into Tibet, advancing to Shigatse and looting Tashilhumpo monastery, the seat of the Panchen Lama. On the verge of a renewed defeat, the Tibetans requested assistance from the Chinese Empire. The Qing intervened and the Gorkhas were driven out of Tibet. Retreating to Nepal, Chinese troops followed them into the Kathmandu Valley. A peace treaty was signed in autumn 1792 in which the position of the Chinese Ambans, the Qing representatives in Lhasa, was strengthened. All future disputes were to be submitted to them. Furthermore, Nepal was to return what was stolen from Tashilhumpo, never again bring up the currency problem, and henceforth pay tribute to the Chinese emperor every five years.[2]

The first decades of the nineteenth century were a period of relative stability (Rose 1971, 122). Kathmandu retained its position, and the bulk of trans-Himalayan trade continued to go through Kuti and Kyirong. Nevertheless, grievances about the defeat in the second Nepal–Tibet war were still lingering. With Jang Bahadur Rana's ascent to power in 1846, Nepal became again more assertive in Himalayan politics. A border dispute, ill-treatment of the Nepali tribute mission to China in 1854, and attacks on Nepali traders in Lhasa served Jang Bahadur Rana as a pretext to launch a third military campaign against Tibet in 1855. This time, the Chinese, weakened by the ongoing Taiping rebellion, stayed out of the conflict. In 1856, a peace treaty was reached that shifted the balance again in favor of Nepali traders in Tibet, providing them with a customs exemption and the right to establish trade marts in Lhasa (Uprety 1998, 71–72). As with preceding agreements, the treaty remained a bone of contention. With Chinese influence waning, friction between Nepal and Tibet only increased. At times, open hostility flared up. In 1873, for example, a Nepali assistant envoy was beaten during an official reception in Lhasa, and in 1883 Nepali shops were looted after a Nepali trader was accused of beating a Tibetan woman whom he suspected to be a thief (Uprety 1998, 90–92).

While trade was important for the ruling elites both in Nepal and in Tibet, it was Nepal that feared losing its privileges and the potential decline of Kathmandu as primary hub for trans-Himalayan trade. The wars and treaties of the late eighteenth and nineteenth century can be read as an attempt by the rulers of Nepal to prevent this outcome. What eventually undermined Kathmandu's role and position was not Tibet but a geopolitical shift beyond the control of both. At the height of the Great Game, the quarrel over spheres of influence between the British and Russian empires, the British became increasingly concerned about the rapprochement between Russia and Tibet. Reports of Tibetan diplomatic delegations at the czar's court in Saint Petersburg raised the specter of expanding Russian influence in Tibet. As a response to this threat, the British troops under Colonel Francis Younghusband marched into Tibet. This infamous invasion in 1903 to 1904, known as the Younghusband expedition, finally "opened" the Chumbi Valley for direct trade between Lhasa and Kolkata (Harris et al. 2013, 32–35). Kalimpong emerged as the main entrepôt for trans-Himalayan trade—the very outcome Nepal had sought to prevent.[3] The privileges for Nepali traders, such as customs exemptions, did not apply to the Kalimpong trade, and Kathmandu's position eroded.

Walung's Positionality

Walung's fortunes were closely entangled with these geopolitical developments. It was in the course of the Gorkha Kingdom's expansion toward Sikkim that Walung came under Nepali rule. And it was Kathmandu's concern to prevent direct trade between Lhasa and Kolkata through Sikkim and the Chumbi Valley that provided Walung with its favorable position. Before Younghusband's military intervention, the route through Walung—the easternmost trans-Himalayan pathway through Nepal—was the shortest connection between Tibet and Kolkata. At the same time, the fact that Nepal's ruling elites had their focus almost exclusively on Kathmandu and the Kuti and Kyirong routes also meant that Walung was granted a certain degree of autonomy. The *lal mohor*, the red-sealed letter from the king of Nepal, gave the *goba*, the village head of Walung, wide-ranging authority in exchange for an annual flat tax, and the Walung traders were relatively free to conduct business on their own terms.[4]

Passing through Walung in November 1848, Joseph Dalton Hooker complained about this absence of state authority. "Equally dependent on Nepal and Tibet, they very naturally hold themselves independent of both," he wrote. Hooker found his "roving commission from the Nepal Rajah was not respected, and the guard of Ghorkas held very cheap" (Hooker 1854, 205). Twenty-three years after Hooker's expedition, Sarat Chandra Das, one of the pundits in the service of the British crown, sought to sneak into Tibet via Walung. However, discussing his plans with a host along the way, he was advised not to try, as he "would be sure to meet with much difficulty" (Das 1902, 24). Avoiding the scrutiny of the Walung goba, he chose the neighboring Yangma Valley instead.

Besides a favorable position in the context of trade politics and considerable autonomy, Walung traders had yet another advantage: Whereas Walung officially belonged to Nepal since the late eighteenth century, it was still very much part of the Tibetan world. According to Brigitte Steinmann (1991, 480), Walung continued to pay some form of tax to Tibet. While some Walungnga that I talked to doubt this claim, and I have not been able to verify it, it is clear that Walung traders were not foreigners in Tibet in the way that Newari and other Nepali traders were. Many Walung families had marital relations with Tibet. For generations, most of the men of the goba family married Tibetan women from Shigatse, for example.

Tamla Ukyab, a former civil servant and Nepal's consul general Lhasa in the 1980s, grew up in Walung in the late 1940s and early 1950s. In those days, people going to Kathmandu would say they were going to *Nepal*, Tamla remembers. "They never used to think of themselves as part of Nepal, you know."

Himself a member of the goba family, Tamla witnessed the bustling exchange and close connections to Tibet that shaped life in Walung. One of the stories he told me, during several days of interviews, is the following:

> I remember vividly, when I was about six years old, two elephants were brought to Walung. They were offered to the Dalai Lama by the king of Nepal. I think it was a present to the Dalai Lama when he came to power. The government of Nepal sent two elephants and they came through my village. My father was in charge of [it]. The elephants were tied in our compound. I still remember their names. Somar Kali and Jatan Kali. And then, they were taken to Tibet. One, I heard, died on the road. One reached Lhasa. When I was consul general, I inquired about the elephant. I was told that when the Dalai Lama left Lhasa [in 1959], the elephant was still alive. It was still there. Ask him.[5]

Even after the gravity of trade moved to Kalimpong following Younghusband's "expedition" at the beginning of the twentieth century, there were still plenty of business opportunities, Tamla explains:

> We used to supply everything [to Tibet]: food grains, sugar, vegetables, fruit, everything. And from Tibet we used to get wool, salt, meat, and horses also. In those days, you know, our people used to trade in horses.

They used to buy hundreds of horses inside Tibet and bring them to a place called Karga Mela in India. And they used to make good profit from that.

China in Tibet and Walung's "Golden Years"

In 1951, the People's Liberation Army (PLA) marched into Lhasa. Facing an imminent invasion, the Tibetan government, under the young fourteenth Dalai Lama, had signed an agreement with the People's Republic of China (PRC). This agreement, known as the Seventeen Point Agreement, accepted Chinese sovereignty in exchange for comprehensive guarantees for regional autonomy, religious freedom, the right of the aristocracy and the monasteries to keep their property, and the promise that there would be no compulsion to reform the political system. The agreement avoided bloodshed and allowed the Communist Party to celebrate the PLA's takeover as the "peaceful liberation" (Shakya 1999, 63–123; Goldstein 2007).

During the first years under Chinese rule, the Seventeen Point Agreement was more or less honored. Life in Tibet did not change abruptly. However, the Chinese takeover had an immediate effect on trade. The United States sanctioned imports from Communist China, which meant that the booming wool trade through the Chumbi Valley came to a halt. As a consequence, Kalimpong's role as the most important trading hub was severely undermined. For Walung, however, this was a boon. Tamla Ukyab recounts:

> I think the best part of the trade happened from 1951 to 1958. Why? Because [when] the Chinese army marched into Tibet, they spent a lot of money. Chinese silver coins. . . . Another thing is that when the Tibetans started fleeing after 1956 . . . there were troubles in Tibet, you know. Then, lots of people started selling their things. So, our people used to go and buy these things. There were more Tibetan refugees than villagers [in Walung], and many of them were our relatives also. They brought with them yaks, sheep. . . . And those living close to the border, they brought all their furniture also. . . . Once the Tibetan refugees came into our village, they started to sell their things because they wanted to leave the village and proceed to Darjeeling, India, and other places. They could not carry all their belongings. They sold many things for very cheap prices. . . . So, I think, the business was at a peak. . . . Many people became very rich during those days.

Amid this boom, Tamla's family sent him to India for education. He accompanied his father on a business trip to Kolkata and a pilgrimage to Bodhgaya. Father and son took the train to Siliguri and traveled by bus to Darjeeling. Tamla remembers vividly how exciting all of this was and how sick he felt in the bus climbing up the curvy road to Darjeeling.

Tamla was enrolled at St. Joseph's School, North Point—one of India's most prestigious boarding schools. He was in the same hostel as the son of Tsarong, one of the most eminent figures in Lhasa and commander-in-chief of the Tibetan Army. The son of the fourteenth Dalai Lama's sister was also there. Tamla met John Kenneth Galbraith, the Harvard economist and leading figure of American liberalism who served as ambassador to India during the administration of President John F. Kennedy; after their encounter, a national Indian newspaper published an article on the North Point student who walked fifteen days to his mountain village during term breaks. In brief, at North Point, Tamla found himself among a cosmopolitan elite that embraced him for his unusual upbringing in the "remote" Himalayas.

While a school like North Point was out of reach for most Walungnga, the importance of education outside the village was widely acknowledged early on. The familiarity with the wider context of South Asia thereby gave the Walung trading families a head start, as Rabten, an elderly Walungnga living in Kathmandu, explains:

> Because [Walungnga] used to go to Kolkata and reach as many places as possible, [they] also had to deal with many different groups of people—such as Bihari, Bengali, and all the others—and even learned their languages. Right! Through their experience and hardship, they acquired practical knowledge. And because of that, our people understood the importance and the need of education for their children.

Politically on the sidelines yet geographically right at the center of the geopolitical shifts of the nineteenth and twentieth century, Walung's fortunes were always tied to its positionality at the margins of Nepal, India, and Tibet. To survive in Walung meant to be able to react to developments on the world stage by finding niches. Walung's remoteness from the centers of power provided it with a degree of autonomy while the prospect of prosperity depended on a continuous investment in connections to the outside world. Brokering relations were the core business of the Walungnga—be it through marital relations, trade, or sending children to schools outside the village to prepare them for their future role as middlemen. In other words, it is this particular nexus of remoteness and connectivity from which the efforts to tie places into the expanding knot emerged.

During the boom years of the 1950s, not all Walung families benefited in the same way, and prosperity was far from universal. Walung featured a high degree of social stratification and sheer inequality—a fact that the focus on the Walung elites, and particularly the goba family, in the few existing ethnographic accounts tends to eclipse (cf. Steinmann 1988, 1991; Fürer-Haimendorf 1975). The vast majority of Walungnga eked out a precarious livelihood at the margins of the lucrative trade in the village.

A typical way to make a living was to work for one of the richer trading families as a helper or servant. Such arrangements would either provide food, lodging, and a modest salary or, instead of an actual salary, a loan on which a helper could do some trade on his own. A servant would, for example, accompany a trader on his expedition to Tibet, carry goods, load pack animals, and cook food for his patron; in exchange, he would receive a loan of salt, which he would then barter for grain in the lower valleys over the winter. The profits he made were considered the compensation for the services rendered.[6]

Over time, reliable helpers would sometimes be entrusted with trading expeditions on their own, which facilitated helpers to carry out more side-business with money loaned from the patron, the waiver of interest being their salary. While bigger traders would often stay in Tibet for months during the trading season, their helpers traveled back and forth, sometimes as far as Kolkata. The responsibilities of trusted assistants could be considerable. One former assistant, for example, mentioned his jobs included carrying the silver coins for his patron. He was even tasked with bringing these coins to a place in Mustang where there was a market to exchange them for paper currency. He remembered vividly the small but heavy backpack he used for this purpose.

In winter, many poorer families would leave Walung for lower altitudes, either touring the villages to barter salt for grain or staying in semipermanent winter settlements where many would make a living by running teahouses, selling *tongba* (millet wine), *chang* (rice beer), and *momos* (Tibetan dumplings). Petty trade on limited or loaned capital and seasonal migration to the lower valleys was often combined with other activities, such as gathering and selling firewood or collecting medical plants. While most livelihood strategies were in one way or another tied into the larger economy of trade, not everyone was always a trader. Rabten, an elderly Walungnga now living in Kathmandu, gives a concise summary of this situation:

> In general, the people of Walung had no fixed occupation, and there also was no agriculture. Most would also not have the capital to trade. Life in those days was a bit weird. People would migrate to the lowlands in winter not because of the cold weather in Walung but to earn a little

money by selling chang and alcohol. With the money earned, they would buy food, grain. And gradually this would be taken back to Walung during the winter, so that they could consume it in summer. There were not many alternatives. All people in Walung used to trade according to the capital they had. Right!

A considerable part of economic activity was based on debt. Loans as small as a few rupees, even within extended families, were carefully recorded on little slips of paper. Signed in duplicate by both parties, they were kept safe and only destroyed once the loan was repaid. When not waived in favor of services provided, interest rates were high: typically a flat 25 percent.[7] These ensuing debt relations are a recurring topic in many Walung biographies. There are ample complaints about how rich families were getting richer on the work of the poor, and how only those with capital were really able to profit from trade.

The End of an Era

In 1956, a border treaty between Nepal and China introduced a passport regime for citizens of both countries. However, the treaty also included an exemption for inhabitants of the border districts "who cross the border to carry on petty trade, to visit friends or relatives, or for seasonal changes of residence." Border residents were allowed to continue crossing "as they have customarily done [heretofore] and need not hold passports, visas or other documents of certifications" (Pyakurel 2017, 3, para. 5.3). The Walungnga were still free to travel to Shigatse and Lhasa.

Around the same time, tensions in Tibet were on the rise. In 1956, the PLA bombed Litang monastery in Kham. In 1958, several armed resistance groups in eastern Tibet established the *Chushi Gangdruk* guerrillas. This Khampa movement gained the attention and support of the US Central Intelligence Agency (CIA). In a secret operation, Khampa fighters were brought to Camp Hale in Colorado for training and were then secretly parachuted back into Tibet. The United States began supplying the anticommunist Khampa guerrillas with arms and equipment (Shakya 1999, 169–196; McGranahan 2006, 2010; Andrugtsang 1973; Dewatshang 1997).

As conflict between Khampa guerrillas and the PLA became increasingly brutal in Kham, the Chushi Gangdruk gradually shifted its operations to central Tibet. In Lhasa, the Tibetan government under the fourteenth Dalai Lama came under increasing pressure to deal with the Khampa rebellion. At the same time, it became more and more obvious that the communists had little intention to follow through with their promise not to push through reforms. In March 1959, triggered by fears that the arrest of His Holiness was imminent, a rebellion erupted in the streets of Lhasa. Amid the uprising, the Dalai Lama fled to India (Shakya 1999, 221–49). In Tibet, the so-called democratic reforms started, burying the guarantees of the Seventeen Point Agreement for good (Shakya 1999, 277–318).

With the "democratic reforms," the old system of trans-Himalayan trade underwent an abrupt change. The trans-Himalayan traders based in northern Nepal, including the Walungnga, now had to deal with Chinese state authorities and fixed prices rather than with private Tibetan businesspeople.

Furthermore, in the spring of 1960, a border agreement (OGBIR 1965, 6) and a "Treaty of Peace and Friendship" (Kansakar 2001, app. III) were signed between the PRC and the Kingdom of Nepal. These accords stipulated the formal demarcation of a borderline by a joint boundary commission. The commission met four times and in October 1961 assented to a principal borderline that became officially recognized in the border treaty of 1961. Remaining details were settled over the next two years and integrated into the existing border treaty on January 23, 1963. For a brief period during these negotiations in 1962 and 1963, border trade came to a complete standstill.

Meanwhile, ever more Tibetan refugees arrived in Walung, following their leader into exile. Among them was a group of Khampa resistance fighters. After the Dalai Lama's escape, the Chushi Gangdruk decided to move their operations to northern Nepal. They established their main base in Mustang and several smaller camps in other places along the border, including Walung. The presence of Khampa fighters in the village led to a series of conflicts that threatened the authority of the old Walung elite. The goba family especially felt the pressure, Tamla remembers:

> I will tell you two things. First, once the Dalai Lama fled from Lhasa, abruptly, the freedom of our people to move within Tibet was restricted. Second, the Khampas started coming. So, there was a lot of insecurity felt by the local population. Lots of murders, looting, banditry happened in our village. . . . Mostly the rich people felt very insecure. Law and order were taken over by [the Khampas] for a few years. From 1962 to 1974 or something like that. They controlled virtually everything. Local people had no choice. These were trained people.

At the same time, the traditional authority of the goba also came under pressure through political developments in Nepal. After dissolving parliament in 1960, King Mahendra introduced the partyless Panchayat system, modeled on the Indian system of local governance. The Panchayat system, enshrined in Nepal's new constitution promulgated in December 1962, did away with the traditional authority of village leaders and replaced it with a village assembly and an elected mayor. In Walung, a member of the goba family was elected to this position. This caused latent tensions between the goba and another rich family to flare up and turn into an open feud. In 1963, Tshewang Damdu Ukyab, now officially the zonal Panchayat representative, was murdered under circumstances that were never fully investigated. Allegedly, he had demanded that the Khampa guerrillas surrender their weapons if they wanted to stay in the village, arguing that people felt insecure. The situation was complicated by the fact that one of the Khampas had married into the other rich family opposing the goba.

When Tamla learned of the murder, he was on his way from Darjeeling to Walung where he planned to spend his vacations. He turned back to Darjeeling, took his final exams, and later settled in Kathmandu. He never returned to Walung.

New Orientations

Amid these sweeping changes, a natural disaster took place: A flash flood, probably caused by a bursting glacial lake, undermined a section of the riverbank on which Walung was built. The flood happened in the summer of 1963. In the following months and years, somewhere between a third and half of the houses collapsed and were washed away.

By the time the flood hit Walung, most of the richer families had already started moving out on a more permanent basis. With the capital accumulated during the golden fifties, they had bought land in Darjeeling, Hile, Taplejung, and Kathmandu and were expanding their business enterprises into new domains. After the flood, middle- and lower-income families gradually followed suit, many of them focusing their efforts on what they had been doing anyway—running restaurants in bazaars or along trade routes, selling chang, or herding animals for the richer families. This kind of moving out is, again, better understood as a shift in the place-knot rather than simply abandoning the village.

The story of Lobsang illustrates this process well. Born into a poor household, he inherited his parents' debts. Working as a helper for a rich Walung family, he came to the conclusion that he would never be able to pay them off. He quit his service, took out another loan to repay the outstanding amount, and found a job as a herder for another rich Walung family. Instead of a salary, he entered into an arrangement called *bowma*, in which he was entitled to 50 percent of the profits from herding—including milk products and offspring—but would also have to bear 50 percent of any loss incurred. This shared profit-and-loss agreement allowed him to build his own herd, become an independent pastoralist, and accumulate capital. At one point, Lobsang owned a hundred female yaks and dzo (crossbreeds of yak and bull). He gave some animals to his daughter and her husband, who entered the same fifty-fifty arrangement with him. He sold the remaining animals and moved with this wife to Pashupatinagar at the border with India, where they opened a restaurant and sold chang. The plan did not work out, however. The place was cold and always foggy, he remembered. To run a restaurant, they had to buy firewood, which ate into their profits. They sold the restaurant after a few years, moved to Kathmandu, and opened a new one. With this and the income from the shared risk and profit arrangement with his daughter's family back in Walung, they now live a decent life.

Lobsang's story is typical for those who weathered the storms successfully. In many of the stories of upward social mobility, pastoralism plays a crucial role—often not as a family trade inherited from generation to generation but as an intermediary step with the goal to accumulate capital that could then be used to start a business. But pastoralism involves high risks. A harsh winter or a disease can always occur and decimate or even wipe out a herd carefully built over the years. This happened several times in living memory.

Walung biographies are littered with stories of setbacks and losses, be it in herding or in trade. One elderly woman, for example, complained that her father experienced one setback after the next. Once, he was arrested in Tibet; once he picked a fight with a Sikh at a train station in Kolkata and had to run away from the police, leaving his goods behind; once he invested in pigs to be sold in Darjeeling, but by the time he arrived, the price had fallen and he incurred a substantial loss. "My father wasted so much money," she said.

Despite the risks and uncertainties, most Walungnga kept one foot in trade. After 1963, business with Tibet picked up again, although in different ways and at a smaller scale than before. For the lower-income families, the exodus of the old elite also provided new opportunities. Those who stayed moved into the empty houses of the big trading families and began to take their place. The Walung houses with their shingled roofs require steady maintenance; shingles need to be replaced periodically, and without the permanent smoke from daily kitchen fires, the roofs start to leak. Such house-sitting arrangements are thus beneficial to both parties involved.

Those who started their own businesses had to adapt to the changing circumstances in Walung as well as in Tibet and the wider world. At times, the ever-changing situation opened unexpected possibilities. While the Cultural Revolution raged on in Tibet, for example, trade in Tibetan antiques became a lucrative business. It met with a global demand. The Tibetan exile community in Dharamsala successfully attracted global attention to the plight of the Tibetan people under communist rule. With Tibet in the news, public interest in Tibetan culture was

The children are told to stay back while the yaks are being unloaded. They wait eagerly to find out what present their father brought them from China. *Source*: Martin Saxer, 2012. www.theotherimage.com /arrivals-then-and-now/.

A yak caravan coming back from Tibet. *Source*: Martin Saxer, 2012. www.theotherimage.com/arrivals-then -and-now/.

gaining momentum in Europe and America. As a result, all things Tibetan, from Buddhist teachings to Tibetan art and jewelry, found buyers around the globe. Collectors were eager to acquire Tibetan antiques. An international market for Tibetan art and religious objects emerged in places like Vienna and New York. While monasteries in Tibet were being ravaged, a steady stream of such objects was pouring out of Tibet—safeguarded from destruction or simply looted, depending on one's point of view.

Meanwhile, people inside Tibet were still very much dependent on grain from Nepal. Poor and hungry Tibetans came across the border, bartering antiques, thangkas, and statues as well as their family jewels for grain. Many of these objects came through Walung. Like in the 1950s, political turmoil in Tibet led to new avenues to make profits.

After the antiques business dried up, other opportunities emerged. When China's economic fortunes began to improve with the economic reforms under Deng Xiaoping, demand for all kinds of consumer goods from India, especially luxury items like wristwatches, was rising. As the border between India and China had been more or less hermetically sealed in the aftermath of the 1962 Sino-Indian War, Nepal regained the paramount position in trans-Himalayan trade that it had lost at the beginning of the century. Remote and comparatively unmonitored border crossings such as Tipta La, the pass above Walung, were ideally suited for such endeavors.

Later, in the 1990s and the 2000s, the trade in wildlife parts became a lucrative business. While trade in fur for festive Tibetan robes and animal parts used in Tibetan and Chinese medicines has a long history in the Himalayas and was hardly considered an illicit activity, rising prosperity in China led to a surge in demand, and the pressure to enforce the Convention on International Trade in Endangered Species of Wild Fauna and Flora (CITES) increased. As a result, the routes of trade moved to more remote and less controlled border areas (Saxer 2013b, 43). Like elsewhere along the border, everything from tiger bones and leopard skins to rhino horns and pangolin scales found its way through Walung. However, this business has recently moved deeper underground (or maybe just further east, to Myanmar)—not least because the Dalai Lama publicly denounced it in 2006 and the Chinese authorities increased their scrutiny.[8]

In brief, with Walung's role and position shifting from a vibrant entrepôt of trans-Himalayan trade to a peripheral and relatively unmonitored border village, business opportunities became increasingly linked to endeavors more difficult to justify, more squarely illegal, and often more risky in new ways. Whereas in the old days, when trading expeditions to Tibet feared roaming bandits and traders always carried arms, the risks today revolve around checkpoints, border guards, and Chinese police.[9]

Besides trade now branded as smuggling or trafficking, other opportunities emerged. Contrary to the situation in the 1950s and 1960s, when Tibetans relied on Nepal for basic provisions, most of what people in Nepal's border region eat, wear, and use in their daily lives is now imported from China. Today, the old ground-floor storerooms in the large Walung houses are filled with shoes, clothes, kitchen utensils, detergent, soft drinks, rice, wheat flour, Lhasa beer, and Chinese liquor to be sold in the valleys further south. In addition, trade in medicinal herbs used in Tibetan and Chinese medicines has emerged as a major source of income over the past decades. In the Walung area, *chiraito* (Swertia chirayita, Tibetan: *tigta*) and *kutki* (Tibetan: *honglen*) are the main species traded. Other income opportunities include weaving traditional Walung carpets that are in high demand in Kathmandu and raising yaks to be sold to Tibet. The latter, however, has recently become more difficult because of a stricter veterinary regime in China. These developments directly affected Walung livelihoods.

Dawa's story is a point in case. He grew up in a herder family in Yangma. When he was around eight years old, the family sold their livestock and moved to Taplejung, the district headquarters. Dawa and his siblings went to school, while his father would go to Tibet for trade and his mother sold chang and dry meat. After three or four years, realizing that they were unable to make progress, the family moved back to Yangma, bought livestock again, and Dawa worked as a herder. Still in his teens, he married a woman from Tibet. The marriage, however, did not work out. In his mid-twenties, Dawa married again, this time a woman from a neighboring village. Since his share of the family's herd was just a dozen animals and not enough to establish a household of his own, Dawa left the livestock with his parents and moved to Walung together with his wife. He started collecting medicinal plants, cutting wood, and selling planks to Tibet. His wife wove carpets. Then, selling the livestock that was still with his parents, Dawa started trading. He would buy red corals in Tibet and sell them in Nepal. With the income from these activities, the family gradually expanded their business. They established a camp site for the odd trekking group passing by and also began raising yak calves and selling them in Tibet.

Where to Go Next?

Walung life continues to evolve in a knot of places—also for those without the means to settle in Kathmandu or overseas. Dawa's biography, moving from a village in the region to the district headquarters and back to the village before settling in Walung, is quite typical. Despite the many crises Walung went through since the late 1950s, the village has not ceased to be an entrepôt. While families continue to leave Walung with the aim to establish themselves outside, other families from surrounding areas still keep moving in or moving back. There is hardly an empty house in Walung today. However, only three or four are still occupied by the same family as a generation ago. As a result, Walung has not become a village of grandparents and young children sustained by outside remittances. While there is money flowing into the village from abroad, Walung is also still a place where capital can be accumulated. Profits from trade continue to flow out and pay for children attending school in Kathmandu.

Most of the families resident in Walung today, however, do not expect to stay for good. The vast majority already has family members living in Taplejung, Kathmandu, or abroad. Most do not see their children living permanently in the village. Unlike in other Himalayan villages where agriculture requires continuous labor—maintaining terraces and irrigation channels, for example—the village itself is less important in the case of Walung. As long as its positionality facilitates upward social mobility, Walung will keep its place in the knot.

The question that haunts most of the Walungnga I met—both in Walung and in Kathmandu—is thus not so much where to settle for good, but where to go next and when. What is the "right" moment and the "right" place for the next step? While economic opportunities are clearly important, many other considerations play a role in these decisions, including the wish to facilitate the best possible education for one's children and the ambition to provide a comfortable life for one's parents—preferably in Kathmandu, where they can spend their old age circumambulating the Boudha Stupa and gain religious merit.

Dawa, for example, toyed with the idea of leaving Walung for Kathmandu so that his children would have a better chance to move abroad in the future. But other considerations were also important, he explained:

> After this year's earthquake, I changed my mind. We are hearing that there is a shortage of gas and petrol in Kathmandu, and people have been cooking food on kitchen fires. So, that too makes me uneasy about the idea of moving to a place like Kathmandu. For the next couple of years, I don't have any plan to move. Maybe, if my children would go . . . but if I go, then at least I must have the money to buy a small house so that I won't have to pay rent. If I have a house to live in, I could make a living as a trekking guide or with some small business. Otherwise, I'd struggle a lot and would always have to appease the landlord. That's what my parents are going through in Kathmandu at the moment. So, I don't like to move to Kathmandu for this very reason as well. I don't deny that it is a good place to gain religious merit, but without a secure income, it would be a disaster to move. For example, my uncle Gyatso moved to Kathmandu, but they came back to Walung this year. He says, he won't return. And Grandpa Ghulik is also not willing to return to Kathmandu. But we forced him and sent him back in a helicopter.

Walung, with its absence of agriculture and paramount importance of business, with its history and positionality, is a special case. It does not represent the general situation of villages in the Himalayan borderlands. What Walung does offer, however, is a particular vantage point that demands a critical rethinking of locality, community, and mobility. Walung's role and position in the place-knot of which it is part is clearly more than a nostalgic attachment to a place of origin. Walung is a place where people move out but also still move in, with the expectation to move up.

The question is whether the notion of place-knots has any analytic value beyond this specific case. To answer this question, we need to turn our attention to Himalayan border areas where trade is equally important but where the investment of labor in agriculture exerts more gravity than in Walung. Chapter 3 takes on this task by looking at Upper Humla in the northwestern corner of Nepal.

In front of Yonten's house, Waltse, Limi Valley. *Source*: Martin Saxer, 2016.

INTERLUDE

A Son's Uncertain Ambitions

"How is he doing? Has he found work on a construction site?" Yonten asks.

We are sitting in a smoky kitchen in Waltse, one of the three villages in the Limi Valley in Nepal's district of Humla.[1] Butter tea is being prepared. The question is directed at a neighbor who has just dropped by. A few days earlier, the neighbor came back from Purang, the county seat across the border in Tibet, where she spent the summer earning money on a Chinese construction site. Yonten, the woman of the house, is eager for news about her son, who is also in Purang.

"He is doing well, but he is not working in construction" the neighbor relays. "He is just helping out in a friend's shop these days."

The neighbor briefly inquires about me and my research assistant—where I am from, where we are heading, how long we are planning to stay. Waltse sees only a few dozen foreigners a year, and most of them set up tents at the campground that the Youth Club in Waltse operates near the health post outside the village. We, however, "do the circle" (*kora kyab*), as people call the system of providing hospitality to outside guests on a rotational basis: one night per house is the village rule, making sure that burden and income are equally shared among the households of the village.

The water is boiling, and Yonten pauses for a moment to churn the tea with butter and salt. She fills the steaming white liquid into a Chinese thermos and pours a cup for each of us. She is agitated. Since we arrived, she has talked about nothing else than her son's uncertain ambitions and all that is at stake. Like many others, her son has studied outside the village at one of the Tibetan Children's

Villages (TCV) in India. A foreigner sponsored his education up to class twelve, for which they were grateful. But now, the sponsor encouraged him to continue his studies and even offered to pay for a university degree. The family finds this turn of events utterly unhelpful. Now it is time for the son to come home, marry, and take up his responsibilities in the village. Yonten is angry about the sponsor's interference. "Should he ever turn up here, I will kill him," she says.

The parents have arranged for their son to marry a beautiful girl from the neighboring village. The arrangement has been in place for seventeen years now. The family invested more than US$2,000 to keep the promise alive. The son has completed his TCV education a couple years ago. Since then, he roamed around, postponing the marriage and showing little ambition to settle down. And now the sponsor's offer has made things even more complicated. The bride and her family are suffering from the limbo in which they find themselves, and they increasingly put pressure on Yonten and her husband.

Marriage, a house, and a place in the community against some useless degree in India—that this was even a choice Yonten finds difficult to understand. The longer teenagers and young adults are away from the village, the higher the chances that they start toying with the thought of leaving for good. What, then, will happen with the house, the land, and the parents? Complaints about young adults who spent long years in Kathmandu or India and then have to be taught even the most basic skills of agropastoral life back home are frequent in the village.[2] Education is important, yes. But gambling the future of the household on this opportunity would obviously not be worth it, right?

Waltse has strict village rules that demand the presence and active engagement of adults in community affairs. An elaborate system of fines makes those who do not attend the frequent and compulsory village meetings pay for their absences.

While Yonten discusses the problem with the neighbor, the story of two boys from Limi studying in Kathmandu comes up. Both fell in love with Tamang girls, and both were immediately called home. Up to now, most Limi men have married within the valley—not because there would be a taboo against marrying outsiders, but rather because parents insist that only a Limi girl is actually useful and up to the task of managing the hard and stressful life up here. One young man from the neighboring village married a German woman. He is referred to as the *chigyal magpa*, the overseas groom, echoing the old Tibetan custom that a family with no male offspring "adopts" a husband into the family, granting him all the patrilineal rights of a biological son. The chigyal magpa left the valley for good. Yonten worries that something similar could happen with her son if she doesn't find a way to bring him back.

Of the roughly ninety households in Waltse, the vast majority has at least one member working on Chinese construction sites in Purang over the summer. The village is almost empty during this time. It is 2016, and thirty-four houses have shut their doors completely over the summer months as all members ventured out to find work outside. Now, it is late September and people are coming back. The next month will be extremely busy in Limi. First, the grass along the barley fields needs to be cut and dried on the flat roofs for the winter; the yaks have to be brought down from the summer pastures; and soon, the barley harvest will begin. Between late November and late April or May, the passes are closed, and the valley is cut off from the rest of Nepal. Right after the harvest, before the snow, many leave again to spend the winter doing business outside the valley or collecting maple burls to make *phuru*—wooden bowls sold for a good price in Tibet—in the jungles of Uttaranchal, the Indian state bordering Nepal in the west.

Yonten refills our cups and inquires with her neighbor about her son's plans for the winter. Will he stay in the valley or leave? She raises the issue of whether to call him home. If she found a way to persuade him to spend the winter here, she reasons, he may find his way back into village life. The winters are cold but also a time of leisure and fun, a time of festivals and marriage ceremonies. However, putting pressure on her son to spend the winter in Waltse may keep him away even more, she fears. Harvesting is hard work, and he might get bored and then escape to Kathmandu. Yonten considers sending a message to him in Purang, saying that she and her husband will manage just fine harvesting barley on their own, and that he should not feel obliged to come and assist them. This, she hopes, may help sway him to spend the winter in Limi and, maybe, develop feelings for the beautiful girl who is waiting for him.

The neighbor takes leave, and Yonten hurries back to her fields to cut grass. We stay in the smoky kitchen for another few cups of tea. Sagar, my friend and research assistant, cannot help comparing the situation to his own village in a valley nearby. He knows Limi well, as he worked here coordinating the projects of a local nongovernmental organization (NGO). He understands what is at stake. Nevertheless, he continues to be startled by all the village rules in Waltse and the pressure put on young people to forgo their educational ambitions in favor of assuming their duties in the village. We talk about Walung and the young outwardly oriented people I got to know there. No comparable village rules limit their ambitions. How come Himalayan villages have developed such different approaches to maintaining the knots of place and community, such different visions of their future?

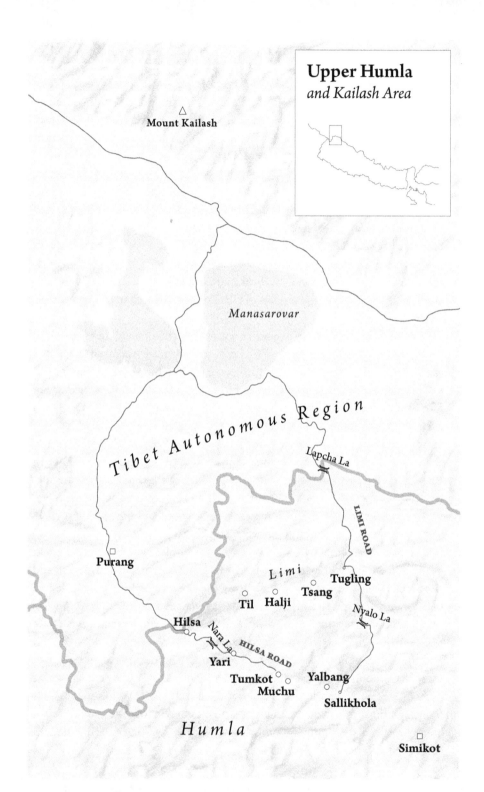

Map of Upper Humla and the Kailash area. *Source*: Martin Saxer, 2019.

BINDING RULES

To some extent, each village and every valley in the Himalayas has its own way of relating to the outside world, of being entangled in place-knots. The closer one looks, the more apparent are the differences and idiosyncratic histories that have shaped the role and position of a place in wider geographical contexts. Walung, as mentioned in chapter 2, is a rather special case for its absence of agriculture and almost exclusive reliance on trade. In this chapter, I juxtapose the case of Walung with stories from Upper Humla, the northern part of the district of Humla in western Nepal, and address the question of how communities are forging place-knots in the context of lifestyles where trade is only one of several strategies to make a living.

However, before starting this endeavor, it is important to step back and stress a number of similarities. Like Walung and the upper Tamor Valley, Upper Humla is home to predominantly Tibetan-speaking communities with long-standing ties to Tibet. Trans-Himalayan trade in salt, grain, wool, and other goods has equally been a mainstay in this region. And like in Walung, trade did not stop after 1959. In fact, the Kailash area of western Tibet bordering Humla has remained dependent on Nepali grain for much longer than the region of central Tibet across the border from Walung.

Walung and Upper Humla also have in common that both have been at the very margin of tourism development in Nepal, which has fundamentally re-shaped other border areas. In the Annapurna and Everest regions, for example, mountaineering and trekking tourism has by and large replaced the erstwhile trans-Himalayan trade as the main source of prosperity. The old trading relations were thereby replaced with new connections to the wider world.[1] Lacking the kind of cosmopolitanism that comes with international mountaineering and trekking tourism, Walung and Upper Humla are typically described as the most remote areas of Nepal. Remoteness is a relative condition not only in relation to urban centers but also the main tourist regions.

Another similarity between Walung and the villages of Waltse and Dzang in the Limi Valley is that all three are said to be founded by seven families from Tibet (Hovden 2016, 45), framing their history as an expansion of the Tibetan world. And, like in Walung, a considerable part of the population lives at least partly outside the region—many of them in Boudha in Kathmandu and Queens, New York, mingling with other translocal Himalayan communities.[2]

The difference between Walung and Upper Humla lies in the ways in which agropastoralism and trade were entangled. In the case of Walung, transportation between the village and Tibet was mainly provided by yak caravans, while south of Walung, goods were mainly carried by porters up and down the valleys. As elsewhere in eastern Nepal, portering still provides an income opportunity that does not require any capital investment. In Humla and most parts of western Nepal, portering never had the same relevance. The transportation of salt and grain was predominantly carried out by sheep and goat caravans that slowly made their way up and down the valleys with the seasons. Their movement was closely tied to the agricultural cycle of the year.

Waltse. *Source*: Martin Saxer, 2011.

After the autumn harvest, the sheep and goats would arrive in the village and graze on the harvested fields for about twenty days, thereby providing manure. The families with small numbers of sheep and goats would allow other itinerant herders to graze in their fields. Then, the sheep and goats would start moving down the valleys to spend the winter in the jungles of the districts south of Humla. A few families would join their herds, pooling labor and sharing responsibilities. Every family would send at least one member—often a young man or women—to stay with the herds over the winter. There are many stories of couples that found themselves building their relation outside the village in the privacy of a nomadic camp.

During the winter, the male sheep and goats would be separated from the females and their offspring. The latter stayed in the forest while the former were taken further down to the plains—the Terai region near the Indian border— carrying the salt bought in Tibet. This salt was sold or bartered for grain. In addition, the herders would offer transportation services when required. Then, in late winter or early spring, the herds were reunited and slowly began moving up the valleys again, carrying grain. They would reach the villages of Upper Humla around May—just in time to spend a couple of weeks on the nonirrigated fields before the summer crops were sown.[3] In late May or June, the sheep and goat caravans would slowly move further up the valleys and cross into Tibet. On the Changthang—the Tibetan Plateau—the herds would again be separated. The females and newborns stayed behind while the male sheep and goats moved back and forth between the summer pastures and the trade marts or the salt lakes where grain was bartered for salt. At the end of the summer, the herds would slowly move down again, reaching the villages after the harvest.

In the villages of Upper Humla, agricultural and pastoral cycles thus met twice a year: around May on the way up and in late October one the way down. As there was no communication between herders and farming villages for most of the year, people relied on signs of nature to synchronize their activities—a specific bird arriving in the valley, for example.

This form of itinerant pastoralist trade requires a more or less steady amount of labor; the agricultural cycle, however, is characterized by several labor peaks. The first such peak is from May to July. First, in May, the fields need to be plowed and the summer crops sown in places where two crops are possible. Then, in June and July, the winter crops need to be harvested and the second crop sown on irrigated fields. This is the busiest period in the villages. From late July to September, people would usually venture out to find paid work or collect medicinal plants. In the second half of September, grass needs to be cut for the winter and the harvesting of summer crops begins—the second labor peak in the cycle. Between October and May, there is not much work on the fields. During this time, people would look for other sources of income. In summary, this means that a substantial part (often the majority) of the population is occupied outside the village for eight to nine months per year.

The rhythms of pastoral and agricultural cycles are, of course, subject to considerable variation in the different villages of Upper Humla, depending on altitude and the possibilities for irrigation. This blueprint of relations between itinerant caravans and sedentary agriculture is based on data from Kermi, a village at an altitude of about 3,000 meters, which has access to a hot spring used for irrigation. In Kermi, two crops per year are possible, and the yields are sufficient to cover basic grain consumption for most families. Overall, however, agriculture and pastoralism do not guarantee subsistence in Upper Humla. Grain produced locally typically covers only four to five months of a family's yearly needs. Of course, there is considerable variation between households in a village, depending on individual landholdings and water rights. For villages where only a single crop per year is feasible, agriculture requires less labor and thus leaves people with more time, but also more urgency, to earn money outside—either by foraging, working as paid labor, or pursuing business opportunities. However, it would be wrong to see itinerant trade as a matter of last resort in a context where agriculture does not guarantee subsistence. Even in Kermi, blessed with a hot spring used for irrigation, every household kept a herd of sheep and goats until quite recently. Those moving up and down with the herds are not called herders but *tsongpa*—traders.

The situation is slightly different in Limi, where the vignette preceding this chapter took place. As the northernmost valley of Humla, Limi lies south of the Gurla Mandhata Massif in Tibet but north of the main passes that separate the southern flanks of the Himalayas from the Tibetan Plateau. Snow cuts off the valley from the rest of Nepal during winter. This is one reason why Limi was always more oriented toward Tibet than other villages in Upper Humla. The three Limi villages traditionally paid head taxes (*mi khral*) to Tibet but land taxes (*sa khral*) to Nepal (Goldstein 1975, 90; Hovden 2016, 39). Only in the process of border demarcation in the early 1960s, Limi was placed unambiguously within the borders of the Kingdom of Nepal. The area was part of an estimated 500 square kilometers of disputed territory that China surrendered to Nepal (OGBIR 1965, 6).

The main trade route between Upper Humla and Tibet passed by the upper tip of the Limi Valley. Limi was thus ideally positioned to engage in trans-Himalayan trade. Several seasonal trade marts operated along this route. However, the border demarcation had a much more direct impact in Limi than elsewhere in Humla. The list of six official border crossings stipulated in the 1963 border protocol did not include the Lapcha Pass on the border between Limi and

Summer pasture on the way to Limi Lapcha, the pass that leads to Tibet.
Source: Martin Saxer, 2011.

Tibet. As a result, trade along this route became illegal. Hilsa, a formerly less important crossing, was chosen as the official border post.

Limi's location in the trans-Himalayas also meant that the winter pastures used by Limi herders were traditionally not in the jungles of the lower valleys but on the Tibetan Plateau. This may seem counterintuitive at first, as the Tibetan Plateau is even higher and colder than the Limi Valley itself. The reason is that the Himalayan valleys receive much snow during the winter, while the windswept Tibetan Plateau remains largely free of snow. This makes it possible for yak and Tibetan sheep to survive. The traditional winter pastures of several Himalayan communities were located within Tibet. The 1963 border protocol led to a loss of access to pastureland on the Tibetan Plateau, which was highly disruptive for agropastoral economies throughout Nepal's Himalayas (Goldstein and Messerschmidt 1980; Bauer 2004).

In Limi, the restrictions on cross-border grazing were introduced gradually. For some years after the demarcation, a system of pasture usage fees (*tsa rin*) continued to allow limited access. However, as Melvyn Goldstein reports, by the mid-1970s, people in Limi were reluctant to continue investing in pastoralism, given the uncertain prospects. Based on data from the village of Dzang, agriculture and pastoralism combined accounted for 57 percent of the village's basic subsistence needs in 1974 (Goldstein 1975, 95). By the end of the 1980s, Limi had lost all pasture rights in Tibet. Cut off from access to winter pastures and with trade rerouted through Hilsa, Limi found itself a remote and literally out-of-the-way place. This change in positionality raised the stakes to find alternative means of income generation.

Salt, Grain, and Labor

As elsewhere in the Himalayas, trade in Tibetan salt and Nepali grain was the backbone of Upper Humla's trading economy for centuries. Like in Walung, Chinese rule in Tibet after the so-called democratic reforms and the demarcation of the border brought a profound change about the region. In Humla, however, this change was less of a rupture compared to other places along the border. The main reason for this was that demand for grain remained high in Tibet for decades to come—not least because army personnel and road construction workers had to be fed along with the local residents. Consequently, caravan trade did not decrease. Christoph von Fürer-Haimendorf visited the area in 1972 and witnessed bustling trade fairs in Upper Humla; Nepalis were allowed to go to Purang, and Purangbas came down to Yari and Yalbang. He noted that the inhabitants in villages on the Nepal side appeared "relatively prosperous," and few sought other employment or business opportunities (Fürer-Haimendorf 1975, 253–56).

Starting around the mid-1970s, a slow decline in trade began. In 1973, the government of India pledged to assist Nepal in fighting the widespread problem of iodine deficiency responsible for the high levels of goiter and cretinism throughout the country (Siva 2010; Commonwealth Legal Information Institute 1973). Tibetan salt was not "fortified" with iodine, and India was the only source of industrially processed, iodized salt. India agreed to bear the cost of 100,000 tons of Indian salt per year, covering Nepal's entire yearly demand. In addition, India also subsidized transport to twenty "inaccessible districts of Nepal"—including Humla (Commonwealth Legal Information Institute 1973, annex 1; Goldstein and Messerschmidt 1980). Consequently, Tibetan salt lost much of its value, and the salt-grain trade became less profitable.

To a certain extent, just like in Walung, other forms of trans-Himalayan trade—in antiques and wildlife parts, for example—replaced the income from the salt trade. Although these new forms of trade in high-value items were no longer directly dependent on sheep and goats for transportation, the caravans continued. Not only Tibet was dependent on grain from the south, but also the villages in Humla themselves. What finally led most families in Upper Humla to sell their sheep and goats around the turn of the millennium were two other factors: community forestry and education.

In the 1990s, community forestry became an integral part of Nepal's strategy to safeguard its forests from what was then seen as an imminent ecological disaster. Handing over the management of forest to community forest user groups promised to put an end to overuse—the classical "tragedy of the commons." The idea, well-tested in other places around the globe, is directly based on the notion of the "local community" and its role as a steward of the environment in which the people live. Community forestry in Nepal is commonly seen as a story of success; it had a measurable impact on the health of forests. At the same time, however, community forestry had the side-effect that itinerant herders lost their traditional winter grazing grounds in the jungles south of Humla. Local forest user groups either obstructed access, demanded prohibitively high grazing fees, or simply expelled the caravans with force. A series of violent confrontations between forest user groups and caravan traders in the late 1990s led most families in Upper Humla to eventually give up and sell their herds (Saxer 2013b, 44–47).

The second reason for the end of caravan trade was education. Sending children to school greatly increased the problem of labor shortage. With rising numbers of teenagers studying at boarding schools outside Humla, it became very difficult for families to ask their children to herd sheep and goats rather than to go to school.

This leads us the question of labor, which is directly tied to income strategies in the triangle of trade, pastoralism, and agriculture. A household engaging in all three needs many hands. During the labor-intensive phases of the agricultural cycle, the caravans are usually not in the village, and the terms of school follow a rhythm that is difficult to reconcile with both. The challenge to synchronize these different temporalities requires decisions: What is central for current livelihoods and future plans and what is less important?

A Humli friend once said while walking up the Karnali Valley during the harvest season that visitors always seem to see only agriculture; those foraging for herbs and mushrooms, or those pursuing business outside the valley naturally remain invisible. The fields present themselves as the center of life, and the people working in the fields are assumed to be first and foremost peasants. The same is true of development work (to which I will come back in part III of this book), which usually focuses on agriculture and the value chains of agricultural output. Moreover, much of anthropological writing on the Himalayas also puts agriculture center stage. Even Christoph von Fürer-Haimendorf's *Himalayan Traders* (1975) or James Fisher's *Trans-Himalayan Traders* (1986) begin with chapters on settlement patterns and the farming economy—despite their titles. In all these perspectives, agriculture is taken as the implicit core of life—*supported* by pastoralism and, if necessary, *supplemented* by trade. Accordingly, Himalayan businesspeople are not seen as "natural traders" but rather as engaged in "enforced trading," as Francis Lim puts it in his study of the Langtang Valley (Lim 2008, 63). Considering that even a village like Kermi, where agricultural subsistence is feasible, engaged no less in caravan trade, that trading villages in the Himalayas are typically richer than those primarily based on agriculture, and that prosperity is generally associated with business in the Himalayas, I believe that this logic is putting the cart before the horse (Saxer 2016b, 109). Today, as families need to raise cash for school fees and to buy basic provisions from China, households have even more reasons not to invest all their labor in farming.

Keeping a Household in Place

In Upper Humla, households traditionally depend on the pooling of labor—especially male labor—to balance the labor needs of agriculture, pastoralism, and trade. The form that makes this possible is fraternal polyandry: the norm that all brothers of a family marry one woman. Ideally, one brother would reside in the village and take care of the fields, while his other brothers would engage in pastoralism and trade, respectively.

Fraternal polyandry in Tibetan societies—and especially in Humla where the polyandric household was, and in Limi still is, the default—has been a source of continuing fascination for anthropologists (Goldstein 1976, 1981; Levine 1988; Haddix McKay and Gurung 1999; Childs 2003; Bauer 2004, 22–23). Fraternal polyandry has mostly been explained from the perspective of population growth and agricultural needs. It is understood as a means to guarantee that a family's limited agricultural resources (land and associated water rights) are not further split into unsustainably small entities through inheritance. This keeps population growth in check and thus helps ensure a balance between ecological constraints and demographic development (Levine and Silk 1997).

The inner workings, advantages, and conflicts arising from polyandric marriages are a topic many of my friends and interlocutors from Humla keep returning to in discussions. Although, except for Limi, polyandry is no longer expected, most of the younger people I know grew up in polyandric households. Many have experienced these households breaking apart, and all have witnessed the strong prejudice against fraternal polyandry within mainstream Nepali society, where it carries connotations of promiscuity and prostitution. However, the many highly emotional conversations I had on this topic never emphasized cultural values or the problem of inheritance; nor was polyandry typically explained to me by a concern for population growth (a point that has lost its urgency anyway as depopulation has eclipsed the former concern with overpopulation). The main advantage of polyandry, as explained to me over and over again, is rather that it keeps male labor in a family and makes it strong and prosperous. The bond of brothers in one household is seen as a precondition to expand a family's reach and diversify its income strategies. While taking care of the fields binds one brother to the village, the others are free to roam and extend their business ventures to new domains.[4]

In Limi, the polyandric norm is also closely related to monastic institutions. Households with two or more sons are obliged to send one of them to the monastery. The present-day remoteness of Limi, one monk from Waltse explained to me, is a problem in this respect: Not being on the circuit of international Buddhism makes it much harder to find potent *jindaks* and enmesh them in sponsoring relationships. Unlike in richer and larger monastic institutions where monks are taken care for, the Limi monasteries fully depend on their monks sustaining themselves. Monks remain part of a polyandric household and have the freedom to spend time outside the villages to earn money.

In Limi, and particularly in Waltse, the largest of the three villages, the norm of polyandry and the necessities of providing for the monastery are woven into a fabric of tight village laws. These laws stipulate a number of rules geared toward keeping the community tied to the village and ensuring that households, depending on size and category, provide monks for the village and that rituals continue to be sponsored.

Astrid Hovden (2016) draws a detailed picture of these villages laws, the system of monk levy, and the taxes and ritual obligations that come with it.[5] Many village meetings are compulsory, at least for the household heads. Absence, for whatever reason, is punished with a fine. The rules (as mentioned in the story told in the interlude preceding this chapter) are of great concern to young adults. Breaking the rules without paying fines implies losing one's rights and privileges in the community.

Village rules do not forbid enterprises outside Limi. Most working-age people from Limi, like their peers from other villages in Upper Humla, spend most of the year outside the valley, even if this means paying fines. Even the monks are allowed to seek employment on Chinese construction sites during the summer.[6] What the rules do is ensure that outside activity remains tied to the village and its resident population.

In other words, fraternal polyandry and village rules appear as a means to keep a village at the heart of an expanding place-knot. They allow for a household to diversify its activities while preventing (or raising the cost of) more permanent out-migration. The polyandric system is thereby neither just a relic of old ways nor a function of ecological constraints. Within the specific context at stake, it simply resonates with a particular socioeconomic situation. It offers one of several culturally adequate responses to the entangled problems of labor, land, and income generation, which necessarily takes place outside the valley.

New Business, Foraging, Labor

Outside Limi, polyandry and strict village rules have more or less dissolved over the past generation. And even in the Limi Valley, the strictness of rules and norms faces increasing pressure. This, I argue, has to be seen against the background of the overall decline of the importance of agriculture and the rise of new opportunities no longer entangled with the agropastoral system: a new form of border trade, foraging, and paid labor. Let me explain these opportunities one by one.

In the early 2000s, many families in Upper Humla found themselves in a crunch. They had sold their sheep and goats; the antiques business had long dried up and the booming trade in wildlife that marked much of the 1990s and early 2000s came under increasing pressure. Around the same time, the construction of the Qinghai–Tibet railway to Lhasa (opened in 2006) and the subsequent upgrading of roads throughout Tibet made transportation of goods to western Tibet substantially cheaper. The new roads in Tibet led to a situation in which Himalayan valleys still lacking road access from the south are now much easier accessible from the north. The Walung area and Upper Humla are only two such cases in point. Consumer goods and staples (e.g., wheat flour, cooking oil, and increasingly also rice) are now imported from China. This latest revival of trans-Himalayan trade began in the mid-2000s and turned into a veritable boom in the early 2010s. Following the same old routes, this new China trade triggered the reemergence of seasonal trade marts at the roadheads in Upper Humla. Many young Humli who had been looking for a life elsewhere decided to come back and seize on these new opportunities (Saxer 2017).

Together with this revival of trans-Himalayan trade, a rush for natural resources swept across the Himalayas. Bolstered by the booming herbal medicine industries in India and China, demand for medicinal raw materials increased manifold. This led to a sharp rise in herb prices and the emergence of a booming resource-based frontier economy. While the collection of fungi and medicinal plants has long been part and parcel of the diverse income strategies of Himalayan households, expectations of quick and easy profits drew many young Humli to rediscover foraging as a promising avenue to prosperity—an avenue that neither requires a degree nor capital.

The commodity that stands like no other for this gold rush is Ophiocordyceps sinensis, known as *yartsagunbu* in Nepal and Tibet. *Yartsagunbu*, a caterpillar fungus sometimes dubbed "Himalayan Viagra" for its alleged properties, became popular in China in the mid-2000s and prices have since skyrocketed. A pound of high-quality yartsagunbu costs up to US$40,000 in Hong Kong; total revenue from Himalayan yartsagunbu is estimated to be more than US$1 billion per year (Winkler 2017, 63). While Humla is not one of the major collection areas many young Humli venture into the neighboring districts of Bajang and Darchula during the collection season in May and June.

Apart from *yartsagunbu*, several other species of medicinal herbs are collected in high volume in Humla and its neighboring mountain districts, including Paris polyphylla (*satuwa*), Nardostachys jatamansi (spikenard, Nepali: *jatamansi*, Tibetan: *pangpo*), and Picrorhiza scrophulariiflora (Nepali: *kutki*, Tibetan: *honglen*).

Moreover, the long-standing business in *phuru*, the wooden bowls turned from the burls of trees, preferably maple, took off. Making phuru was originally a hallmark of Limi craftsmen. The burls are a rare find in Humla today. Phuru collectors expanded their foraging expeditions to Darchula and the Indian state of Uttarakhand. Collection has become increasingly risky. In most places where maple burls can still be found, their harvesting is now outlawed by the regulations of national parks, conservation areas, and community forests. The burls collected in India are no longer made in Limi; they are roughly shaped by a couple of professional wood-turning workshops in one little town in India and then carried across the border as processed wooden items. The finishing is now mostly done by a few workshops in Kathmandu. From Kathmandu, the finished phuru are then brought back to Humla and sold in Purang across the border in Tibet. The phuru business, thus, has transformed from a local craft into a transnational business based on foraging and centralized semi-industrial production.

The average price of a phuru in Tibet is between 300 to 500 in Chinese yuan renminbi (CNY) or US$44 to $72; the highest-quality phuru are sold for several thousand dollars in US currency. According to one collector who participated in six phuru expeditions and knows the business well, profits from five months of foraging are about US$5,000 per person—a substantial cash income in Upper Humla. In 2014 and 2015, an estimated 10,000 phuru reached the Tibetan market. The Limi villages no longer play an active part in the production of phuru; trade, however, remains predominantly in the hands of Limi businesspeople.

In Limi, the most important source of income today is paid labor on the Chinese construction sites in Purang. This labor market is a direct outcome of the Chinese development agenda. At the turn of the millennium, the People's Republic of China (PRC) launched the Great Western Development Program (*xibu dakaifa*) to narrow the growing gap between China's booming coastal region and its western hinterlands. The program established a policy framework in which substantial investments, predominantly in infrastructure, were channeled to the western part of the country. In 2006, Beijing embarked on the "Building a New Socialist Countryside Campaign" to modernize rural villages and county seats. Initially, these programs had little momentum in western Tibet. After the Lhasa uprising of March 2008 and violent clashes in Urumqi in 2009, however, the initiative was pushed at a tremendous pace, and the state's investment in infrastructure triggered a sharp rise in the demand for manual labor. Restrictions on mobility in Tibet following the 2008 incident and a general mistrust among Chinese authorities against Tibetans led to a labor shortage in Purang County. In this context, more and more people from Limi found work on construction sites in Purang.

Construction work in Purang is well paid. Workers from Limi earn between CNY 150 and 180 per day—substantially more than in other places in China and several times an average salary in Nepal. In a month of work in Purang, a Limi laborer earns up to CNY 4,000—the equivalent of 60,000 in Nepalese rupee (NPR). By comparison, a teacher's salary in Nepal is about NPR 9,000. Working in Purang quickly became the main source of income in Limi. By 2011, almost every household had at least one person working in construction; by 2016, the vast majority of able-bodied Limi residents spent the summer helping build a new socialist China. Within the span of merely five years, the Limi Valley became fully integrated into the Chinese economy. Not only do people earn their money in China, they also spend it in China—buying whatever life in the villages requires: rice and flour, tools and household utensils, clothes, shoes, detergent, soft drinks and alcohol to cater for guests.

Everybody I talked to in Limi unanimously agreed that labor in Purang was a boon for the valley. This is especially true for the poorer households, and in particular the single-woman (*morang*) households, which are a corollary of the surplus of unmarried women that fraternal polyandry creates. Labor in Purang provides equal opportunities—women and men alike find work on Chinese construction sites and all are paid the same salaries. Here, unlike in the system of trade combined with agropastoralism, the pooling of male labor is not a precondition for upward mobility. With hard work, poorer households can earn more or less the same as richer ones.[7]

However, concerns that the present situation is not to last are growing in Limi. There is only so much that China can build in a local county seat. Construction will inevitably slow down in the future. Moreover, the Limi construction workers technically do not have a work permit. They enter China on a border pass that allows them to stay in Purang and do business without the need for a visa.

This situation could change at any time, people fear. In 2016, after an accident on one of the construction sites and unclear responsibilities regarding payment of the hospital bill, the local authorities encouraged the formation of a Limi "labor association"—not so much to encourage them to stand up for their rights but rather to shoulder some of the risks of employing foreign workers. In this context, it was also announced that labor opportunities for non-Chinese citizens would slowly be phased out over the next few years.

The labor boom, like the foraging booms, is not a stable source of income. No longer embedded in the system of trade plus agropastoralism, these new sources of income are subjected to the logic of boom and bust that is so characteristic for frontier economies. People are acutely aware of this. In 2011, when I asked about the risks of being dependent on China, I was usually told that people in Limi were used to the vagaries of Chinese policies and that they would always find some niche to survive. In 2016, the answer to the same question was rather bleak: "Without labor in Purang, we will die."

The questions that loom large are thus: How to address such uncertainties as a community? What does this mean for the village rules and the future of the monasteries?

What Comes Next

We are guests at the *goba's* house in Dzang, the uppermost of the three Limi villages. Drolma receives us with tea and a never-ending stream of stories. She is alone in the house these days. Her husband and children are away, and there is so much to be taken care of: a ritual tomorrow to prevent the birds from eating the ripening barley, and a house far too big and too old to keep up. Drolma would actually like to go to Bodhgaya this winter to see the Dalai Lama, but someone has to take care of clearing the snow from the roofs of the monastery and the house. Drolma's husband, Tsering, is doing business between Purang and Kathmandu. He is trading in phuru, silverware, and religious objects—things made in Nepal and India and sold in China.

Drolma tells us about her intentions to renovate the old house and make it beautiful again. Money would not be an issue, and many other rich families have done so long ago. The goba family, much like the wealthier families from Walung, has property in Kathmandu. But "why invest here in the village in times when people are moving out?" her husband keeps saying. Eleven out of some sixty households have recently left, and two more are in the process of moving. The goba family owned thirty barley fields and plenty of livestock. Now, they only cultivate four of the fields, and all but six yaks were sold. For big families like theirs, wealth and status has long been derived from other ventures. Rather than relying on foraging and labor, their fortune is based on trade between Purang and Kathmandu.

Drolma's reasoning reminds me of what a Limi friend doing business in Kathmandu said about the slow shift of households away from the village. In the old days, the village was the center of accumulation. Precious and expensive things were purchased outside and then brought to the family's village house. Later, people started investing less in their houses and instead opted for buying land and building a house in Kathmandu or elsewhere. With the new houses in the city, attention and care also moved. As a result, the houses of the rich families in Limi often do not look well-off. Why bother when the center of the place-knot is gradually moving to Kathmandu?

"We are also no longer willing to be goba," Drolma continues. Leading the village implies too much work, too many responsibilities—and most of those responsibilities rest on her shoulders because she is the only family member spending longer stretches of time in the village. Last year the family called a village meeting and asked to be relieved of their role as goba (which has been informal anyway since the introduction of the Panchayat system in the 1960s). The village declined their request, but the goba family insisted that they would henceforth only perform the duties of the other "big houses" (*trongchen*). And so it is now, although everybody in the village still calls them goba. "Ah, what to do?"

It is September 2016, and these are crucial days in Dzang. A group of sixteen monks is on the way to the village. Decisions have to be taken. The households moving out are not just "small houses" (*trongchung, mirey*) and single-women households (*morang*); four of them are big houses (*trongchen*).[8] Anybody has the right to move out. The problem is breaking the monastery rule, which demands a monk from each family with more than one son. The rule specifies a fine for an absent monk. Earlier, the fine was one yak per year, then NPR 7,000. But what if a family leaves for good? Should a monk of such a family continue paying? Those in the United States, Canada, and Taiwan don't pay, the leaving families argue. "So why should we?" Thus, last year, the rule was broken and the families that moved out did not pay fines. This summer, the monks called a meeting. The meeting took place in Purang, where most of the monks, as everybody else, spend the summer working on construction sites, making money and paying the fines. From their perspective, all of this seems utterly unfair. Stark action was decided, and a new rule was laid out: The families moving out for good would have to pay a one-time fine of NPR 800,000 (about US$8,000). Nobody agreed to pay. Thus, another meeting was called and all monks living abroad—most of them no longer living as monks but simply pursuing their lives and careers—were urged to participate. All but one, whose legal status in the United States did not allow him to exit the country, followed the call. "The meeting will take place in twelve days," Drolma says.

While she tells us this story, Drolma prepares a meal: rice from China, greens from the garden, and dried yak meat—"the last yak meat ever," she says with an ever-so-slight ironic undertone. The monk assembly in Purang not only took a decision regarding fines—they also declared the village a no-kill zone, following the call of Pema Rigzel Rinpoche, the influential lama in the neighboring valley. As elsewhere in the Tibetan world, a new form of green vegetarian Buddhism is gaining momentum. It provides yet another reason to abandon pastoralism for good.

The declining importance of agriculture and pastoralism, together with the increasing importance of foraging and labor as sources of income, puts the old system of rules under pressure. Dzang is economically the most successful of the three Limi villages. It is no wonder that the tensions revolving around local rules meant to maintain the ties in the knot are most accentuated here. In Waltse, the biggest of the three villages, there are no signs that the rules would be relaxed anytime soon—on the contrary, if anything, they have become stricter and more abundant. This, I believe, is not a story of one village clinging to cultural traditions while another went with the winds of time. Both communities are equally translocal, engaging in an extension of the place-knots within which they operate. Waltse, however, experienced a major setback some twenty years ago, when two collective investments into trade deals went bust and wiped out the accumulated capital that households had built up over the years. Several Waltse families had to sell their property in Kathmandu and start from scratch. Keeping the community together through strict rules is considered more important here than elsewhere. The strictness of rules is also a reaction to a crisis that can only be weathered collectively.

It is not surprising that the means and strategies to keep a translocal community together are somewhat different in Walung and Limi. Agriculture requires presence and a kind of practical social organization, with meetings and community decisions, even when agriculture is only a minor part of household incomes. Taking care of fields and irrigation systems also creates an affective relationship to land that is quite different from a pure trading village like Walung. However, the question is whether the rigid rules of Limi could backfire. When membership in a community is tied to strict obligations, those moving out on a more permanent basis may well be forced to cut or at least weaken ties with the community. This would lead to the opposite of the intended effect.

Such reasoning is not uncommon in Limi. We later learned that the outcome of the meeting in Dzang was much less draconian than what the monks suggested. The following was decided: Each year, five monks shall be chosen to run the monastery and perform all the necessary ritual duties. They shall be compensated with NPR 200,000 (US$2,000) per year. The absent monks will pay NPR 10,000 per year, but there will be no fine for those staying permanently abroad. Discussing these decisions with people from the neighboring villages, I sensed much skepticism about whether this will work out in the long run. Where will the money to pay the monk salaries come from? Now, donations are being collected, and people apparently do pay up—including those residing in the United States, India and Taiwan. But will they be willing to continue offering donations year after year?

In summary, we see that also in an agropastoral context like Upper Humla, community is not *local* in the ways in which the trope of the local community suggests. In villages like Waltse or Dzang, much of the population spends most of the year outside the valley. This is even true for a village like Kermi that allows for agricultural subsistence. Like in Walung, community in Upper Humla takes place between different localities: the village, Purang, Kathmandu, a forest in India, and maybe a neighborhood in New York or Taipei. Community both depends on and is derived from the effort of tying and retying places into a knot.

The transformations of cross-border trade—from salt and grain to antiques and wildlife and eventually to Chinese goods and Himalayan herbs—bear many similarities between Walung and Upper Humla. The challenges that Upper Humla and Walung face, however, are not the same. Trade in Walung was never as deeply embedded in a system of agropastoralism as it was in Upper Humla. Walung never faced the problem of distributing labor between agriculture, pastoralism, and trade; at the same time, Walung families do not have the safety net that agriculture provides, nor do they have access to well-paid seasonal labor across the border in China.

It is no surprise, then, that approaches to these challenges vary. Limi's strict rules, monastic obligations, and the norm of polyandric households are absent in Walung. And even within the Limi Valley, there are notable differences: While in Waltse the system of rules is very much held dear, in Dzang these same rules are being dismantled. The aim can thus not be to establish correlations between challenges and approaches, or to focus on particular environmental or historical differences to explain the choices communities make. Both in Walung and in Upper Humla, sociocultural, environmental, political, and economic challenges are moving targets, and the ways in which different communities deal with them is necessarily in flux.

However, the basic task of tying places into knots, and at times keeping them from falling out, is at the core of translocal communities both in Upper Humla and in Walung. Positionality, movement, and exchange between the places in the knots thereby play a paramount role. Despite episodes of decline and border restrictions, trade has never ceased to be one of the prime avenues to prosperity.

This leads us to part 2 of the book on the business of wayfaring, the stubbornness of old pathways, the power of borders, and the labor of distribution.

Part 2
PATHWAYS

THE BUSINESS OF WAYFARING

If places are tied into knots through repeated movement between them, these iterations *take place*—quite literally—along the paths that link them. Itinerant iteration leaves traces not only in the stories that bind places in a knot but also in the landscape. Trails gain form as an "accumulated imprint" of repeated journeys, and the landscape becomes a "taskscape made visible" (Ingold 1993, 167).

Trails in eastern Nepal, like the one that leads up to Walung, feature resting places every few hundred yards. Hip-high stone walls on the side of the trail let porters rest their heavy crates without putting them down, allowing them to catch their breath. In Upper Humla, whenever the trail opens up to a flat place outside a village, there are traces of caravan camps where several hundred sheep and goats would spend the night.[1] The animals need fodder, and the herders need to keep them away from the fields surrounding the villages whenever they are not needed for manure. Seasonal trade marts pop up at temporary roadheads and become bustling centers of activity for a few years, leaving traces that can be seen long after they moved on. Movement inscribes itself in the landscape; it shapes the terrain on which it takes place as much as it is conditioned by it.

Tim Ingold calls this form of movement wayfaring. The wayfarer, he writes, "has to sustain himself, both perceptually and materially, through an active engagement with the country that opens along his path" (Ingold 2008, 35). The wayfarer makes his way *through* this world rather than *across* it from point to point (Ingold 2008, 37). Wayfaring is an apt description of the caravans that move up and down the Karnali Valley and their continuous engagement with the environment they encounter on the way. The sheep and goats graze and digest the world through which they move; the caravan traders look out for the arrival of a particular species of migratory bird to synchronize their movement with the agricultural cycle.

Wayfaring also captures much of what is at stake in pilgrimage and trekking tourism. What counts is not arrival but the experience of being on the way.

To make his point, Ingold juxtaposes wayfaring with transport. Transport, he argues, refers to the experience of passengers in an airplane or a bus. They are passively transported from place to place. Transport is concerned with point-to-point connections, shipping goods and people between a port of origin and a port of destination in a network superimposed on a Cartesian imagination of the world as surface. For the wayfarer, on the other hand, the world is not a surface that needs to be traversed; wayfarers are "instantiated in the world as a line of travel," Ingold writes (2008, 35). In other words, they *are* the movement. Unlike the straight point-to-point connections in a network, the meandering lines of movement along which a wayfarer proceeds form a *meshwork*.

The terminological pair of wayfaring and transport does not suppose a clear-cut distinction. Its usefulness lies in highlighting a tension. In the case at hand, this tension arises in the context of the ongoing road construction frenzy in the Himalayas. On the one hand, trekking tourists, who hike along old Himalayan trails that are in the process of being upgraded to dirt roads, curse such developments. Choking in the dust picked up by vehicles crawling by, they find their wayfaring experience annihilated by the sad arrival of petroleum-driven modernity. On the other hand, residents of roadless valleys often actively support road construction. Roads, they hope, will replace the burden of wayfaring with means of transport. For them, wayfaring is not a recreational activity but an integral part of their business. Himalayan trade, historically as well as today, is a business of wayfaring in the service of transport.

As way of life and source of income, the business of wayfaring forges identities. A case in point is the story of the Humli-Khyampas, an itinerant group of caravan traders. According to Hanna Rauber (1987, 1980, 1981), the group emerged in the second half of the nineteenth century as a loose conglomerate of households from different origins who left their land and villages behind to become itinerant salt and grain traders. Numbering approximately 1,000 members by the late 1970s, the Humli-Khyampas became a distinct group, speaking their own western Tibetan dialect, marrying endogenously, and displaying identity through dress and jewelry. In other words, Rauber argues, they underwent a process of ethnogenesis and became recognized as a distinct ethnic group by their neighbors. Only about half of the Khyampa households leased land from

Goat carrying Chinese wheat flour in Upper Humla. *Source*: Martin Saxer, 2011. www.theotherimage.com /series/wayfaring-business/.

The road from Hilsa to Nara La. *Source*: Martin Saxer, 2016.

sedentary farming communities at the border between Humla and Bajura, which provided some modest additional income. The Khyampas predominantly lived on trade, and their identity was formed around constant movement rather than being rooted in a certain place. Their lives revolved around the business of way-faring. Today, the Khyampas no longer travel between Nepal and Tibet. Iodized salt, subsidized grain, and the problem of winter pastures increasingly under-mined their business. What eventually rendered their itinerant lifestyle unsus-tainable, however, was their *lack* of a domicile. Ironically, not being residents of a village in Humla District excluded them from obtaining border passes that grant visa-free access to Purang County.

The landscape in which wayfaring takes place is also a political one. Forces far beyond the scope of the landscape condition the business of wayfaring. This was obvious when I first came to Humla in September 2011. Together with my research assistant Rinzin, his uncle, his aunt, and a couple of pack horses, we walked up the Karnali Valley from Simikot toward Hilsa, the settlement at the Tibetan border. Wherever we came, there was a sense of excitement and oppor-tunity in the air. The new China trade was just picking up, and the trails were extremely busy with people shuttling back and forth between Purang and their native villages. Some came from the neighboring district of Mugu, traveling in small groups and carrying baskets brimful of clothes, shoes, and blankets back to their villages. Others drove sizable herds of sheep and goats. These caravans were not from Upper Humla, and they no longer carried salt and grain but cheap Chinese liquor—six bottles per animal. Empty mule caravans would regularly overtake us, rushing up toward the border to fetch another load before the Hindu festival season. We witnessed dozens of yaks and dzos carrying wooden beams up to Hilsa, destined for the construction sites in Purang. At times, there were veritable traffic jams on the paths. Mule caravans would try to cross herds of sheep and goats coming down; those driving them would hustle back and forth, seeking to prevent the animals from venturing off the trail and trample the fields almost ready for harvest.

We crossed Nara La, the pass that separates the agropastoral villages of Upper Humla from the dry highland desert of the western Tibetan Plateau, and started our steep descent to Hilsa. The winding trail down to the border settlement afforded me with a panoptic glimpse of the situation: On the Chinese side, there was a neat black strip of new tarmac coming down from Purang and leading right up to the border. The border itself was marked by nothing else than an open gate. There was no visible presence of customs, immigration, or police. At the gate, vehicles coming from Tibet were unloaded. Porters were carrying boxes and bags across the narrow suspension bridge over the Karnali River to Nepal, funneling a never-ending flow of Chinese goods into Humla's economy of wayfaring.

Pathways

Tim Ingold's reflections on wayfaring are derived from his observations in the Arctic of the movements of reindeer, herders, and hunters in the snow. Their tracks make for a concise illustration of what he calls a meshwork. Ingold fleshes out his argument with insights from other "remote" areas, such as the Australian Outback, where the Aboriginal people would cross the continent following invisible lines preserved in songs and stories. In the examples Ingold solicits to make his point, transport (and the infrastructures built to foster it) herald the end of wayfaring.

This is one way to read the situation at the suspension bridge in Hilsa: smooth transport on new Chinese roads on one side, wayfaring on the other side. Here, however, the arrival of transport did not trigger the end of wayfaring; it rather drove the business of wayfaring and led to an astounding yet fragile revival of trans-Himalayan trade. The Himalayas, with their legacies and continuing importance of trade that put wayfaring in the service of transport, invite us to rethink these modes of movement and their entanglements. To do this, we need to turn to the particularities of the terrain in which Himalayan wayfaring and transport take place.

Compared to the vast open landscapes of the Arctic or the Australian Outback, movement in the Himalayas is conditioned by a much more rugged topography. The steepness of a valley, the altitude of a pass and the amount of snow it gathers in winter, the availability of fodder for pack animals—all have a direct effect on the lines of movement. Movement in and across the Himalayas neither conforms to the image of straight lines between points in a network nor the meandering lines entangled in what Ingold calls a meshwork; rather, Himalayan lines of movement are bundled along a limited number of routes conditioned by terrain. I propose to call them *pathways*.

As argued elsewhere (Saxer 2016b), a pathway is not just another word for a trail or a trade route. While trade is often an important dimension of life along a pathway, it is all but one mode of exchange. Life along a pathway is shaped by things, stories, rumors, and people passing through—by motion. A pathway describes a configuration that is at once geographical and social and that affords the business of wayfaring.

A pathway, as I use the term, is thus something more specific than Pnina Werbner (2007, 19) has in mind. For her, the term pathway denotes the routes along which people, goods, and ideas travel. Her interest lies with flows between points in a network rather than the kind of movement I am concerned with.

While the fortunes of pathways rise and fall with the vicissitudes of border making, geopolitics, and visions of development, they also have a capacity to weather such storms. Embedded in the fixity of Himalayan topography, pathways can witness revivals even after longer phases of decline. In this respect, pathways provide a point of reference and an element of continuity in Himalayan history. Borders are made and unmade, regulations transform over time, booms come and go—but Himalayan pathways survived centuries if not millennia. At times, they lost out, but then reemerged when conditions allowed.

Pathways couple terrain and history, only not in the way the school of geographic determinism had it. Pathways don't precondition particular social, cultural, economic, or political forms, just as the high mountains do not "act as barriers preserving cultures" (Fürer-Haimendorf 1981, ix). What Himalayan topography does, however, is define where people walk. As pathways of exchange and movement are embedded in a particular environment that usually changes only over the very *longue durée* of history, they possess a certain stubbornness that helps them outlast regimes and polities. At the same time, this stubbornness is also what makes pathways strategically important and casts them time and again right into the center of political turmoil.

My aim is not to elevate my notion of pathways to a general theory applicable around the world. Yet, this partial and nondeterministic coupling of terrain and history is not exclusive to the Himalayas. It is also at work in other "remote" areas lacking dense networks of roads and railways. Consider, for example, the continuing importance of rivers in Siberia. Used as waterways in summer and roads when frozen in winter, rivers have a long history of channeling routes of exchange (Zatsepine 2008). The same can be said of rivers in Amazonia or Borneo, even when roads are increasingly taking their place (Tsing 1993, 2005; Harvey and Knox 2015; Penfield 2019). However, the routes that river systems forge are directional.

They connect "upstream" hinterlands with "downstream" centers and ports. The same can be said of logging roads driven into primary forests in Amazonia, Indonesia, or Myanmar: They are directional, connecting a resource frontier with a global market. Reflecting on an abandoned logging road in Kalimantan, the most desolate of places, Anna Tsing writes that "it doesn't go anywhere, by definition" (2005, 29).

Herein lies a difference to the pathways I am concerned with. Himalayan pathways are thoroughfares. They always do lead somewhere. In this sense, they are more akin to the routes crossing the Sahara from oasis to oasis (Scheele 2012; Lydon 2009)—they do not start somewhere *connected* and end somewhere *remote* but provide potential passageways for the business of wayfaring in both directions, even if they are abandoned for a period of time.

In the Himalayas, pathways are engrained in terrain and continuously made and remade through social relations, infrastructure, and environmental factors. They highlight two important aspects of the socio-spatial configuration in which the business of wayfaring takes place: the relations between places directly along a pathway and places further away, and the competition between pathways that drives (and is driven by) infrastructural interventions. I will unpack these two aspects one by one in the next two sections.

Hinterlands and Hidden Valleys

Taking pathways into account provides us with a better sense of the socio-spatial texture of remoteness and connectivity. In the Himalayas, distance to an urban center is often less important than proximity to a pathway of exchange. Valleys that are not used as major pathways tend to orient themselves toward a pathway rather than an urban center somewhere in the lowlands. Pathways, in other words, create asymmetries between places that lie along them and their own "hinterlands." These hinterlands are typically tied into the economies of trade and exchange that emerge along pathways—for example, by rearing pack animals, serving as collection sites for herbs and mushrooms, and specializing in particular crafts such as saddle-making or, in the case of Limi, the production of *phuru*. The dynamics of pathways and hinterlands help account for relations between different areas in Nepal's Tibetan borderlands.

The socio-spatial dynamics between pathways and the hinterlands they create thereby shed new light on the notion of the "hidden valley" (*beyul*). The hidden valley plays an important role in Himalayan Buddhist imaginations and is a common motive in sacred Tibetan geography. A beyul affords protection in times of destruction, war, and threats to religious practice. Hidden valleys are sacred and can only be found by those in need with a pure heart and mind. They are typically associated with Padmasambhava, the Indian tantric master who brought Buddhism to Tibet (cf. Brauen 1985; Childs 1999; Diemberger 1996; Ehrhard 1997). A sacred hidden valley is quintessentially remote. Its power of protection depends on isolation and the spiritual "border regime" that provides access only to those truly seeking refuge.

The Himalayas have, indeed, a long history of serving as refuge for all sorts of people. Himalayan valleys became home to hermit monks, prosecuted believers, fugitives, and bonded peasants unwilling to bear the heavy taxes or corvée obligations they were subjected to. The rise of the Mughal empire in India, the establishment of Gelug power in Tibet, and the arrival of the People's Liberation Army in Lhasa all sent waves of people to the Himalayas in search of refuge. The idea of moving to mountainous terrain in search of freedom and protection gained new currency with the debate about "Zomia," the highland areas of South and Southeast Asia that James Scott (2009) describes as zones of refuge in the context of expansionary valley states.

There is little doubt that the notion of beyul is grounded both in Buddhist spirituality and in historical Himalayan experiences. As a figure of thought, however, the "hidden valley" has become a synonym for the Himalayas in general. It serves as a valuable notion for tourism marketing. Limi, for example, is frequently advertised as a hidden valley—one of the last truly unspoiled gems tucked away in the mountains. The Limi Youth Society, a welfare organization and registered nongovernmental organization (NGO) based in Kathmandu, even chose "Limi hidden valley" as the address of its now-defunct website.

This emphasis on remote and hidden valleys may seem to contradict the outward-oriented world that I described over the previous chapters. The notion of pathways, however, allows for a more fine-grained answer to reconcile the history of cosmopolitan trade with the continuing importance of hidden valleys. The Himalayas are neither a universal contact zone nor are they a world of isolated hidden valleys. The simple insight that movement congregates along certain lines also implies that there are places away from these arteries of exchange. The beyul and the pathway are two positionalities in the evolving texture of Himalayan remoteness and connectivity. At times, they are situated far apart; at times, they come in contact with each other.

A couple of weeks after catching an initial glimpse of the hustle and bustle along the Hilsa route, I found myself in such a place where these two positionalities, the pathway and the "hidden valley," came in contact. In Tugling, a camp at the upper tip of the Limi Valley, the first Chinese trucks from Tibet had arrived. In the months preceding my visit, a dirt road from the Tibetan border had reached the camp. A Limi businessman had built a teahouse and shop, catering to the Limi villages. He bought a satellite phone link—at that time, the only one in the upper part of Limi—to coordinate his business.[2] Tugling quickly became the center for all the new ambitions linked to the prospect of reviving the Limi pathway. The place had a distinct Wild West atmosphere to it. Residents from Dzang would come to place phone calls to the world, while nearby herders would gather to play cards through the night and drink cheap Chinese liquor. A pack of wild dogs circled the camp, coming closer each day, it seemed to me.

People would hang around and wait for trucks to arrive from China, bringing household items, carpets, furniture, and winter provisions to Limi. Phuntsok, the shop owner's younger brother, was running the place. He would spend afternoons showing DVDs on his solar-powered Chinese TV set. Among the films, there was a documentary that he and his friends from the Limi Youth Society had made the previous year. It was an ambitious project and an impressive accomplishment. On the one hand, the filmmakers worked hard to present an unbiased and comprehensive insider's view of Limi; on the other hand, the film was meant to promote the "Limi Hidden Valley," its stunning beauty and sheer remoteness, for tourism. A young American woman spoke the narration.[3]

While we were watching monastic rituals and marriage ceremonies, the satellite phone rang. One of Phuntsok's clients expected the call; he answered immediately and began reporting on the current state of affairs. The caller's voice added a second narration to the film's American voice-over. Lhundup's truck was stuck in the river, and Mangal had gone to help pull it out. They had already tried to free the truck yesterday, but the hook had broken off and the truck was still in the river. Yes, the diesel had arrived from Tibet, but the iron stove was not here. Some of the goods had fallen out on the way. Yes, they would go back and find them tonight. The reporting was calm, factual, and without the slightest sign of being worried about any of the things that had gone wrong. These were all small problems, frequent but minor obstacles, in the larger scheme of things. In Tugling, an incipient revival of an old pathway met with the native filmmakers' honest portrayal of Limi as a remote and hidden valley.

Both the prospect of direct trade with Tibet and the promise of more trekking groups in search of their beyul are directly linked to the business of wayfaring—for traders between Purang and Limi, for the truck driver stuck in the river, and for trekking guides.

Competition and the Role of Roads

The notion of pathways not only sheds light on the socio-spatial dynamics in one area, but it also invites us to think about the relations between different val-

The Hilsa border. *Source*: Martin Saxer, 2016. www.theotherimage.com/happy
-beauty-lucky/.

leys in the Himalayas. Local Himalayan histories are often embedded in a wider
competition between pathways. The rising importance of one pathway frequently
induced a decline along another one.

Consider the Limi Valley: The main pathway of exchange that passed by the
upper tip of the valley was outlawed in the context of the border demarcation in
the early 1960s. As a consequence, the neighboring pathway following the Karnali
and crossing Nara La to the border at Hilsa became the main avenue of exchange.
Quite literally, Limi became an out-of-the-way place and a newly "hidden" valley.
Consider also Walung's positionality: Once it was the main route between Shigatse
and India. Then, Colonel Francis Younghusband's 1904 military campaign in Tibet shifted the center of trade to Kalimpong, a few hundred kilometers east of the
Tamor Valley. In the 1950s, when the US ban on "communist wool" undermined
Kalimpong's standing, Walung witnessed a revival that led to what Tamla Ukyab
described as the "golden times" of business. More recently, Walung's positionality
once again came under pressure. A new road in the Tibet Autonomous Region to
the border village of Kimathanka in the neighboring Arun Valley led to a clear
decline in the importance of the pathway through Walung. The Chinese road
turned one of Walung's former "hinterlands" into a bustling hub for trade.

Competition between pathways also plays out at larger scales. Consider the
three wars Nepal fought against Tibet to prevent the main arteries of trade from

moving to Sikkim. Keeping the Chumbi Valley off-limits was seen as a precondition to safeguard the importance of the Kyirong and Kuti routes. It is not surprising, then, that the competition between pathways has remained a much-contested topic throughout the Himalayas. When the border between Tibet and Sikkim reopened for limited trade in 2006, for example, there was a heated debate about which pass should become the official crossing. Kalimpong pushed for Jelap La but lost out against Gangtok favoring Nathu La (Harris 2008, 2013). Geopolitics and strategic considerations directly weigh on such decisions and thereby alter the careers of pathways and the economies surrounding them.

Infrastructure plays an increasingly important role in this respect. Roads, customs facilities, and dry ports affect the careers of pathways and the competition between them. This has far-reaching consequences for the business of wayfaring.

Nepal's Strategic Road Network plan 2015–2016 lists ten existing or planned roads up to the Tibetan border.[4] From east to west, they include the H07 to Walung and Tipta La; the F053 to Kimathanka; the F106 to Lapcha; the H03 Araniko-Friendship Highway; the F021 to Rasuwaghadi; the F042 to Mustang and Kora La; the F196 through Gorka to Larke Pass; the F145 to Hilsa; the F195 through Bajhang to Saipal; and the H14 from Darchula to Tinkar La. All ten roads follow well-established pathways of historical trans-Himalayan trade. Mustang, Rasuwa–Kyirong, and the Araniko-Friendship Highway currently feature roads that cross the Himalayas and link Nepal with China; the other three routes still lack connections to Nepal's road network in the south.

On the one hand, Nepal's Strategic Road Network is embedded in notions of integrating remote border areas into the state. On the other hand, the three existing roads, and to a lesser extent the seven planned routes, have also become enmeshed in the larger vision of establishing trade corridors between China and South Asia. Epitomized in China's Belt and Road Initiative and its promise to pour hundreds of billions of US dollars into transportation infrastructure over the coming years, the new Silk Road fever has reached Nepal.

The best example to show the effects of these visions on the ground is the Rasuwa–Kyirong corridor, which according to official plans was designated to become the main route of trans-Himalayan trade in the near future (Cowan 2013, 101–102). In Nepal, the revival of the old Kyirong route was heralded as the beginning of a new chapter in bilateral relations with China, pivoting away from Kathmandu's traditional reliance on India (Campbell 2010; Murton, Lord, and Beazley 2016). Around 2010, China started building a somewhat oversized customs and immigration facility that rendered this vision in concrete. China also helped Nepal extend the road from the border into Nepal. Eighteen kilometers were built from the border in Rasuwaghadi to the district headquarters of Shyabru Besi. In the anticipation of future volumes of trade, outside actors

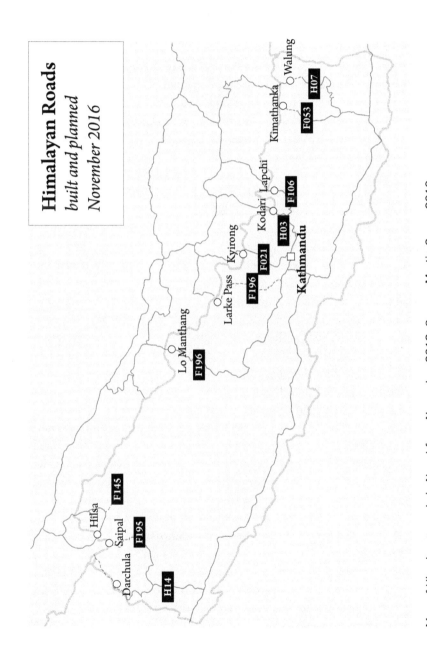

Map of Himalayan roads in Nepal from November 2016. *Source:* Martin Saxer, 2019.

began to flock into the region, trying to position themselves for the boom in the making. In 2014, Chinese foreign direct investment overtook India's for the first time (Murton 2016, 7). Land prices along the road from Rasuwa to Kyirong began to rise exponentially.

The massive double earthquake that shook Nepal in 2015 and hit Rasuwa particularly hard accelerated this transformation in many ways. Although the border bridge and the Chinese customs and immigration facilities suffered considerable damage, the competing Araniko-Friendship Highway was hit even harder, shutting down for years to come. As immediate reconstruction efforts focused on the Rasuwa–Kyirong route, China took the chance to further its agenda. A world that ever more closely resembled the vision of a "modern" trade corridor started emerging from the rubble. The customs house and border bridge were rebuilt and work on a dry port started.

Some profited substantially from these developments; others, however, were beginning to feel sidelined. Initial hopes for an economic revival became overshadowed by doubts about who would be in the position to benefit from all of this. The hustle of reconstruction brought more outside actors to the scene. While restaurants and roadside shops provided new income, residents of Timure, a village close to the border, protested against unfair land grabs (Thapa 2016).

In brief, the old Kyirong pathway is reimagined as a *corridor* that will eventually overcome the friction of terrain. Couched in the fantasy of pure transport, it is meant to allow for cost-effective flows of goods between centers of production and consumption. The implicit aim of upgrading an old trade route to a corridor is to put an end to inefficient wayfaring.[5]

Moreover, the slow movement of goods together with people and pack animals was always difficult for states to read, understand, and control. The idea of a modern trade corridor carries the promise to better establish state authority in the borderlands. In this sense, the dedicated purpose of corridors goes beyond the simple quest to overcome the friction of the terrain. The aim is to replace the social and geographical configuration of existing pathways with man-made infrastructure facilitating the storyless movement of goods and (to a lesser extent) people.

Corridors are the obvious infrastructural answer to the vision of flows and networks. This answer includes bridges and tunnels to smoothen out terrain and straighten the lines between points in the network; dry ports, special zones, and logistics hubs to replace unruly entrepôts and seasonal trade fairs; and customs-cum-immigration facilities capable of managing future flows at larger scales. In other words, planning a corridor can be understood as an attempt to create an artificial pathway unencumbered by the existing social and environmental fabric.

In practice, of course, this is a much messier enterprise than such visions of smooth flows would suggest. The narrative foundations on which corridor fantasies rest—the end of remoteness and the daily drudgery that comes with mountainous terrain, the idea of progress once a landscape is flattened—quickly become more complicated. As any engineer would agree, building a road through rough terrain is a challenge that is intrinsically tied to the socio-environmental fabric it is meant to cut through. Landslides destroy roads halfway built, earthquakes alter the very foundation on which they rest, and people along the way may resist the comprehensive transformation from pathway to corridor or try to co-opt infrastructural interventions for their own agendas.[6]

Furthermore, corridor infrastructures, once built, require massive maintenance that is an order of magnitude more expensive than maintaining simple trails. Left unattended, roads are taken back by jungles or buried by landslides; tarmac inevitably grows potholes; and trucks, unlike porters and pack animals, are highly susceptible to the faintest of obstacles.[7] A stone or a fallen tree can stop their movement until heavy machinery arrives to clear the way. Unlike the socio-environmental configuration of old pathways, corridors need continuing outside investment and effort to weather the ravages of time. As a result, the state necessarily becomes more present.

The situation in the Himalayas is more complex, however. The fact that development efforts focus on the most promising corridors triggers a paradox: Those who make a living along a roadless pathway not selected to be turned into a corridor in the near future find themselves at a disadvantage. For those engaging in forms of wayfaring in the name of trade, building a road is increasingly seen as a precondition to keep a pathway alive. A road—once "opened" as a rough but motorable dirt track—may not herald the end of wayfaring for the sake of smooth transport. However, as a single truck can replace dozens of caravans and scores of porters, it has a profound impact on who continues to participate in the evolving economy of a pathway.

Those living along a corridor in the making realize that roads do not always have the anticipated effects. They may lead to more traffic, but they also change where people stop. In Mustang, for example, the road to Tibet has attracted scores of young Nepali adventurers driving up to Lo Manthang on motorcycles. Transporting provisions to the Upper Mustang, both from Tibet and the lowlands of Nepal, has become much easier. But the road has also changed the pace of movement and thus the choices of those traveling for business or leisure regarding where to stay overnight. Historical junctures like Kagbeni—*kag* literally meaning stop in Tibetan—saw their role and position change. Kagbeni residents complain that "nobody stops and stays anymore," Galen Murton writes (2018, 315). A road may increase traffic, but traffic may just pass by or be out of reach for those without the means. "If you are poor," Murton quotes from a conversation he had in Mustang, the road "makes you (feel) poorer" (2018, 320).

Road corridors lead not only to uneven mobilities along one pathway, but they also affect the relations between pathways. Corridors usually come with increasing scrutiny and state presence. In the face of dry ports and fancy Chinese border facilities guarding transit, business that is for one reason or another not fully legal begins to move to pathways at the periphery of the state's field of vision—such as Walung and Hilsa, but also Kimathanka in the Arun Valley, Saldang in Dolpo, Nubri and the Tsum Valley in Gorkha, or the Lapchi area in Dolakha. The relative "remoteness" of these pathways becomes an asset that again drives certain forms of connectivity. The construction of corridors along selected routes triggers a fragile, risky, and ephemeral window of opportunity for the business of wayfaring along other pathways.

The notion of pathways renders visible such socio-spatial relations between long-standing arteries of exchange and the hinterlands they foster. It offers a perspective on the competition between different areas with their routes of trade. And it helps us keep in view the layers of history accumulating along pathways vis-à-vis the vicissitudes of borders and political regimes. In this sense, pathways suggest a starting point to explore the manifold outcomes of the current infrastructure frenzy against the backdrop of the longue durée of history.

While this frenzy is rhetorically tied to visions of transport as an antidote to cumbersome wayfaring, the story I seek to tell is not the nostalgic tale of the end of wayfaring and the arrival of smooth corridors of transport. The story at stake is more complex, and the distinction between wayfaring and transport is less clear-cut. Wayfaring in the service of trade is always already tied to the problem of transport; and in the rough terrain of the highlands, transport often continues to rely on wayfaring—despite new roads. For those living along old pathways, new roads built along them may promise a revival of old trades; others, however, find themselves sidelined from the business of wayfaring.

These dynamics are at the heart of what I witnessed in Humla and Walung. The quest for local roads with their side effects, conflicts, and unexpected outcomes for the business of wayfaring are the topic of chapter 5.

A QUEST FOR ROADS

In 2011, when I first visited the border settlement of Hilsa, the Nepali state was largely absent. There was no customs office, and the few police stationed at the border seemed only interested in checking the trekking permits of the odd tourist passing by. The Chinese border and customs facilities were located in Purang, some 25 kilometers from Hilsa. The border gate was usually unattended. Humli traders were able to enter and exit China freely on their border passes. To export goods from China to Nepal, the only document necessary was an export permit, which was easy to obtain in Purang. Exports from Nepal to China—mainly herbs, timber, and *phuru*—underwent little scrutiny. For all practical purposes, Hilsa was a "free trade" border. Only the Maoist Youth League, present in the border settlement with a solemn red flag on a dilapidated house, was handing out pamphlets stating that the export of timber and the import of liquor were, in fact, illegal.[1]

The black strip of tarmac coming down from Purang right to the border provided access to the quickly expanding network of Chinese transportation infrastructure. The road to the Ngari region of western Tibet had been upgraded, cutting travel times between Purang and Lhasa by half. Since 2006, Lhasa was connected to the Qinghai–Tibet railway. In 2011, an extension to Shigatse was under construction.[2]

As a gateway to the Chinese network of roads and railways, Hilsa was of utmost importance to the region. It provided access to cheap manufactured goods and, most importantly, food products. The decline of caravan trade—starting with subsidized salt in the 1970 and going through several phases until most families sold their sheep and goats around the turn of the millennium—had left Humla with an acute shortage of basic provisions, particularly rice. By 2011, the remaining caravans, which were usually owned by people from Lower Humla and neighboring districts with access to community-managed forests in the south, were no longer bringing grain to Upper Humla. Instead, they were mostly carrying cheap Chinese alcohol down to the valleys. A series of severe winter droughts in western Nepal added to the crises. Agricultural yields, which were already far below subsistence levels, dropped even further. According to alarming reports by the World Food Programme, the resulting food shortage reached a magnitude comparable to the worst cases in sub-Saharan Africa; three-quarters of Humla's population was classified as "highly food insecure" (NeKSAP 2009, 2; WFP 2010, 3). To mitigate this crisis, the World Food Programme and the Nepal government were distributing rice. This direct food aid, however, did not cover basic subsistence needs. The import of wheat flour from China was the main means to cover the gap.

Against the background of the evolving food crisis in Humla, the question of transport and infrastructure gained further importance. Simikot, the seat of Humla's local administration, is one of the two remaining district headquarters without road access to the rest of Nepal. Limited resources and difficult terrain make it unlikely that this will change in the near future. The lack of a road connection to the centers of Nepal meant that the World Food Programme and the government of Nepal had no other option than to fly rice into Humla, using the airstrip in Simikot. As this was a tremendously expensive enterprise, Nepal's Department of Local Infrastructure Development and Agricultural Roads (DoLIDAR) started looking north—to Hilsa and China—for an alternative solution.

Work on a feeder road from the Tibetan border down to Simikot started in the mid-1990s. The project was funded by the Asian Development Bank (ADB), the Swiss Agency for Development and Cooperation (SDC), and the World Food Programme (WFP). The WFP contributed to the road project with a food-for-work program. In a twist of irony that has largely gone unnoticed, local residents, reimagined as poor farmers rather than former caravan traders, were offered rice to build a road to feed Humla along the very pathway they had used to provision the region for centuries. The vision of transport for the sake of rural connectivity eclipsed any understanding of the business of wayfaring.

Many in Humla, however, had far greater ambitions than to work on the road in exchange for some rice. When, in 2011, the road had crossed the Nara Pass and reached the village of Yari, some 30 kilometers from Hilsa, a group of young Humli saw an opportunity. They bought a used Chinese truck, tossed it across the Karnali River to the Nepal side, and started offering transportation services between the Hilsa border and Yari. In the same year, another group of young Humli established a seasonal trade mart at the roadhead and began selling goods imported from China. I knew one of these pioneers, Paljor, from my previous work on medicinal herbs and the industry of Tibetan medicine (Saxer 2013a). Paljor had been the secretary of the Himalayan Amchi Association, a nongovernmental organization (NGO) based in Kathmandu. Now, I met him again, when he was running a tent shop at the roadhead in Yari.

As one of Nepal's poorest districts, Humla is known as a region that those with ambitions sooner or later leave. It is not usually imagined as a place that attracts young, entrepreneurial minds. Meeting Paljor, I was surprised to learn that he had given up his job in the capital to become a roadside trader at the end of a dusty dirt track in Upper Humla. I quickly learned, however, that the improvised trade mart run by Paljor and his peers was based on a deep understanding of Humla's needs and market. Although the prices for flour, kitchen utensils, soap, and manufactured goods were slightly higher in the roadside camp than in Hilsa or Purang, their business thrived. While many of their customers had a border pass that allowed them to cross into Tibet without formalities, many preferred paying the moderately higher prices over the hassle of traveling to Purang. The Nara Pass between Yari and Hilsa is a weather divide, separating the green valleys of Humla from the arid Tibetan Plateau. After the pass, there is no grass for pack animals, which makes it difficult and expensive terrain for caravans. Furthermore, caravans are forbidden to enter Tibet.

What Paljor and his friends did was to revive an old Himalayan institution geared toward addressing precisely this kind of issue: They set up a seasonal entrepôt. Historically, such seasonal trade marts played an important role in trans-Himalayan trade. To revive this venerable Himalayan institution at the roadhead in Yari turned out to be a rewarding endeavor. Paljor's profits over the season averaged about US$2,400 per month—some thirty times more than the salary he earned in his former NGO job. These profits, he stressed, were meager compared to what his friends operating the truck between the border and Yari made: Their net profits hovered around US$12,000 per month. A good secondhand truck cost about US$14,000 in Tibet—an equivalent of thirty-five days of profit. The season lasted for more than five months.

These figures may not be accurate; they were Paljor's best guess. Maybe his truck-owning friends were bragging; maybe they were talking their business smaller than it actually was. Regardless, the tales of such lucrative roadside trade spread quickly throughout Humla. These stories of fortune attracted more young entrepreneurs willing to start similar businesses. When I returned to Humla a year later, the roadhead had moved a few kilometers further down. The old camp that consisted of a half dozen tents was abandoned. Scattered pairs of old Chinese canvas shoes marked the place where Paljor had sold new ones the year before.

At the current roadhead in Pani Palbang, however, a veritable tent city had emerged. I counted fifty tent shops. Rather than one single truck, thirty vehicles were now shuttling between Hilsa and the temporary entrepôt. There were restaurants and even an improvised service station. Within a year, the new China trade had become a mainstream phenomenon. Walking through Humla with Rinzin, my friend and research assistant, we met several of his former classmates. All of them had either started businesses or were planning to do so. The new road captivated the hearts and minds of many young Humli. It gave the venerable pathway a new breath of life.

The Limi Road

This revival of trans-Himalayan trade in the slipstream of China's rapid economic development made Humla's general predicament all the more obvious. Just a generation ago, hungry Tibetans from Purang came begging for food, one elderly Humli remembered. Now, Purang was rich and Humla poor. While in Tibet new roads were being constructed at a breathtaking pace, Humla was lagging behind. In sixteen years, a mere 30 kilometers had been built between Hilsa and Pani Palbang. The construction project went painfully slow—despite funding from ADB and WFP and the support of SDC. People complained that the Hilsa Road was deeply mired in corruption.

With all this in view, Tshewang Lama, a former member of parliament who had also served a stint as assistant minister in the last king's government, came up with an idea: Why not build an alternative road following the other pathway through Limi? Although the border crossing at Lapcha La was closed since 1962, there were signs that the Chinese authorities might be willing to renegotiate this issue. From a Chinese perspective, there was nothing wrong with cross-border trade between Tibet and Nepal. It promised a source of income for Tibetan counties near the border and thus fed directly into the party state's conviction that underdevelopment was the primary cause for all the trouble in Tibet. At the Hilsa border, Tshewang observed, the Chinese authorities were quite flexible and pragmatic. He reasoned that this general attitude toward trade in China could be leveraged to open the Limi route as an alternative to Hilsa. Building a road along this old pathway would help bring back prosperity to Limi, Tshewang argued.

Compared to the Hilsa Road, the route through Limi offered a number of advantages in terms of construction. From the Chinese border, the old pathway crossed the southernmost outskirts of the Tibetan Plateau. The terrain was mostly flat. Opening a road would require only minimal effort. The route then descended to Tugling at the upper tip of the Limi Valley before gently climbing toward the

Nyalo La. The pass, at 5,000 meters above sea level, was a major obstacle, and crossing it would be a challenge. But behind the pass, the road would again follow relatively easy terrain—no bridges, no cliffs—down the Salli Valley to Sallikhola, at the confluence of the Salli River with the Karnali. In Sallikhola, the Limi Road would one day meet with the planned Hilsa Road to Simikot.

Tshewang, himself from the Nyin Valley near Simikot, pitched the idea to the three Limi villages and found strong local support. A road construction committee was established, and a proposal drafted. With the help of Tshewang's good relations to government offices in Kathmandu, the committee managed to secure US$200,000 in seed funding, earmarked for further prospecting and planning. Furthermore, the Limi Village Development Committee (VDC) decided to spend 80 percent of its annual budget on the road (Hovden 2016, 145). The road construction committee, however, had no intention to spend the money on feasibility studies or the like. Their aim was to build a road and not siphon off money for consultancy fees. With the government's pledge in hand, the committee members approached a major Nepali construction company and talked them into putting an excavator at their disposal. Then, they managed to persuade the Chinese authorities to let them ship the excavator through the Araniko-Friendship Highway and the newly black-topped Ngari Road a thousand kilometers across the Tibetan Plateau to western Tibet. From there, the excavator made its way to the Lapcha border and to Limi.

Tugling, Limi. *Source*: Martin Saxer, 2011.

Construction began in 2010 with nothing but this single excavator and much enthusiasm. By the end of the summer 2010, the road reached Tugling at the upper tip of the Limi Valley, about 30 kilometers from the border. In one season, the Limi Road had covered as much terrain as the Hilsa Road in sixteen years. An official Chinese delegation came to attend the inauguration ceremony for this first section of the project. A sense of pride and achievement lay in the air.

Meanwhile, however, Nepal was stumbling from one political crisis to the next. Amid this turmoil, the funding earmarked for the project was not released in time. This was critical because the daily expenses—rental fees for the excavator, the salary of its operator, and the cost of a steady flow of diesel from China—were substantial. Yet the road construction committee was not willing to wait for things to settle in Kathmandu. They were anxious about losing their momentum.

Moreover, some of the committee members, including Tshewang, also had personal stakes in the project. They had taken out a government contract to deliver food-aid rice through the unfinished Limi Road—for a price much lower than the going airfreight rate. With this contract, they hoped to prove the value of the Limi Road and secure further government support. To fulfill the contract, road construction had to be continued. Thus, despite the unclear funding perspective, the committee decided to push ahead. With private loans, work continued. In summer 2011, the road crossed the Nyalo Pass. By the end of summer, within less than two years, more than 60 kilometers were completed. The word of this achievement spread throughout the region. People started dreaming, preparing, and planning for the new road.

In Tugling, the camp where I watched the Limi Youth Society's "Hidden Valley" documentary, Limi entrepreneurs bought two Chinese Dong Feng trucks. Dong Feng means "eastern winds"—an apt name for the China-driven developments in Limi. The world of motorized transport, however, was new to the truck owners. They yet had to acquire the necessary skills to operate them. Trucks got stuck fording rivers and Tibetan mechanics had to be called whenever one of them broke down. The Limi Road was still an improvised dirt track. In late September 2011, a convoy of Chinese trucks carrying good for the valleys further south tried to cross Nyalo La. The road had just been opened, and the bends were still precariously narrow. Most of the trucks gave up. They abandoned their load just before the pass. When we passed a few days later, we witnessed bags of rice and wheat flour, thick Chinese blankets, bundles of shoes and winter cloths, as well as the missing iron stoves that we had heard about in Tugling (described in chapter 4). The abandoned goods dotted the field of debris below the pass, like strange mushrooms from a different world.[3]

Making use of the new Limi Road was a hazardous adventure. Skilled drivers were difficult to find, and getting fuel was a constant hassle, as the Chinese au-

Crossing Nyalo La. *Source*: Martin Saxer, 2011.

thorities only allowed a limited amount of diesel to be exported for the dedicated purpose of building the road.

On the other side of the Nyalo Pass, I spent a couple of days in a place known
as Tsongsa. Tsongsa literally means marketplace in Tibetan—a testimony to its
erstwhile function as a seasonal entrepôt. The area was used as a summer pasture by herders from a neighboring valley. The road construction committee had
set up camp here to embark on the last stretch of road down the Salli Valley.
I made friends with the operator of the excavator hired from the Nepali construction company. It already looked quite beaten, and I wondered whether it would
ever return to its lowland abode. The operator was a Nepali from Pokhara. He
had learned his skills in Dubai and also doubled as impromptu engineer and
construction supervisor. In the morning, he would walk the stretch he intended
to "open" during the day. He would then head back to the excavator, do a short
prayer, gently pick up one of the blue diesel barrels with his shovel, and head off
to carve a brown line into the mountainside. Going to bed in the evening, I would
still see the headlights of his machine and hear the rumbling of boulders rolling
down the steep slope.[4]

Despite the difficult circumstances and all the uncertainty, people in the camp
were optimistic. They felt that the Limi Road set a process in motion that could

not be stopped. With some luck and perseverance, those daring to be pioneers would eventually be rewarded for their efforts.

Over the winter 2011/2012, however, the road project faced a new challenge. The government official in Kathmandu who had supported the project and promised seed funding was ousted. His successor had no intention to live up to his predecessor's pledge. He argued that the road construction committee acted in violation of government rules. According to these rules, local road construction on the village level was to be carried out without the help of heavy machinery.

The Swiss Agency for Development and Cooperation had pushed for this rule. Based on decades of experience around the globe of what can go wrong with contractors building roads, SDC argued that village-level roads should be built exclusively with manual labor in order to prevent corruption. Between 1999 and 2014, SDC ran the highly regarded District Roads Support Programme (DRSP), where it successfully tested this labor-intensive approach to road construction (Starkey, Tumbahangfe, and Sharma 2013).

Sepp Zimmermann, a veteran development professional who was deeply involved in the program, explained the advantages to me. The main focus was not even the roads themselves, he said, but rather rural income generation. The program provided millions of man-days of labor, paid by cubic meter of earth moved rather than hours. It was well managed and strictly supervised. No money was wasted, many young women found employment in the project, and during the People's War even the Maoists liked it. Sepp had a passion for this kind of pragmatic, inclusive, and hands-on development work. He showed me photo albums, sketched the various kinds of gabion walls on the backside of an envelope, and talked at length about the importance of bioengineering, training in stone masonry and gender sensitivity.

Among development professionals, there is a certain ambivalence about road construction in the Himalayas. On the one hand, the importance of roads is widely acknowledged; on the other hand, many express fears that new roads would destroy the fragile ecology and heritage of the mountains and thereby undermine the tourism potential of remote "hidden" valleys. To address this ambivalence, SDC and the German Society for International Cooperation (GIZ) developed guidelines for "Green Roads" in the Himalayas (Acharya et al. 2003). The "Green Road" approach aims at building eco-friendly roads that minimize environmental damage and rely on locally available resources for labor, material, and finances. "Green Roads" are based on simple engineering techniques to keep erosion in check and "social principles" of creating employment and ownership (Klatzel 2000, 2–3). ICIMOD, the International Centre for Integrated Mountain Development, headquartered in Kathmandu, expanded this vision of the good, green road with an additional emphasis on safeguarding heritage along historical

Himalayan trails (Shrestha et al. 2010). "In the recent past," the ICIMOD authors write, "poor governance and lack of environmentally sound road engineering led to the construction of least-cost but unsustainable mechanically 'bulldozed' road tracks in many Nepal mountain areas" (Klatzel 2000, 8).

Wearing one of his many hats, Tshewang is listed as one of the coauthors of the report. Tshewang's aim in Humla, however, was not to turn an erstwhile trade route into a heritage trail for happy Western tourists. His ambition was rather to revive the old pathway here and now. "Once, we were in the center . . . but now we have become very, very backward," he said. The agendas of development agencies, with whom he maintained good and close relations, now became a problem. In principle, the Limi Road initiative ticked many of the right boxes: It involved local participation, finances, and ownership; the road construction committee was also aware of the problem of erosion; and the committee certainly had a much deeper understanding of the region's sacred landscape and heritage than any Kathmandu-based development organization. The only problem was the excavator. Following the advice of SDC and GIZ, the Nepali government had decreed that road projects involving excavators and other machinery were to undergo a nationwide web-based tender process known as "e-bidding."

The Limi Road clearly fell into this category. For this reason, the promised seed funds were deemed a misappropriation for unlawful construction. After months of attempts and pleas, the Limi Road was finally upgraded to district level, and a pragmatic solution was found for the sections already built. This helped limit private losses. However, for the remaining section, tenders had to be won through e-bidding.

Meanwhile, the Nepali company from which the road construction committee had leased the excavator became increasingly concerned about arrears in payment. Losing hope that it would ever retrieve its machine from Upper Humla, the company was eager to find a way out. Eventually, the company sold the machine to a group of local businesspeople with close ties to the road construction committee. As there was only one excavator in Upper Humla at that time, its new owners were in the pole position to win the tender. Construction continued in 2012 with the same excavator and more or less the same people in charge, but the work was no longer under the road construction committee.

By October 2012, the road reached the Karnali Valley at Sallikhola, the juncture where the Limi Road and the planned road coming down from Hilsa were to meet one day. Within less than three years, more than 100 kilometers of mountain road had been built.

Regardless of this remarkable achievement, the troubles of the previous year left their scars. The anonymous e-bidding process undermined trust among former partners. One of them had bid against the others behind their back.

Furthermore, disputes about maintenance obligations and the schedule for the promised road extensions to nearby villages eroded the sense of working toward a common goal. The government rules to strengthen local ownership clearly had the opposite effect.

Boom and Bust

As the accomplishment of the Limi Road echoed throughout Humla, it put those responsible for the slow pace of construction on the Hilsa Road under substantial pressure. How could it be that this officially sanctioned road project progressed so painfully slow after all the money and official support that it received? With an increasing number of young and vocal Humli tying their ambitions and futures to the China trade, roads became a political issue that no longer could be ignored. Public perception and rumors of corruption put the political futures of the local officials in charge of the Hilsa Road on the line. As a result, they intensified their efforts and lobbied for more money in Kathmandu. Funding for the Hilsa Road increased and construction slowly gained momentum.

In addition, 2012 was a year of boom along the Hilsa route—not just for the trade mart at the roadhead in Pani Palbang but also for the herb business. This boom mainly revolved around China-bound trade in Paris polyphylla, a medicinal herb known as *satuwa* in Nepal and as *qiyeyizhihua* in China. Satuwa roots are used for treating fever, headache, and livestock poisoning. In China, a variety of other conditions, including ulcers, tonsillitis, and rheumatism, are treated with a decoction of the root (Madhu, Phoboo, and Jha 2010).

Satuwa grows at medium altitudes throughout the greater Himalayan region. It was traditionally collected and used in Humla. It was also sold to Tibet, although on a comparatively smaller scale than other commercially traded species. In 2012, however, a Chinese businessman allegedly began buying large quantities of satuwa through a representative in Purang. A rumor started that he was willing to invest up to 30 million in Chinese yuan renminbi (CNY), the equivalent to US$4.9 million, and buy all available stock. Within months, demand outstripped local supply. As the price for satuwa was rising, traders began sourcing the root in the major South Asian herb markets of Delhi and Amritsar. By late summer, even these supplies dried up. According to one Humli businessman, the wholesalers in Delhi and Amritsar began importing satuwa from abroad, allegedly even from Pakistan and Afghanistan.

Because of the lack of a road to Humla from the south, satuwa had to be flown to Simikot. In October, I witnessed chartered airplanes arriving in Simikot on a daily basis, their small cabins turned into cargo holds for satuwa. The brown gunnies (the term used for the inexpensive jute sacks used in the wholesale trade in South Asia) gave away their Indian origin. At the airport in Simikot, these gunnies would be strapped onto the backs of mules and transported up to the Tibetan border—a trip that takes five to six days. While, in 2011, most of the pack animals I witnessed going up to the Tibetan border were empty, now all of them were carrying satuwa. Caravan after caravan was moving up the valley. Demand seemed bottomless, and the starting capital required to set up a satuwa deal was readily available. The opportunity was so good that several people around me considered investing. The margins for Humli traders were substantial. After all expenses, including charter flight and mule transport, net profits were in Nepalese rupees (NPR) around 200 (US$2.35) per kilogram.

Satuwa is considered rare and vulnerable, yet it is not officially a threatened species. It is neither listed in the appendixes to the Convention on International Trade in Endangered Species of Wild Fauna and Flora (CITES), an international treaty both China and Nepal have signed, nor is it included on the Red List of Threatened Species from the International Union for Conservation of Nature (IUCN). Trade in Paris polyphylla is thus technically legal, given customs procedures are followed and the plant is not collected in a protected area. Why, then, did the pathway through Humla become a major artery to ship South Asian satuwa to China? Transport by sea or through the Araniko-Friendship Highway between Kathmandu and Lhasa would have been substantially cheaper than chartering aircraft and hiring mule caravans. Nevertheless, the roots were channeled in massive quantities through the remote border crossing at Hilsa.

There were several reasons for this. First, the Humli traders had a working agreement with Chinese customs authorities that facilitated import without formalities, bypassing Chinese customs and import procedures. The latter would normally imply sampling, testing, and plant quarantine. And second, the pathway through Humla offered a combination of basic infrastructure—an airport, mules, and road access on the Chinese side—with an abundance of Humli entrepreneurs willing to invest and take risks. In other words, not only did the relative remoteness of the Hilsa border promise a degree of illegibility, but the pathway economy, with its long history and current revival, allowed transportation to scale up to industrial-level demand. Humla, in 2012, was predestined to become an arena for this kind of resource-based "frontier capitalism" (Tsing 2005, 27–50). It offered transportation services in a context where the business of wayfaring was still necessary—both to bridge the gap between Simikot and Hilsa and to tame import regimes with social relations.

The business of wayfaring in the service of transporting large quantities of a particular medicinal herb required adaptation. Schedules of chartered aircraft had to be met, and speed was crucial as nobody knew how long this window of opportunity would remain open. The slow movement of the last remaining sheep and goat caravans was utterly incompatible with the rush of the boom. Wayfaring, in this context, no longer had any connection with agropastoral cycles and seasonal migration.

The wayfarers able to profit from the satuwa boom were those with mules. Unlike yaks, dzos, horses, sheep, or goats, mules have only one purpose: carrying goods. Their meat is not eaten, and they have no wool that could be sold; a mule does not make for a good ride, nor is it a suitable wedding present. Possessing a mule does not inspire pride and status in the way owning a good horse does. Unlike herds of yak, sheep, and goats, mules do not serve the purpose of a rainy-day fund that can be converted into cash in times of need. Mules do not produce offspring—they just get old and lose their value. Mules, then, are in many ways like trucks: an investment that needs to be put to use and deliver a return. Like trucks, their lives can be extended by taking good care of them. But one day, they will perish.

Given these utilitarian parallels between mules and trucks, it is no surprise that the importance of mules grew with the development of road infrastructure in Humla. Following the logic of capital investment, mules extend roads where they have not arrived yet. With feeder roads reaching deeper into Humla, the prices for mules tripled over the span of merely a few years. In 2012, a good mule cost around US$1,300 in Humla. Mules were more expensive than horses, and they were increasingly difficult to get amid the boom.

The satuwa boom, however, lasted for only one season. In November 2012, the arrangement bypassing Chinese import procedures came to an end. Entire shipments of satuwa were returned, and people began stocking the herb in Hilsa, waiting for a chance to complete their transactions.

The traders around me saw these developments as a temporary hiccup. They were used to sudden shifts in the border regime and knew from experience that such ruptures were best dealt with by just sitting them out. Surely, the customs officer in charge would flee the cold of the Tibetan winter and leave for a long vacation to the mainland, one businessman predicted. Things would then go back to normal, at least for a while.

I have no doubt that traders will continue to find answers to the vicissitude of border regimes. Nevertheless, in hindsight, I now see the end of the satuwa boom as more than just a hiccup. It portended a series of developments that nobody was able to foresee. In November 2012, right around the time when it became clear that the satuwa bubble had burst, the Eighteenth National Congress of the Communist Party of China took place. Xi Jinping emerged as the new party secretary and almost immediately began a far-reaching anti-corruption campaign. Initially, many observers saw these efforts as a means to eliminate rivals and consolidate power. Over the years, however, it became increasingly clear that Xi's ambitions are far greater. The anti-corruption campaign, and later the Belt and Road Initiative, with its grandiose vision of new Silk Roads, set developments in motion that would reverberate throughout the borderlands of northern Nepal.

In Humla, it took a few years until the effects of these developments became palpable. At first, the dynamics triggered by the new roads seemed to take their course. Good progress was made on the Hilsa Road. In 2014, it reached a place called Tumkot at the banks of the Karnali River near Muchu, one of the larger villages in Upper Humla. In Tumkot, a semipermanent trade mart emerged. Tent shops were increasingly replaced by improvised shelters, and the market began operating year-round. In 2015, Tumkot Bazar had sixty-five shops. When I came back in 2016, however, the number of shops had fallen to thirty-two. Around the same time, the price of mules started to decrease again. A general sense of crisis overshadowed the spirit of opportunity. There were several storms brewing simultaneously, closing in from different directions.

The first reason for the crisis was the exchange rate between Nepali rupee and Chinese yuan. In 2011, one yuan was 11 rupees; in September 2016, the rate was 16 rupees per yuan. Consequently, all Chinese products became a third more expensive by default.

Second, in 2016, Tumkot suffered from a side effect of a sudden increase of Indian Kailash pilgrims traveling through Humla—itself a corollary of the 2015 earthquake in Nepal. Before the earthquake, the majority of Indian Kailash pilgrims used to take the Araniko-Friendship Highway from Kathmandu through Kodari/Dram to western Tibet (the same route along which the Limi excavator was shipped to the Lapcha border). Heavily afflicted by the earthquake, the Araniko-Friendship Highway remained blocked for years. With the Kyirong–Rasuwa and Mustang routes closed to foreign tourists, travel agencies organizing Kailash trips began to reroute their clients through Humla. Large groups of Indian pilgrims were flown to Simikot and helicoptered onward to Hilsa, where Tibetan tour operators would meet them at the border. Between 8,000 and 10,000 Indian pilgrims traveled along this route in 2016. Six helicopter companies moved their aircraft to Humla, offering shuttle services between Simikot and Hilsa. As these helicopters often flew back from Hilsa to Simikot empty in order to pick up the next batch of pilgrims, they started accepting cargo. The going rate was NPR 30 per kilogram—less than half the price of truck and mule transport and with the added benefit of guaranteed delivery in fifteen minutes instead of five or six days. The market in Tumkot suffered from this unexpected competition. Suddenly, there was a form of pure point-to-point transport that rendered the business of wayfaring moot.

Third, and most importantly, Chinese customs authorities began tightening import and export regimes and placed new restrictions on several types of goods.

One such restriction concerned Chinese wheat flour, the staple on which most families in Upper Humla relied. Chinese wheat flour used to bring a large number of customers from Lower Humla and neighboring districts to the trade mart in Tumkot. In Purang, a special kind of product was available—namely, wheat flour beyond its official shelf life. This flour was sold at discounted prices, which made it a much sought-after commodity in Humla. Preserved by the dry and cold Tibetan climate, it was also generally safe and of good quality. Nevertheless, the Chinese authorities moved to ban the sale of expired foodstuff in Purang. Accordingly, the price for wheat flour rose substantially. While customers from Upper Humla had no choice but to swallow the higher cost, those who used to come from far away (and thereby also stocked up on other things available in the roadside market) were evaluating other options. Together with the unfavorable exchange rate, the market in Simikot selling goods flown in from Nepalgunj became competitive again.

Another restriction targeted trade in alcohol. Demand for cheap Chinese liquor and beer was substantial in Humla—especially since local beer and brandy are made from grain, of which there was a shortage anyway. After an initial phase of practically free trade, the Nepali police began patrolling and confiscating alcohol on the trails. However, they were far from being able to stop the lucrative business. Eventually, the Humla government appealed to the government of Purang County. The local Chinese authorities took action and started controlling the export of larger quantities of beer and liquor. Since then, the alcohol trade has greatly decreased. In 2016, none of the shops in Tumkot Bazar had Chinese liquor on display.

Interestingly enough, there is no law that would forbid the import of Chinese alcohol into Nepal. Import simply requires a license. In 2015, the Nepal government issued such a license to a trader from the neighboring district of Bajura. The license, however, stipulates an import tariff of 300 percent, and the trader never used it. A fully legal business is simply not profitable under these conditions.

Perhaps the most consequential restriction concerned trade in medicinal herbs. What started with the intervention into the satuwa business in 2012 became solidified in policy. By default, Chinese regulations treat medicinal herbs the same as vaccines or antibiotics. Import requires quarantine, sampling, and testing in authorized facilities. During my research on the Tibetan medicine industry in Tibet between 2007 and 2009, I witnessed these regulations being implemented at the Kodari/Dram border on the Araniko-Friendship Highway. Since 2015, they seem to become relevant on the Hilsa border as well. Customs authorities make the point that Purang is not an "authorized port of entry" for medicines; it lacks quarantine and testing facilities (Saxer 2013a, 110–113).

In principle, the Chinese Drug Administration Law allows for small quantities of herbs used in traditional Chinese medicine (TCM) to be traded locally across borders. These exemptions, I suspect, provided the legal umbrella under which plant trade along the more remote border crossings between Nepal and Tibet thrived. Today, it seems, the authorities in Purang are no longer willing to see the substantial business of medicinal plants as small-scale local trade.

The rules on the import of medicinal herbs are not uniformly implemented along the Sino-Nepali border. In Walung, for example, plant trade went on unabated. The people I talked to in Humla in late 2016 still hoped that these restrictions were temporary. If this stricter regime were here to stay and be expanded to other minor border crossings, it would certainly put a dent into the revival of trans-Himalayan trade. Herbs make for a substantial part of what Nepali traders export to China, and if you have nothing to sell, there is not much you can buy.

The restrictions on flour, alcohol, and medicinal herbs are a testimony to the increasing presence of the state—on both sides of the border. During my last visit in 2016, Hilsa had a customs office, and China was building substantial new border facilities, including an oversized customs and immigration building, a hydropower plant, and additional fencing with night-vision cameras overlooking the border gate.

Dependence

The efforts to rein in a freewheeling enterprise in the gray zone of legality were also felt along the Limi Road. Tshewang's initial assumption was that once the road was built, the Lapcha Pass could be upgraded to an official crossing, but that belief turned out to be overly optimistic. By 2016, the Chinese authorities were clearly of the opinion that Hilsa was for international trade and Lapcha La was simply for local consumption—tolerated as a humanitarian gesture for the time being. The hope that the Limi Road would lead to a revival of the old pathway has faded away.

The three Limi villages still import their winter provisions by way of this road, but now there is much scrutiny to make sure this scheme is not misused. Shipping a single truckload from Purang to Limi requires permits from a half dozen different offices in Purang. Each and every matchbox must be listed, and products are carefully checked for their expiration date. Each truck is then escorted to the border by customs authorities and border police. The Chinese authorities made their stance perfectly clear to the people of Limi: If you break rules, engage in illegal activities, or help Tibetan refugees, we will shut down the border for good. In this sense, roads, especially when crossing borders, may become vehicles for disconnection.[5]

This open threat to shut the border was effective. In 2015, two Tibetans working in Purang's tourism sector arrived in the Limi Valley—perhaps with the intent not to return, or maybe just because they had lost their way, as they insisted. Shortly after their arrival in Tugling, somebody called Purang. Promptly, the Chinese police came to apprehend them. The vehicle the two alleged "refugees" had used was left behind and later given to those residing in Tugling as a reward for their cooperation. The fact that Chinese police operated on Nepali territory without any legal basis did not raise an eyebrow. The road brought not only Chinese goods to Limi but also Chinese rule.

The import of Chinese rule is certainly linked to Limi's growing dependence on labor and consumption in Purang. However, there is more at stake. Dependence is not simply an unwanted corollary of the current socioeconomic asymmetry. Quite to the contrary, dependence is often actively sought. Dependence and autonomy are strangely interlinked at the interface of Nepal and the People's Republic of China. To keep a degree of local autonomy requires strong ties of dependence to state powers on both sides. Dependence creates interdependent moral obligations, a form of deep neighboring (Zhang and Saxer 2017), which, people hope, will add a dimension of stability to the vagaries of life in the borderlands.

This is not just true for the acceptance of Chinese police operating in Limi, but also for the road projects discussed in this chapter as well as Upper Humla's relations to Kathmandu in general. On the one hand, the roads brought in the state, which put existing businesses at the margins of legality under pressure. On the other hand, the roads created a relationship of dependence between Upper Humla, Kathmandu, and Purang that allows for claims to be made. These dependencies are conceived as ways to highlight the district's rightful place within the nation of the Nepal and as China's intimate neighbor. Dependence, in this context, is as much a strategic effort to foster relations as it is a result of asymmetric power relations. It helps tie places into knots.

Mangal Lama, one of the initiators of the Limi Road project, made this point with utmost clarity when I asked him about the current crisis in late 2016. For Mangal, as well as several other Humli businesspeople I talked to, the ban on medicinal herbs was not set in stone but simply part of the evolving relations. Local authorities in Purang, Mangal argued, were very much in favor of upgrading the Hilsa border to an authorized point of entry for medicinal herbs. According to the chief of customs in Purang, such a request had already been made by the Nepali government and was pending in Beijing.

At Mangal Lama's construction camp near Nara La. *Source*: Martin Saxer, 2016.

Mangal was part of the group that bought the excavator initially leased from a Nepali construction company. After completing the Limi Road, the group successfully bid for a tender on the Hilsa Road and became one of a half dozen contractors working there.[6] In his role as contractor, Mangal got involved in the newly established Humla Chapter of the Nepal China Chamber of Commerce and Industry. In 2015, a delegation from Tibet was invited to Simikot to formally sign the chapter into being, with Mangal as its first president.

The daring Limi Road initiative, despite the failure to achieve its initial goals, was nevertheless a valuable asset, Mangal argued. He was optimistic that the Lapcha border could still be opened one day on a more formal basis—if not for trade then for tourism. It could provide Kailash pilgrims and tourists with the possibility of a round trip through the greener valleys south of the Tibetan Plateau. Such an opportunity could fit well with Chinese visions of development.

The People's Republic clearly has bigger plans for Purang. In 2016, construction of a fancy new trade zone meant to house Nepali businesspeople began. A signboard depicting a vision of the future zone shows a series of multistory buildings grouped around an edifice resembling a Tibetan stupa. The Chinese agenda is not to curb exchange across the border but rather to expand it in an orderly and managed fashion. Explaining all this to me, Mangal expressed confidence that with enough wit and relentless efforts at fostering relations, many things could be accomplished in the future. The trick was to push for more inter-dependence rather than trying to keep oneself independent.

The stories of the Hilsa and Limi Roads are just two of many such tales of infrastructural dynamics in the Himalayas today (Rankin et al. 2017). Roads are currently under construction in all border districts of northern Nepal. Some of these projects are pushed by powerful lobbies in Kathmandu and ignore local concerns (Lama 2013). Others—like the Limi Road—are grassroots initiatives driven by the feeling that government-sponsored road projects either take too long or follow the wrong route.

In general, it is certainly true that road construction is associated with state interventions rather than private initiatives. However, in places where trade has historically been a main source of income and where a pathway suffered a phase of decline, private grassroots initiatives appear to be the most logical thing to do. The Limi Road is not the only example in this respect. The road in Upper Mustang connecting Lo Manthang to Tibet began as a private initiative (Murton 2016, 2017a, 2018), and so did the project to extend the road from the Chinese border to Walung. Frustrated by the absence of progress, communities take matters in their own hands.[7]

Tenzing Ukyab, the New York based businessman and cosponsor of the *phutuk* festival described in chapter 1, argued along the very same lines as Tshewang Lama. Today, a road is a precondition for the revival of trade, which, in turn, is crucial for the survival of a "remote" mountain village. In other words, pathways need roads to sustain the business of wayfaring, and the business of wayfaring keeps a place tied into the expanding knot. Like Tshewang in Limi, Tenzing in Walung was well aware that such a privately initiated project only had a chance by creating a momentum and public attention. To this end, Tenzing organized community sessions in Kathmandu, raised private funds to start manual construction in Walung, and lobbied the press to cover the story of the seventy Walungnga working on *their* road with nothing but picks and shovels. And just like the Limi Road construction committee, Tenzing knew that a road is not just a problem of engineering. It comes into being through social relations as much as through the work of an excavator. The letter Tenzing had shown me when we met on a bench in Union Square in New York City was crucial in this respect. The letter, requesting help from the authorities of Riwu County in Tibet, had traveled through Kathmandu, Beijing, and Lhasa to Riwu County, gathering social and political weight at each step along the way. Once it reached Riwu, it facilitated a local Chinese construction company that was to undertake the work inside Nepali territory.

In early 2017, just a few months after the 2016 phutuk festival, a rough track was finished from Tipta La to Walung. At the time this book was being written, there were no signs yet of a tightening border regime. It remains to be seen whether the road construction in Walung gets caught up in the same dynamics as the Limi Road in Upper Humla. The Walung Road does have certain advantages: it is part of Nepal's Strategic Road Network planning, and Tipta La is an official border crossing.

That new roads have the capacity to both boost the business of wayfaring but also undermine its very foundations may not receive enough attention by those enthusiastically pushing for their construction. This paradox can be observed beyond the Nepal–Tibet border. In Central Asia, for example, the opening of the Chinese border in the 1990s heralded an era of small-scale shuttle trade. Initially, this shuttle trade was dominated by borderland communities that possessed the necessary skills of language and cultural etiquette to succeed. With better roads, larger logistics companies and actors with better ties to capital and authorities moved in and took over (Steenberg 2014, 2018; Alff 2016, 2017). In many parts of Central Asia, the business of wayfaring was indeed pushed aside by the logic of transport. It may well be that eventually this process repeats itself in Upper Humla or Walung.

But perhaps it does not. The tightening of border regimes that came with the roads, and the crises it triggered in Upper Humla, are certainly not the end of the story. While new roads often fail to live up to their promise, in Humla they clearly also served as devices for communities and their elites to establish closer relations with the state—often by actively seeking dependence in the hope of attaining interdependence. In this sense, a road is not just a way for the state to extend its reach into the borderlands; it also helps borderland communities to reach into the state.

Sheep caravan in Sallikhola, Upper Humla. *Source*: Martin Saxer, 2012.

INTERLUDE
A Mound of Rice

Sallikhola, at the confluence of the Salli and Karnali rivers in Upper Humla, is the crossroads where the paths from Limi and the Hilsa border meet. On a little clearing above the deep and forested gorge, about a dozen people are gathering around the open fire in an improvised kitchen shelter. Tshewang, the main initiator of the Limi Road, set up camp here a few months ago. We eat a Tibetan noodle soup, which Tshewang's wife has made from Chinese wheat flour—labeled in Arabic and Chinese, ISO 9001 certified, and well within its shelf life. The skins of two sheep butchered the other day are lying in a corner. Sweetened Nescafe, honey from Humla, and Chinese liquor go around. We are here to guard twenty tons of rice just outside the shelter, a mound of yellow polypropylene bags three meters high and covered by a blue tarp. Tshewang and his wife pitched their tent right next to the rice to make sure they would hear if a thief were to lift the tarp.

Rice has been stolen before, which makes things even more complicated than they already are. It is October 2012. After a season of troubles and tension surrounding the e-bidding requirement (described chapter 5), the Limi Road has just reached Sallikhola. In addition to finishing the road, Tshewang and four of his associates took out a government rice contract to prove that delivery of food aid through China and the Limi Road would cost less than airfreight. Last year, they placed a bid at a rate of 64 Nepali rupees per kilogram of rice, calculated on the basis of 55 rupees per kilogram of actual costs and 9 rupees profit. Their bid was substantially cheaper than what other contractors offered to fly food aid to Humla. They were awarded a contract to ship 300 metric tons of rice from Kathmandu to Simikot.

After winning the bid, becoming a government rice contractor required first a down payment of 5 percent of the full value of the rice. To actually receive the rice for shipment, full collateral needed to be provided. Contractors are only paid once their contract is fulfilled. The stakes are high, Tshewang explains. Family houses in Kathmandu have been used as collateral, and since the contract has not been fulfilled yet, they are now in jeopardy. A combination of unexpected complications at the Chinese border and an early winter meant that last year only half the rice could be shipped across the border from Tibet and stored in Tugling, the camp at the upper tip of the Limi Valley. Of these 150 tons, Tshewang and his associates only managed to bring 70 tons across Nyalo La and onward to Simikot before it started snowing.

However, 15 out of these 70 tons never arrived at the government rice depot. People just took their share along the way, arguing that it made no sense that the rice destined for them would first need to be brought to Simikot before being handed out. They had ample experience with government food aid. There was never enough rice at the depot to fulfill the quotas. When a shipment finally arrived in Simikot, it was crucial to react quickly and queue up. Those without a house and family members in the district headquarters would often end up empty-handed. Taking rice directly to the villages seemed only fair. For Tshewang and his associates, trying to fulfill their contractual obligation to deliver rice from Kathmandu to the depot in Simikot, this was a disaster. They spent considerable time and effort tracking down lost rice bags in individual households, getting paid and organizing food aid coupons to document the transactions in retrospect. Even after all this work, their loss was substantial.

For the remainder of the contract, Tshewang thus decided to take matters into his own hands. Over the past few months, assisted by his wife, brother, and a handful of trustworthy helpers he paid to deal with the many problems requiring simultaneous attention, he has been babysitting the remaining rice now trickling in across the Nyalo pass by way of the Limi Road and micromanaging its onward transport to Simikot.

I am spending a couple of weeks with Tshewang and the rice. The camp at the crossroads of the two pathways is a hot spot for news and stories traveling through the valleys. Hanging out during the day and huddling around campfires at night, I sometimes feel I am pursuing anthropology by rumors. Everybody has a story to tell in this improvised caravansary and nobody knows what to believe. Yesterday, a young man came to the camp and started bragging about the rhino horn he was smuggling to China. That, however, was an easy case to judge, everybody agreed—had he really carried any expensive wildlife part, he would certainly not have bragged about it among people he barely knew. Too dangerous, too many potential thieves.

The mound of rice in Sallikhola. *Source*: Martin Saxer, 2012.

Sealing a bag with needle and thread. *Source*: Martin Saxer, 2012. www.theotherimage.com /moonlight-departure/.

It is the peak of the *satuwa* craze, discussed in chapter 5. While trying to organize transport for the remaining contract rice, we witness caravan after caravan going up to the border laden with the precious roots and coming down with shoes, cloths, kitchen utensils, and winter provisions. Empty mules are difficult to find these days. And despite Tshewang's efforts to employ only caravans he felt he could trust, the last mule driver from his own valley marched right past Simikot, taking the rice, once more, to his village instead of delivering it. Tshewang curses his fellow valley folks and swears that he will only trust outsiders from now on. Mule drivers from Mugu, for example, have a much more professional attitude, he claims, echoing his frustration more than his belief.

Then, two of the last remaining sheep and goat caravans arrive in Sallikhola on their seasonal migration down to the winter grazing grounds in the community forests of Lower Humla and neighboring districts. They do not carry any salt and agree to help out. At first, Tshewang is excited, but then complicated negotiations ensue. Unlike mules, the sheep and goats cannot carry the heavy polypropylene bags. The rice needs to be repackaged into the traditional salt and grain bags designed for sheep and goats. This means that the rice bags need to be opened. Tshewang fears that some of the grain will inevitably be lost in the process and that the rice may also be contaminated with dirt, grass, or other foreign matter. Moreover, the traditional salt and grain bags are made of natural fibers rather than plastic. The rice will dry out and its net weight decrease, which will amount to further losses. This is a risk Tshewang and his associates are neither willing nor able to take. Their job is to deliver a certain number of bags to the depot—sealed, clean, and with a standard weight.

On the other hand, however, Tshewang has plenty of sympathy for the venerable sheep and goat caravans. He was involved in this type of caravan trade himself and also wrote a book about Humla in which the caravans feature prominently

(Lama 2002). Finally, an agreement is reached with one of the two caravans, while the other one leaves empty. We carry the agreed number of rice bags to their camp. The caravan herders open them and begin to repackage the rice into the small bags for their pack animals. Closing the bags means sewing them up by hand. The men work for two entire days.

On the second day, an empty mule caravan arrives. They are outsiders from Mugu willing to offer their services and Tshewang agrees. They stay for a quick lunch and then strap two of the heavy bags on each of their two dozen mules. Within twenty minutes, the caravan is ready to leave.

Late in the evening, the sheep and goat herders are sewing up the last bags. They light a fire and seek some rest. After midnight, they start loading their caravan, and around two in the morning they set off. This is the old way—walk during the night, rest and graze during the day. Now, with all the traffic jams on the narrow paths caused by the revival of trade with China, traveling at night has become even more important.[1]

While I watch the caravan make its way up the steep forested flank of the gorge, the men's headlamps searching like ghost lights for the way amid the sound of animal bells, Tshewang joins me. He smiles and shakes his head. "Like in the old days," he says. "But the world is turned upside down. Now the salt comes from the south and the rice from the north."

THE LABOR OF DISTRIBUTION

The story of Tshewang's venture of becoming a government rice contractor raises an important issue that has received little analytic attention in the highlands of Asia: distribution. In this chapters I argue that distribution, which was already an integral part of Himalayan livelihood strategies, has become even more important in the age of subsidies and food aid—yet not always in the ways foreseen.

The term *distribution* covers a range of related aspects that pertain directly to our case. In a business sense, distribution refers to the effort of making a specific good or product available to potential consumers. In other words, distribution is concerned with the logistics of transport and markets, putting the former in the service of reaching the latter. In economic sociology, distribution means something rather different. In this context, distribution deals with questions of socioeconomic inequality, distributive justice, and the politics of redistribution—for example, through taxes, tax exemptions, subsidies, and other forms of government spending targeted at specific populations. It serves as a measure of the way in which a certain property—income, wealth, or capital—is shared between the members of a society. Distribution thus describes a result, often in statistical terms, rather than the activity of distributing as such.

The work of Tshewang and his associates delivering food aid to Humla concerns both business and logistics as well as the politics of subsidies and redistribution. As contractors tasked with shipping subsidized rice to the distribution center in Simikot, they found themselves right in the middle of the problem of distribution and its different meanings.

When Tshewang complained about his countrymen *stealing* rice, he was referring to distribution as a question of logistics and business. As a contractor, he was responsible for timely delivery to the depot in Simikot but explicitly exempt from dealing with questions regarding the fair and equal distribution of subsidized rice. When people took rice from the pile that we were guarding in Sallikhola or when those tasked with transport decided to bypass Simikot and instead proceed directly to their villages, they were clearly foregrounding the aspect of distributional justice. From this perspective, their actions were maybe not strictly legal or fair to Tshewang and his associates; however, they did not perceive their act as *stealing* but rather as *securing* a fair share of what was legally and morally theirs anyway. Given their past experiences—that once the rice would be registered at the distribution center in Simikot they would find themselves at a disadvantage vis-à-vis Simikot residents when it came to actually obtaining it—taking rice home directly was certainly justifiable. For them, this was a matter of distributive justice rather than logistics.

Guarding the mound of rice in Sallikhola, Tshewang was acutely aware of this. He knew that potential theft was not simply a desperate act in the face of the acute shortage of rice. Despite his complaints about the hopelessly corrupted character of his countrymen, he also knew that this was not a question of culture. Rather, what was at stake was a quarrel about different understandings of what distribution was all about and how it should be carried out. When Tshewang raved about the professionalism of outside mule drivers—like those from Jumla and Mugu—his hope was that they would have less trouble distinguishing between the type of distribution at stake and the larger matters of the rice crisis and distributive justice in Humla. Although a mule driver from outside would be practically impossible to hold responsible if he decided to abscond, Tshewang's judgment was that such a mule driver would be much less likely to do so because he had no rightful claim on the rice himself.

There was clearly a moral obligation that came with being a rice contractor. Tshewang and his associates were well aware of this. As contractors, they were seen as part of the system of redistribution rather than simply providing logistics services. To counter this notion was an uphill battle. When they toured the villages in search of missing rice bags, they were careful to negotiate and find solutions that would be acceptable to those in possession of the rice. They did not present their case as a clear-cut matter of stealing, but rather tried to subtly educate their counterparts about the problems they had caused them and the losses they would have to bear privately; that, in other words, it *was* a matter of stealing in the end—not from the government but from them personally.

The problems Tshewang and his associates faced were rooted in a longer history. In pathway economies, distribution is notoriously difficult to distinguish from exchange, as both are embedded in the same set of social and environmental relations. Consider, for example, the old system of caravan trade in Humla and its embeddedness in agropastoral cycles, village rules, and the norm of polyandry. The traders moving up and down between the lower valleys and the Tibetan Plateau were engaging in distribution—bringing salt from its source to the market in the hills and, in exchange, grain back to the higher valleys and the Tibetan Plateau. At the same time, their work was also tied to the issue of a fair sharing of risks and benefits within their households and translocal communities. When business was good, they would bring wealth back to the village; when business was bad, they would rely on agropastoral income generated in their native valleys.

State-sponsored distribution, first of subsidized salt (to combat iodine deficiencies) and then of subsidized rice (to fight the evolving food crisis), altered both the logistics of bringing food into the mountain valleys and the sociopolitical structure of distributional justice in general. Ironically, as we have seen in the previous chapters, it was precisely this intervention that turned the existing system of distribution into a question of logistics and transport. Neither in the old caravan trade nor in the current era of subsidies and contractors can the logistics of distribution, the work that goes into moving goods, be separated from the socioeconomic questions of distributional outcomes.

Already Karl Marx saw this double nature of the problem of distribution. In *Grundrisse*, his critique of the political economy literature of his time, he discusses different layers of distribution. Only in its most shallow sense, he argues, is distribution the distribution of products, because the distribution of products is always *dependent* on more fundamental types of distribution—namely, (a) the distribution of the means of production and (b) the distribution of the members of a given society in different types of production (Marx [1857–1858] 1983, 31). For Marx, the process of distribution (the actual problem of moving goods) is just an outcome of the existing structure of distribution in terms of means and labor. However, the distribution of means and labor, Marx contends, is part and parcel of the production process itself. Distribution, thus, cannot be understood independent from production. Accordingly, for Marx, distribution is "a product of production" (24)—both in substance (regarding goods, as only what is produced can be distributed) as well as in form (as the structure of distribution is defined by the structure of production).

In addition to production and distribution, Marx also briefly discusses exchange and consumption in *Grundrisse*. In its most simple conception, Marx notes, *production* converts raw materials into things of use; *distribution* concerns the shares derived from participating in this production; *exchange*—which in our case concerns what I described as the business of wayfaring—allows individuals to sell or barter parts of this distributed share for other things they need;

and *consumption*, finally, closes the cycle. While consumption is less important for our discussion here, the question of exchange pertains directly to pathway economies. Marx explains that the relation between production and exchange is similar to the relation between production and distribution. The exchange of skills, he writes, is an integral part of production itself and thus not independent from it. The exchange of goods, he continues, is determined by the development and structure of production. Exchange, like distribution, is thus either a part of production itself or determined by the very processes of production (Marx [1857–1858] 1983, 33–34).

In summary, Marx concludes that production, distribution, exchange, and consumption are not identical but "parts of a totality" or "distinctions within a unity." While he does not deny the interdependent effects of production, distribution, exchange, and consumption onto each other, he clearly sees production as taking precedence over and impinging on the other three (Marx [1857–1858] 1983, 34). This analytic stance found reflection in the widespread hostility of socialist regimes against the business of trade. In the Soviet Union, for example, trading was often branded as speculation—a form of profiteering that ignores the hard labor of those actually producing something.[1]

Marx had good reasons to see production, and thus control over the means of production, as paramount. His view implied that the glaring injustice and stark inequalities of nineteenth-century capitalism could not be solved by a more equal and fair system of distribution; only radical change in terms of ownership and control over the means of production could better the plight of the working class.

Putting production center stage, however, also creates blind spots—intellectually, analytically, and politically. While Marx, for instance, explores the relations between production and distribution as well as between production and exchange, he does not give any concern to the relation between distribution and exchange. For him, distribution and exchange are just the two particularities linking the generality of production to the singularity of consumption, with exchange being more closely related to individual needs and distribution to society.

The ties between distribution and exchange, on the contrary, have been implicitly at the core of the reflections on "the gift" by Marcel Mauss (1923) and many anthropologists inspired by his groundbreaking work. While Mauss never actually used the term distribution in a sense comparable to Marx, the ceremonial distribution of wealth in potlatch rituals or circulatory systems of exchange, such as in the Kula ring, became points of reference in anthropological theory.

A fuller discussion of Marx and Mauss and their understandings of distribution and exchange would take us too far away from the issue at stake. Suffice it to say that there is ample ethnographic evidence from a variety of contexts around the globe showing that distribution is not a corollary of production but rather deeply integrated in processes of exchange. This certainly holds true for the distribution of subsidized rice in the example I have given. In simple terms, one could argue that in the old Himalayan trade, the distribution of lowland grain in the villages along the route was embedded in the logistics of caravan trade. In other words, distribution was a modality of exchange. In its subsidized form, rice is explicitly defined as a good for redistribution. Exchange and the logistics or transport, then, become a modality of distribution. In both cases, the significance of production is relatively minor.

Tshewang's efforts to partake in the government's distribution of subsidized rice required him to push aside the very relations of exchange. At the same time, however, these relations remained indispensable for successfully fulfilling the contract. While the role of a contractor implies a commitment to pure transport in the service of distribution, the social reality of Upper Humla required Tshewang and his associates to practice the kind of wayfaring described in chapter 4. As contractors, they were still in the business of wayfaring, so to speak.

What made matters even more complicated was the fact that the deep social relations necessary to fulfill the contract were the same that had been instrumental for the construction of the Limi Road in the first place—the very infrastructure on which the rice contract depended. Without exchange, and the promise of exchange in the context of a pathway's envisioned revival, the Limi Road would never have been built. The pure form of transport determined by the contract was difficult to reconcile with this history. Finding themselves in this dilemma, Tshewang and his associates decided not to seek any further rice contracts.

Tshewang's dilemma, despite its specificity, helps us unpack a set of larger issues regarding the labor of distribution. First, it highlights the role and scope of subsidies in Nepal and the highlands of Asia in general. Second, it raises the question of why subsidies and the politics of distribution have received relatively little academic and public attention in debates about the present and future of the greater Himalayas. And third, it points to the actual work of distribution and helps unmoor the discussion of labor from its strong associations with production. Let me follow up on these three issues one by one.

Subsidies, Distribution, and Aid

The history of food subsidies in Humla goes back to the early 1970s, when a drought in the Karnali region triggered an acute food shortage and the army reacted by air-dropping sacks of lowland rice. Since then, the government of Nepal has maintained at least minimal provisioning of the region. According to Adhikari (2008), the Maoist conflict (1996–2006) and a series of droughts since 2006 exacerbated the situation. By 2008, the National Food Corporation—the government organization tasked with the problem—annually supplied about 10,000 tons of food to thirty districts (Government of Nepal 2009, 99–100). In principle, every household in Upper Humla is entitled to five kilograms of subsidized rice per month, which only covers a part of household needs. The rice brought in as food aid is white and different in taste from the varieties of red rice grown in the lower hills of the region. White rice not only became a staple that gradually replaced the red rice and other local grains but also a status symbol, adding another layer to the problem (Grocke and Mckay, 2016, 306). In addition, China is delivering food aid on a more informal basis to the border districts in Nepal.[2]

The story of subsidized salt started even earlier. The distribution of industrial iodized salt lies in the hands of the Nepal Salt Trading Corporation, founded in 1963 (Karmakar and Pandav 1985). As mentioned in chapter 3, the Indian government provides assistance to Nepal, bearing both the cost of the iodized salt and "transportation by rail, road, and air; packing, stamping, and labeling of bags and expenditure on salaries and allowances of liaison officer and staff employed specifically for distribution of iodized salt in inaccessible areas" (Commonwealth Legal Information Institute 1973, art. III). The agreement, originally signed in 1973, has since been renewed several times (Government of Nepal 2011; Jayshi and Haidar 2014). Iodized Indian salt is readily available and sold for a minimal price in Humla as elsewhere in the Himalayas. Given the relatively small amount of salt a household needs compared to grain, these subsidies are only a minor contribution to household budgets.

Distribution, however, does not stop at cheap salt and five kilograms of subsidized rice per month. In one way or another, most of the nontrade income opportunities are tied to the politics of subsidies and distribution. With the food crises came the nongovernmental organizations (NGOs), singling out Humla as a worthy receiving end in the context of global distributive injustice and channeling money from Europe and America to the area (Citrin 2010). Currently, there are more than a hundred NGOs present in Simikot—a small fraction of the 40,000 NGOs registered in the country between 1977 and 2014 (Karkee and Comfort 2016). Most of them are local organizations established as implementation partners of Kathmandu-based development agencies.

Learning the language of international development and establishing an NGO is a common strategy for educated young Humli. While the founder of such an NGO would typically be based in Kathmandu, this strategy usually includes establishing a physical presence in Simikot, ideally by building a house, where the organization has its offices and some members of the founder's family live. Apart from better access to subsidized rice, a house in Simikot affords proximity to schools as well as other potential benefits of aid distributed through Humla's only airport. Simikot has seen a veritable construction boom over the past decade, fueled by the influx of donor money.

The politics of distribution are even more accentuated on the Tibetan side of the border. Today, around 70 percent of household incomes in Purang County are derived from subsidies, according to an estimate by a Chinese researcher familiar with the situation. Regardless of the accuracy of this estimate, it is clear that subsidies have come to play an increasingly important role in Tibet as well as other parts of western China (Fischer 2011, 2015; Global Times 2017). These subsidies, which I will come back to in more detail, consist of a combination of environmental compensation for the reduction of herd sizes on rangelands deemed ecologically fragile, poverty subsidies, and border bonuses. On top of these direct monetary contributions, a series of newer development policies are now used in China, including the subsidized construction of new housing for rural families as well as cheap credit for business.

These subsidies on the Chinese side of the border have a profound impact on Upper Humla. Most economic activity in the region is at least indirectly tied to these subsidies and the politics of distribution within China. The demand for seasonal construction labor in Purang on which most Limi families rely is driven by subsidies; the new houses built in this context are often decorated by Humli thangka painters and equipped with furniture made in Nepal; the boom for ritual objects and precious things such as maple *phuru* coincides with the rising availability of cash through subsidies in Tibet; and cross-border business in the roadhead entrepôts is often based on credit granted by Tibetan or Chinese businesspeople who themselves found ways to tap into this flow of money pouring into western Tibet.

With some variations, this is true not only for Humla and western Tibet but all the areas straddling the border between Nepal and Tibet. The politics of distribution—from food aid and poverty subsidies to development projects and government schemes—are at work throughout the region. Subsidies and the question of distribution are a crucial part of both the livelihood strategies and the dreams and ambitions of people living in the highlands. In this context, production—in agriculture, crafts, and construction—is increasingly determined by the politics and practices of distribution rather than the other way around. Distribution (a) provides investment for production and (b) shapes the basic structure of production processes. The primacy of distribution not only turns Marx's logic on its head, but it also has the capacity to reverse the directions of exchange along a pathway: salt from the south and rice from the north, as Tshewang noted when watching the sheep and goat caravan leave.

Productionism

Distribution and subsidies are pervasive and, if anything, have gained rather than lost importance. Yet they often remain invisible. "Give a man a fish and you feed him for a day; teach a man to fish and you feed him for a lifetime"—so goes the saying that has become a meme in global development discourse. James Ferguson (2015, 36) calls out the "productionist premise" that undergirds this slogan. It identifies the problem of underdevelopment in a deficit of production based on a lack of skill and outlines a solution: training to improve and increase production. Following this logic, distribution—giving a man a fish—is not only depicted as futile and unsustainable but potentially even counterproductive.

This logic can be seen in the numerous workshops offered by NGOs in the Himalayas, ranging from hospitality training to microcredit management, from farmer business schools to marketing classes for women cooperatives producing handicrafts. Even if attendance in a training workshop is paid and being included in a "pilot project" usually comes with direct and substantial support, the idea is almost always that the respective development project does not set up a structure of distribution but rather helps kick-start income generation through one or another form of production. Or—returning to the refrain of man and fish—a development project may chip in a fishing rod or two, or even build a fishpond and hand out nets, yet it remains rhetorically tied to the promise of self-sustaining future production.

Following this logic, even outright food aid needs to be repackaged as some form of honest and productive labor—for example, in the form of food-for-work programs, in which aid recipients provide their labor to help upgrade a road or build a hospital. Without at least some productive yield, the fear is that aid might just foster laziness and keep a *man* dependent. The standard narrative is that men should work, produce, and provide; only women rearing children have an excuse to be dependent. Ferguson calls this gendered perspective a "patriarchal productionism," which continues to form the ethical and analytical basis of global development (Ferguson 2015, 36, 41–47). Dependence has no room in these debates.

This productionist bias glosses over the fact that dependence is sometimes actively sought, as we have seen in the previous chapters. Seeking dependence can be a form of establishing and maintaining relations that are a priori asymmetrical—be it between a local road construction committee and a government office in Kathmandu or between a monastery and a welfare association abroad.

In other words, dependence is part and parcel of the process of tying place-knots. Rather than a defect that needs to be mended, dependence is, in Ferguson's words, a "carefully cultivated status," and "declarations of dependence" are a powerful sociopolitical tool (Ferguson 2015, 107–8).[3]

The premise of production also limits the scope of what a development initiative is able to address. None of the development projects I have come across in the Himalayas has focused on developing brokerage or trade, for example. Giving a village a truck (or an excavator, for that matter) is not among the options on the table. The business of wayfaring and existing forms of distribution remain on the fringes of international development agendas. Development agencies would much rather spend money on developing a logo and a branding strategy for potential future products to be sold on imagined future markets than supporting existing forms of exchange and distribution; they would rather sponsor workshops on how to cook for potential future tourists than help traders deal with the bureaucratic complexities of contemporary cross-border trade.

What we find is a productionist rhetoric of essentially distributive interventions. This rhetoric thereby masks the real productive role of distributive development interventions in local economies—namely, not by teaching future fishermen to fish but rather through the very language and logic of global development interventions, which provide career perspectives, access to powerful social networks, and the potential to attract more funds in the future. In this context, "being local," at least in the eyes of the global development industry, gains in importance and provides one more reason for the stickiness of remote villages in place-knots. Once a village becomes a case for a pilot project, chances are high that it is selected for future projects as well. Here, the agents of development themselves become the fish, and those allegedly in need of training have long learned how to catch them— carefully, silently, avoiding any noise that could drive them away.

The slogan of teaching a man to fish rather than giving him a fish is attributed to a Chinese proverb or a Confucian saying. Ironically, today, it is the People's Republic of China that hands out the most fish in the form of subsidies. Many of these subsidies are related to the willingness of people to abstain from production for the greater good of environmental protection. Rangeland management policies or regulations that outlaw agricultural production on slopes steeper than twenty-five degrees usually come with compensation schemes to ease the economic impact on affected populations. But even these subsidies are wrapped in a layer of future production rhetoric. They often point to heritage tourism as a potential productive domain: dancing for tourists will replace the drudgery of farming or herding, so the promise goes.

Last but not least, the productionist bias goes hand in hand with the sedentarist bias described in chapter 3. Just as the notion of community remains tied to land and locality, labor continues to be imagined as first and foremost productive rather than distributive. Productionist and sedentarist imaginaries create an echo chamber for a certain kind of development vision: the remote and poor local communities that, through training and expertise from outside, find a way out of underdevelopment through local production while maintaining their role as guardians of cultural heritage and stewards of fragile environments.

This vision of sedentarist productionism also defines the scope in which the current food crises in western Nepal is analyzed—namely, as crises of domestic food *production* (NeKSAP 2009, 3). This crisis of production is attributed to a number of factors, including poor seed varieties, insufficient irrigation, climate change, population growth, and paradoxically, the lack of male labor because of out-migration and depopulated villages. The solution suggested, for example, by Oxfam (Kilpatrick 2011, 3), includes support for micro-irrigation schemes and seed banks through cash-for-work programs, the promotion of better seeds, training for improved farming techniques, and building market linkages between communities and traders (as if such linkages had never existed). What is absent from this analytic perspective and the policies derived from it is an understanding of distribution and exchange—both historical and contemporary.

The Labor of Distribution

This gap in mainstream analytic perspectives also means that the entire economy of pathways remains out of sight.

In standard economic terms, the labor of distribution that is directly concerned with transport and logistics is subsumed under the category of services. As such, it is part of gross domestic product (GDP)—the standard measure of *production*. Nevertheless, the labor of distribution that facilitates these services is rarely a focus of development agendas in the highlands of Asia. Transport and logistics are the business of outsiders or wealthy Kathmandu-based elites rather than "local communities." The lens of sedentarist productionism tends to highlight harmful or at least problematic forms of mobility, such the trafficking of protected species or precarious labor migration.

As distribution remains hidden behind the sedentarist and productionist bias, the actual work invested in this domain is neither much appreciated nor well understood. I fully agree with Ferguson who proposes "an analytical focus" on what he terms "distributive labor." As he writes, "To appreciate the way that distribution can be the object of labor, I will suggest, we must be prepared to sever what has become an unthinking and dogmatic coupling of the concept of labor with the process of production" (Ferguson 2015, 97).

Let me summarize the point I seek to make. In pathway economies, like in Upper Humla, prosperity is not primarily linked to production but to business derived from exchange. The long-standing exchange of salt and grain took place between two ecological zones—the arid Tibetan Plateau and the fertile valleys of lower Nepal. Following Marx, we could say that this form of exchange was structured by the unequal production of salt and grain in these different ecological zones. For the trading communities engaged in this exchange, it was not only a form of business but also an important means of distribution within their translocal households—distribution as a modality of exchange.

With the state-sponsored distribution of salt and rice, the profitability of this traditional trade came under pressure. Subsidized rice and salt, and more recently the manifold cash subsidies in Tibet, further cut production out of the equation. Once a product is subsidized, the importance of its physical distribution—and thus the issues of logistics and transport—become the focus of attention. Exchange, in this context, increasingly becomes a modality of distribution.

This fuzziness between old exchange in the service of distribution and distribution as part of long-standing relations of exchange made Tshewang's work as a rice contractor so difficult. Distribution in this context is never simply a matter of distributive justice; it is always also a practical challenge conditioned by social relations, difficult terrain, the border, and the weather. Distribution, thus, requires labor: the work of contractors, NGO employees, and participants in food-for-work programs. In Purang, the subsidies and distributive state programs even created a new labor market, as we have seen, bringing about a form of frontier capitalism that revolves more around distribution than production.

The politics and practices of distribution are obviously crucial, yet they tend to be eclipsed by sedentarist productionism and the idea that a man should never just be given a fish. This leads to a series of fundamental misunderstandings—namely, that remote peripheral communities need training in value chain development, agricultural improvement, and tourism, and that they have to be shown ways to avoid rural–urban migration. This is all well intended and maybe useful for some. However, the resulting picture of the challenges, ambitions, and livelihood decisions taken in the highlands is incomplete, at best, and often rather far removed from any reality on the ground. In the context at stake, the labor of distribution is necessarily work carried out along a pathway. And, in the age of subsidies, working in a pathway economy is increasingly tied up in the labor of distribution.

The world of global development, entangled in the business of distribution while trying to foster production, and its effort to cure mountains and people are the topic of the third and final part of this book.

Part 3
INTERVENTIONS

ICIMOD workshop, Kathmandu. *Source*: Martin Saxer, 2016.

INTERLUDE
Kailash—Truly Sacred

Hotel Himalaya, Kathmandu. The parking lot is full of fancy SUVs with blue diplomatic number plates.[1] The last days of monsoon bring intermittent rains. A hotel employee equipped with a large umbrella is waiting to bring visitors from the parking lot to the hotel's ballroom where the workshop is taking place.

The International Centre for Integrated Mountain Development (ICIMOD) has invited its partner organizations in Nepal, India, and China for a three-day review and planning session for its Kailash Sacred Landscape Conservation and Development Initiative—KSLCDI, in ICIMOD speak. The initiative's aim is "to achieve long-term conservation of ecosystems, habitats and biodiversity, while encouraging sustainable development, enhancing the resilience of communities in the landscape, and safeguarding cultural linkages among local populations."

I just started a stint as a visiting researcher at ICIMOD. I still feel lost in the jungle of acronyms swirling around. The review and planning session, I hope, will help me become familiar with the language and logic of the initiative and its components. More than fifty people—delegations from the seven project partners in India, Nepal, and China—have come together to discuss progress and schedule activities for the final phase of the initiative.

The conference venue features large round tables; it is designed for weddings rather than for conferences. There is no seating order, but the Nepali, Indian, and Chinese delegations don't mingle. Each delegation gathers around a couple of tables of their own. A sea of national isles emerges in the lavish ballroom of one of Kathmandu's best hotels. Along the wall, a line of tables provides exhibition space for the various brochures, maps, and publications. These "knowledge products" are the harvest of the initiative's first three and a half years.

The agenda today includes "planning of human resources and fieldwork consolidation," "strategies on converting outputs to outcomes and impacts," "disseminating knowledge products to create impact," and "augmenting the initiative's communication strategy."

The workshop begins with a pair of presentations on the management philosophies that ICIMOD currently subscribes to: Theory of Change and Impact Pathways. Both are well-known frameworks in the development industry. They are closely related to each other. Both aim at working backward from a long-term goal to envisioned outcomes and the activities necessary to achieve them; both stress plausibility of assumptions, feasibility of the planned interventions, and testability of the indicators chosen to evaluate outcome and impact. So-called SMART criteria—specific, measurable, attributable, realistic, and time-bound—are part of the highly structured toolbox to help design interventions in the name of development and conservation. Nevertheless, Theory of Change and Impact Pathways understand themselves as participatory approaches that involve stakeholders throughout the process.

Stakeholders is another term that I only now begin to understand. The stakeholders here are not the people living within the territory defined as "Kailash Sacred Landscape" but the seven partner organizations. All of them are well-established research institutes and government agencies of the three countries joined in the initiative. Improving *their* participatory, transboundary collaboration is the goal of the event. However, the seating order in national isles that emerged so naturally hints at one of the problems identified in an evaluation by the German government's Gesellschaft für Internationale Zusammenarbeit (GIZ). ICIMOD's transboundary initiative lacks "transboundariness," the report bemoans. The problem needs to be addressed in order to maintain a perspective for future funding. This is not an easy task given the political sensitivities involved. In the Kailash region, not all borders are settled yet. The project area includes territory claimed by India, Nepal, and China. One of the challenges is thus to establish *transboundary* cooperation without talking about *borders*.

Tensions flare up for a moment when one of the new "knowledge products" is presented—a vegetation and land-use map of the project area. Compiling the map required considerable resources. The members of the ICIMOD's Geospatial Solutions Group are proud of their achievement. During their presentation, a member of the Chinese delegation stands up and raises his hand. He says that the map is indeed a valuable knowledge product, but unfortunately, he would never be able to show it to his government because it lacks borderlines. "You have to understand my government," he adds.

There is no time to address the conundrum of borderlines—first carefully omitted and then dearly missed—or to "understand" the sensitivities of the Chinese government. The workshop's program is dense. Review and planning require discipline. The three-day workshop consists of tightly scheduled five-minute presentations on each activity. Time is of the essence, and the task at hand is to evaluate progress and plan the coming seventeen months according to the Gantt charts with their looming milestones.

It is, again, the Chinese delegation that faces most criticism: Reports were not delivered on time, and the outputs so far are difficult to reconcile with the framework in which they have to fit. Members of the Chinese delegation try to translate between the development visions of "their government" and the logic and language that governs the workshop. As happened before, when the issue was the disqualifying lack of borders on the vegetation and land-use map, their translation efforts are lost in the stream of short presentations.

In the breaks between the sessions, the male participants of the Chinese delegation gather outside the ballroom for a smoke. I join them and listen in. The anecdotes they share concern the messy but ultimately benevolent interventions of "their government." Five years ago, there were hardly any private cars in Purang, one of them says; now there are 120 registered vehicles, but there are only a couple of driving licenses. At that, the group erupts in laughter. The yak herders who offer rides to Indian pilgrims around Kailash make a fortune, yes, and they were already well-off because of the subsidies they get—subsidies for poverty alleviation, for border residents, and for limiting the number of animals to conserve the fragile mountain pastures. . . . True, but most herders have not reduced their herds; rather, they learned how to evade inspectors. . . . Exactly, the delegates all seem to agree. Whenever an inspector is about to show up, the animals are gone, one of the members of the Chinese delegation observes, smiling.

Such tales of witted evasion and the overall stunning economic change that brought prosperity to a remote region, told on the sidelines of a planning session that is too tightly scheduled and too focused on a particular outlook on the world to be heard, make me think of the people I met in Upper Humla. My Humli friends are similarly impressed by the economic developments in western Tibet; yet they also take a more critical stance toward the "benevolence" of the party state. Their trading partners in Tibet sometimes refer to themselves as birds in a golden cage—well-fed but unable to fly.

The day ends with a session on communication. A new logo is presented: *Kailash—truly sacred*. As a geographical indication, it will be used to advertise products made on the territory of the Kailash Sacred Landscape. Then, an ICIMOD communications officer, a German woman, makes us stand up, move our legs, and physically take a stance on a number of contested topics by positioning ourselves in space. After some initial reluctance, the delegations part from their table isles and participate. We all shake off the long hours of sitting. A light-hearted mood fills the ballroom.

Finally, the delegations from each country are asked to brainstorm ideas for better communication strategies. We gather around flip charts and listen to what each delegation has come up with. The Nepali partners make three suggestions: print publications, local FM radio and TV shows, and newsletters to all stake-holders to be published twice a year.

The Chinese delegation stresses the importance of tea breaks for informal dis-cussions, e-mails for formal communication, and most importantly, the use of WeChat, the omnipresent Chinese messaging platform. The Indians propose quarterly meetings and field visits called "Landscape *Yatras*" (the Hindi word for pilgrimage). To the Chinese WeChat proposal, they respond, "And for elec-tronic media we are having some other means of communication."

CURATION AT LARGE

International organizations and development agencies have had a tremendous influence in Nepal. The introduction of iodized salt to combat goiter was an idea advertised by the World Health Organization; community forestry and the rules for using excavators on rural roads were pushed by development agencies; the food-for-work programs were championed by the World Food Programme. All these initiatives found entry into official state policy. The global development industry has steered and guided Nepal's political economy of development to a far greater extent than in most countries in Asia. Nepal is, at once, a laboratory where approaches in the vanguard of global development are being tried out and an arena from which "lessons learned" are being distilled. These lessons learned, in turn, feed back into the evolving visions of global development.

In this final part of the book, I juxtapose different outside interventions and explore their outcomes and legacies. I approach this task ethnographically—by describing the world in which such interventions are taking shape.

For Mountains and People

Between August 2016 and January 2017, I worked as a research fellow at the International Centre for Integrated Mountain Development (ICIMOD) in Kathmandu. ICIMOD is an intergovernmental institution that seeks to unite its eight member countries—Afghanistan, Bangladesh, Bhutan, China, India, Myanmar, Nepal, and Pakistan—in finding ways to develop sustainable and resilient mountain communities. Its tagline reads "For Mountains and People." Founded in 1983 with seed money from international development agencies, ICIMOD straddles the boundaries between intergovernmental policy think tank and the world of the global development industry.

One of ICIMOD's initiatives is called "Transboundary Landscapes." It aims at fostering cross-border cooperation for sustainable development and conservation in five mountain regions in the greater Himalayas. These five transboundary landscapes include the two regions this book revolves around: the Kanchenjunga area where Walung is situated, and the Kailash area of which Humla is part. I was eager to join ICIMOD because I wanted to learn more about this initiative and, somewhat naively, thought that what I had learned over the preceding years might be of use and could, perhaps, help shape future interventions.

In summer 2016, I moved to Kathmandu with my family. We found a flat close to the British school where my daughter was enrolled. This part of the city, called Lalitpur, is home to many diplomats and staff members of nongovernmental organizations (NGOs). It is known for world-class cuisine, organic café latte, German bakeries, farmers markets, and yoga classes. Every morning, walking my daughter to school, I would navigate the traffic jam that built up in front of the school when the rich Nepali families, embassy corps, and development professionals dropped off their children.

Then, just around the corner, I would wait for the ICIMOD bus to take me to the organization's campus and headquarters in the outskirts of the city. Working at ICIMOD came with considerable prestige and perks, like a company bus. The air-conditioned ride was a relief from Kathmandu's notorious dust and pollution. Most of my colleagues would wear face masks waiting for the bus. Once embarked, they would take them off and start talking about their current assignments or the latest gossip.

The majority of ICIMOD's roughly 250 staff members were South Asian, most of them Indian or Nepali. Some were seasoned professionals in key management positions, and some were recent graduates aspiring a career in the world of global development. What they shared was a deep love for the mountains and an honest concern for conservation issues. None of my colleagues, however, was from the Tibetan-speaking borderlands of northern Nepal. Thus, despite ample South Asian expertise and close ties to regional governments, ICIMOD's transboundary initiative in the Kailash and Kanchenjunga areas was not based on intimate knowledge or experience. Like most outside interventions born and bred in the offices of development organizations or state ministries, ICIMOD's initiative started from a certain set of assumptions about the problem at hand: that there was a need to balance conservation of nature and heritage with sustainable income generation; that training could help unlock hidden potentials;

and, especially in the case of the transboundary initiative, that healing a landscape split by borders required international cooperation. These underlying assumptions did not stem from a detailed analysis. They were embedded in a particular outlook on the world and cast in a specific aesthetic vision of what a healthier future for mountains and people would look like. And, despite the enthusiasm and love for the mountains, there were asymmetries of knowledge and power in play that could not be glossed over.

Bikas, as development is called in Nepali, is often criticized both for its failure to materialize and for the kind of inequality it reproduces. The majority of politicians and government officials in Nepal are Brahmin or Chhetri, the high caste Hindu elite. Even the leaders of the Maoist revolution came from this background. The same is true for the majority of Nepali development professionals. In his 1991 book *Fatalism and Development*, Dor Bahadur Bista links Nepal's continuing "backwardness" directly to the cultural disposition of its ruling class. The Brahmin-Chhetri elite, Bista argues, regard rent-seeking and government appointments as a natural privilege. Education is not about skills but status. Becoming an important person, an *afno manchhe*, is the primary goal. His argument is a culturalistic one: India's caste structure imported into the Hindu Kingdom of Nepal poses an obstacle to development. The country's potential would actually lie with those outside this elite—the hill and mountain people, he argues. Regardless of whether such cultural explanations suffice to explain Nepal's history with development, Bista's scathing insider critique echoes through contemporary debates in Nepal.[1]

Based on my previous research on the creation of a Tibetan medicine industry in the People's Republic of China (PRC), I had certain assumptions about how development driven by elites that consider themselves to be the center of civilization plays out among those seen to be at the margin. Large-scale interventions, regardless of how benevolent their intentions, become enmeshed in subtle forms of resistance on the ground. For me, the work of James Scott has been a great source of inspiration to think about such processes. I owe many insights to his conceptual groundwork.

In *The Moral Economy of the Peasant* (1976) and *Weapons of the Weak* (1985), Scott analyzes everyday tactics of peasants in Southeast Asia in their dealings with state interventions. Such tactics include obfuscation, foot-dragging, and forms of resistance that only occasionally turn into open rebellion. Following up on this theme, Scott highlights the "hidden transcripts"—the subtle and secret discourses of the powerless that undergird the art of resistance (Scott 1990, 2002)—and the ways in which such "hidden transcripts" relate to the "public transcripts" of official rhetoric.[2] In *Seeing Like a State* (1998), Scott turns to these public transcripts and the "thin simplifications" they are often based on in order to explain how major schemes to improve the human condition have failed time and again. His examples for such schemes range from scientific forestry in Germany to the creation of modernist cities and the catastrophes resulting from forced collectivization of agriculture. High-modernist planning and the quest for legibility, combined with a strong state and a weak civil society, are a recipe for disaster, Scott argues. Statistics, surveillance, and the invention of the passport (Scott 2002) are the tools of choice in the state's quest for legibility and control. In *The Art of Not Being Governed* (2009), Scott explores how this conflict played out in the mountainous regions of the Southeast Asian Massif. Following Willem van Schendel (2002), Scott calls this region Zomia. According to Scott, the rough terrain of Zomia long served as a refuge for people consciously "opting out" of the taxes, corvée obligations, diseases, and wars that characterize rice-growing valley states. From this perspective, egalitarian political organization, agricultural techniques, and cultural forms in Zomia are not ancient relics of indigenous groups that have not yet embraced the civilizational achievements of their lowland neighbors; they rather appear as a conscious strategy of avoiding state control by settling in the mountains.

Scott's work, pursuing bold arguments for the sake of clarity, has been highly influential. At the same time, it also attracted a continuous stream of criticism (cf. Edelman 2005). My aim here is not to invest in the debate about whether Nepal, the PRC, or intergovernmental organizations such as ICIMOD "see like states," or whether Scott's take on Zomia provides a useful perspective on the Himalayas (Michaud 2010). My concern lies with a more fundamental question that has remained on the sidelines of the debate about how people in highland margins are dealing with their states. Evasion and subtle resistance are only two ways of reacting to outside interventions. Equally important are strategies of tapping into distributive flows, forging relations, and even dependence. What is at stake, then, is more than just power and forms of resistance. From a highland perspective in the twenty-first century, the problem at hand is less about the desire "not to be governed." The questions are rather how to make the best use of being governed; how to co-opt the forces of incoming money, language, and power; and how to use them as avenues into state structures, both local and central (Zhang and Saxer 2017). The lines of friction are less clear than suggested when casting powerful states and elites against powerless local communities—not despite the obvious asymmetries of power but precisely because of the dependences and the fleeting opportunities that come with them.

An organization like ICIMOD certainly does not pursue the kind of high-modernist projects that Scott describes. While funded by states, it rather "sees" like an NGO. ICIMOD tries to stay clear of top-down "schemes to improve the human condition" (Scott 1998); it subscribes to a fair, bottom-up, participatory approach. International organizations in Nepal are truly trying to learn from the experiences and failures of development and conservation around the globe. Whether they live up to the lofty promises of the "public transcripts" on their websites is not my primary concern. The question that keeps puzzling me is simpler: How to understand interventions in the name of development and conservation in an era of subsidies, participatory development, and honest concerns for cultural heritage?

To explore this question by analyzing asymmetries of power, wealth, and knowledge is important but not sufficient. To understand development and conservation in the Himalayas at this particular historic moment, we need to take such asymmetries into account, but we must also consider the genuine attempts of those planning and implementing initiatives to do better than their predecessors.

For some, the Himalayas are a sensitive border zone; for others they are quickly turning into a resource frontier. For international organizations, however, the Himalayas are first and foremost a salvage frontier (Tsing 2005, 32)—a sensitive socio-ecological system that needs care. The notion of *curation* has become an important term for me in trying to understand Himalayan development and conservation initiatives. The idea is not mine alone; it has emerged in a process of collectively thinking through materiality and connectivity in a series of workshops at LMU Munich (Saxer and Schorch 2020).[3] Let me sketch out this idea before we proceed.

Curare—to Heal, to Cure

Curation at large has little to do with the work of a museum curator. I take the term in its original meaning of *curare*—to cure. On the one hand, to cure means to heal, to remedy, to make better. On the other hand, to cure also denotes efforts to cleanse and preserve, to prevent a raw substance from rotting and infecting its surroundings. Understood in this broad sense, curation is part and parcel of contemporary interventions in the name of fair, participatory, bottom-up development and conservation. It offers a perspective on such interventions and their attempt to pursue a more circumspect form of assistance.

Describing interventions in the name of curation as "curatorial" or "curative" does not fully capture the semantics of the original *curare*. The adjective "curatorial" conjures up the work of a curator; "curative" implies the ability to heal but not necessarily to cleanse. I therefore call such interventions *curational*.

The rhetoric of curation undergirds both high-modernist schemes and the various civilizational missions that roared through colonies and peripheries of empires and nation-states. Consider, for example, the system of tribute through which the Chinese empire aimed to govern its unruly frontiers. Tribute, on the one hand, implied a declaration of submission by a "tribe" at the edge of the empire, acknowledging the emperor's supremacy and right to rule. On the other hand, tribute was not just a form of tax but rather a system of exchange. Regular missions from the borderlands would bring tribute to the court and return with a wealth of gifts, which often exceeded the value of the goods they brought. Tribute structured the relations between "civilized" center and "barbarian" peripheries (Fairbank and Teng 1941; for a more critical approach see Hamashita, Grove, and Selden 2008; Tagliacozzo and Chang 2011). The imperial administration thereby distinguished between "raw" and "cooked" barbarians, referring on the surface to the type of food that barbarians were imagined eating and more generally to the question of whether they had tributary relations with the center and thus had declared their dependence. The implicit civilizational project at the heart of this distinction was to "cook"—or to "cure"—barbarians by implicating them in the system of tributary relations (Fiskesjö 1999).

Of course, just like the high-modernist schemes that Scott describes, this civilizational mission hardly ever played out in the ways foreseen. However, it provided the moral and political basis for powerful interventions couched in a language of curation. Arguably, this kind of curational ambition still has currency in the PRC's contemporary development efforts, which combine a demand for loyalty to the Communist Party with forms of alimentation through subsidized exchange and distribution. In imperial tribute, as much as in current Chinese development, such curational rhetoric is obvious.

Curation does not offer a clear-cut distinction between different types of interventions. It is rather a matter of degree. In some interventions, curational ambitions are explicit; in others, curational rhetoric serves as a smokescreen. Rather than defining a new category of intervention, the notion of curation helps direct our attention away from spectacular schemes like the construction of dams, road corridors, or special economic zones toward the long-term agendas and forces of which such projects are typically part.

Curation, then, is more akin to constant gardening: It involves singling out a plot and a crop, preparing the ground, sowing and watering, weeding and preventing pests from taking their toll. Like gardening, curation has a long-term goal. It necessarily includes setbacks and involves humans and nonhumans, tools and ideas, side effects and feedback mechanisms. Only in its initial design, a curational intervention is self-sufficient. As a process, it necessarily becomes entangled with its surroundings. Its success depends on co-opting these surroundings for its overarching goal. Curation, thus, is always already part of the world it seeks to foster and cure.

It is important to stress that my aim with the term curation is not to depict development schemes in the rosy language of their "public transcripts" or to buy into their self-understandings as ultimately benevolent. The story I seek to tell is more complex. A curational intervention is not devoid of power; it is itself a relation of power. Like crops and weeds in a garden, the objects of curation are rarely asked for their consent. Their value is assessed according to their contribution to the gardener's ends. The notion of curation is meant to shed light on the pragmatic and messy ways in which ideology—broadly understood as a morally underpinned and future-oriented set of ideas—takes shape in the social and material world by creating and fostering an environment conducive to a certain kind of experience. This experience, the curators hope, will lend the formative ideas behind a curational ambition their gestalt and bring into being the envisioned future. The emerging social and material world, the other way around, leaks back into the very vision that drives it.

Take, for example, the narrow alleyways in the old neighborhoods of Beijing and other Chinese cities. They are called *hutong*. While most hutong were torn down to make room for high-rise buildings of glass and steel, some were preserved, "cleansed," and enmeshed in new curational initiatives: heritage combined with tourism and commerce for twenty-first-century China. The experiences gained from this curational intervention became a template for the safeguarding of cultural heritage in the People's Republic. This template is used to embellish—or, in most cases, re-create—other old towns throughout the country (Steenberg and Rippa 2019; White 2010; Saxer 2012, 2014; Kolås 2008; Nyíri 2006). It is geared as much toward fixing dilapidated "backward" neighborhoods as it is toward healing the nation's wounds left behind by the destruction of everything old since the Cultural Revolution (Anagnost 1997). On a global scale, the Chinese approach to heritage found entry into UNESCO conversations. Some see it as a model; others consider it the ultimate anti-model.

Curation goes beyond architecture and human-built environments. Giving ideology a certain gestalt conducive to particular experiences is also at stake in national parks and conservation areas. Endowed with certain kinds of facilities and equipped with a particular set of rules, national parks and conservation areas fit the notion of curation well. Their underlying curational ambitions are twofold: to conserve plants and wildlife and to make the experience of "nature" accessible to visitors. These experiences, then, will hopefully foster a response that further strengthens the call for environmental conservation. Usually, clear pedagogical goals come with national parks and conservation areas. The absence of infrastructure—except for basic facilities to provide access and reduce the footprint of visitors—resonates with the image of the wilderness to be healed

Signposts in Simikot. *Source*: Martin Saxer, 2012.

and cleansed from damaging practices, such as logging or the commercial collection of medicinal plants.

Consider also the introduction of community forestry in Nepal, which played a central role in the decline of sheep and goats caravans in Humla. The initiative's explicit goal was to heal the wounds of a series of former policies and interventions. In the 1950s, Nepal nationalized all private forests. On the one hand, the government justified this step with increasing forest degradation; on the other hand, nationalization was a policy to rectify the unfair distribution of forest resources. During the Rana regime (1846–1951), the so-called *birta* system rewarded officials with forestland for their services (Pokharel et al. 2007). Nationalization, however, curtailed customary use rights and undermined "indigenous" systems of forest management. Because the state had no capacity to replace these management systems, the result was extensive logging and further degradation. The looming "tragedy of the commons" (Hardin 1968), experts agreed, could only be addressed by handing the forests over to "local communities." The explicit mission of community forestry is to heal the ailing jungles and to cleanse them from predatory outside actors. The idea is that forests and local communities as their natural stewards can only regain their health together (Ives and Messerli 1989; Saxer 2013b).

Similar arguments can be made for the introduction of iodized salt to cure goiter or the rice subsidies alimenting the population of Humla and other Himalayan districts of Nepal. Both are meant to cure an ill.

Curation, in the sense suggested here, is thus neither pure ideology nor rhetoric; rather, it involves the practice of mobilizing things and people to shape a social and material environment. In other words, curation concerns the domain where ideology becomes palpable. This endeavor depends on a degree of collaboration by the "patient." In other words, curation relies on co-opting an existing social and material environment for this purpose.

What, then, is not considered curation?

There are many interventions that cannot be adequately described as curational. One example where curation fails to capture what is at stake are interventions that first and foremost aim at coercion and control. Consider, for example, the history of forced collectivization in the Soviet Union or the Great Leap Forward in China. Both schemes were clearly driven by ideology: integrating peasants into the project of building a communist society. Both schemes tried to create socio-material environments conducive to this end. However, despite the fact that their explicit goal was to cleanse and thereby cure what Communist Party elites identified as "ills," these sweeping interventions had little concern for existing social and material environments. They rather conjured up a radically new world. Extraction of surplus, coercion, and control took precedence over the kind of constant gardening that the term curation is equipped to describe.

Consider also the internment camps that China has established to deal with the perceived threat by Uighur nationalism (Amnesty International 2018; Wang 2018). These camps, officially called "vocational education and training centers," may be couched in a pedagogic rhetoric that could be called curational; yet, in practice, the ambition of reeducation to cleanse is far greater than to heal (see, for example, Amnesty International 2013).

Furthermore, extractive timber industries combined with subsequent agribusiness projects—planting rubber, palm oil, or soy on cleared forest land—have little to do with curational ambitions as understood here. Despite engaging in the creation of a particular material environment, such schemes are primarily extractive. They lack aspirations for a long-term positive effect and rather focus on immediate profit. Of course, they may still use curational language. In our present era, extractive or coercive schemes often face international media uproar when the ugliness of their actions becomes too obvious. It is thus no surprise when such schemes phrase their ambitions in distinctly curational terms. But even if curational rhetoric plays a role in such schemes, the socio-material environments created in the process are seldom geared toward engendering echoes and feedback loops between ideology and experience.

And finally, many worlds take shape with little curational intervention. The slow "organic" growth of a settlement, be it a village or a city, is one example.

While it may partially be the result of phases of planning and pockets of dedicated curational ambitions (each house its own little world), curation plays a minor role in their overall gestalt.

Partial Erasure and Affective Collaboration

Regardless of the degree to which an intent is curational, interventions typically start with the identification of an object and a problem. In conservation, the object can be a biodiversity hot spot, the habitat of an endangered species, a pristine jungle, or degraded pasturelands; the associated problems, then, are biodiversity loss, the fear of logging, or the process of desertification, respectively. In heritage making, the object of curation can be a temple, an old town, or an "ethnic" village; the associated problem is identified as a potential loss of history or cultural diversity. In debates on state security, the object may be a particular border region inhabited by a potentially rebellious population; the problem is uncertain loyalty that could become a threat to national unity.

Inscribed in this simultaneous identification of object and problem is often a solution that appears obvious. This solution typically stems from the very same ideological framework that led to the identification of object and problem in the first place. The solution to endangered biodiversity is a conservation area; the answer to the loss of history is a heritage site (ideally featuring on a UNESCO list). In other words, there is often a shortcut between identification of problem/object and suggested cure. Curational aspirations for a better future guide the identification of a "patient" and an "ill." The initial designs of interventions therefore tend to jump to conclusions.

This shortcut involves a reinterpretation of the object of curation and the partial erasure of existing relations with its surroundings. The national park-to-be is reimagined as a wilderness on the verge of disappearance. Current patterns of land use are the problem to be solved. A heritage site in the making is stripped of its present and recent history to make room for the preservation of a reimagined older history.

Mapping plays a crucial role in this respect. As I will discuss in more detail in chapter 9, outside interventions are often concerned with distinctly cartographic hopes and anxieties (Saxer 2016a; Billé 2016). Mapping correlates with a notion of space that is a priori Cartesian and flat. Curational strategies rely on defining a *proper*, as De Certeau would say (1984, 36)—a bonded zone that can be guarded from its surroundings. Zoning is an important first step because it allows for special rules to be applied. The spatial separation of an object of curation from its surroundings thereby amplifies the partial erasure of exiting relations.

Extractive or high-modernist schemes also involve zoning and erasure. Typically, they reimagine an existing socio-material environment as a "wasteland" or "frontier" waiting to be discovered and developed. However, while such schemes typically entail a complete erasure—a tabula rasa—to make room for something radically new, curational interventions rather start from a selective erasure of erstwhile relations. The object to be healed or preserved needs to be isolated from the noise surrounding it rather than razed to the ground. Or, to come back to the image of gardening, selective erasure with the purpose to cure tries to separate the weed from the crop. This work requires a consensus about what weeds and crops look like.

In this respect, curation touches on the affective qualities of governance. Affect, here, is more than a mere "smokescreen of rule" or a "ruse masking the dispassionate calculations that preoccupy states" (Laszczkowski and Reeves 2015, 2). Affect is not just epiphenomenal to the political, but it is the very substance of politics. Corporeal, tactile, and sensory, it connects human subjectivity with governance and the material environment (Laszczkowski and Reeves 2015, 2–5; Stoler 2004, 6; Navaro-Yashin 2012; Thrift 2008).

As curational interventions seek to foster vibrant socio-material environments, they are inseparable from this affective dimension. Based on the ethics of participation, inclusion, and long-term sustainability, curation cannot rely on strict planning and coercive control. It requires a certain degree of collaboration. Conservation does not work without local sensibility toward environmental issues; heritage making implicitly touches on questions of cultural identity, history, and belonging.

Affective collaboration, however, also plays a role in everyday life beyond the purview of development. Affect and collaboration are at the heart of tying places into knots, and they are key to exchange along pathways. Yet the efforts to heal mountains and people that I became part of at ICIMOD had little regard for translocal communities, the business of wayfaring, or the work and money invested in reviving an old pathway. The topologies of the socio-spatial relations that I described in parts I and II of this book are outside the organization's field of vision. The Boudha-based welfare and youth organizations that are such an integral part of translocal Himalayan communities, or the relations between monastic institutions in Kathmandu and the Himalayan valleys, remained out of sight.

Despite such blind spots and partial erasures, curational interventions like ICIMOD's Kailash Sacred Landscape Conservation and Development Initiative operate in the context of pathways and place-knots. While those designing and

pursuing projects in the name of conservation, heritage, and development con-
ceive of them as *outside* interventions, these projects are always already part and
parcel of the very object they intent to cure.

Sometimes, the ills identified to be cured are the direct result of other curational efforts—prior or ongoing. Much like in gardening, the materials mobi-
lized and the very environments curational interventions seek to cultivate hardly
ever behave as intended. They "speak up" and require further intervention to prevent them from undermining the agendas at stake. Whether we conceptualize
this "speaking up" as a form of agency in an actor-network (Latour 2005) or
whether we simply acknowledge that curational interventions are necessarily
part of a living environment and as such both animated and animating (Ingold
1980, 2010) is less important here. What counts is the fact that keeping a curational gestalt in play requires constant maintenance and care.

There is always a risk that the driving ideological impulse dies or is superimposed with a new one. Once this happens, the curated worlds begin to crumble
and what remains are ruins of former curational efforts. These ruins of yesterday's tomorrows (Corn and Horrigan 1984), then, become context and target of
today's curational ambitions. The result is a layering of curational interventions
that reminds me of a palimpsest: written over again and again, the traces of past
interventions continue to shimmer through—as scars, as lingering tensions, as
nostalgic memories, or as hopes that have not lost their appeal.

LANDSCAPES, DREAMSCAPES

In an era when global concerns for biodiversity and cultural heritage are layered on top of questions of security and expectations of development, interventions seldom stand alone. It is precisely the overlap and friction between interventions that defines the political arena in which they take place.

The subtle dissonances that surfaced during the review and planning workshop were not just related to state anxieties about a sensitive and unsettled border area; nor were they limited to different styles of communication. The deeper problem, I believe, is the fact that in this one curational intervention—the Kailash Sacred Landscape Conservation and Development Initiative (KSLCDI)—different curational ambitions rubbed shoulders.

On one side, there were the staff members of the workshop's organizer—the International Centre for Integrated Mountain Development (ICIMOD) based in Kathmandu—and their colleagues from the Nepali and Indian partner organizations. While sometimes critical of the initiative, they principally agreed with the initiative's outlook and style. They also benefited personally from ICIMOD's prestige. Being part of KSLCDI would look good on their résumés and might open further career paths. On the other side were the members of the Chinese delegation trying to square their government's broader visions with the initiative's framework and approach. This was an uphill battle, and much detail was lost in translation.

In this chapter, I explore the encounter of these different curational ambitions in the Kailash initiative. First, I need to discuss the "landscape approach" that inspired the initiative and the training materials produced to cure mountains and people. Second, I describe the Chinese development efforts that formed the context in with ICIMOD's *Kailash Sacred Landscape* was being implemented in Tibet. And third, I come back to the problem of partial erasure.

The Landscape Approach

At the heart of ICIMOD's curational ambitions is the "landscape approach," championed by the Global Landscapes Forum and adopted by a growing number of nongovernmental organizations (NGOs) and leading development agencies. Landscape approaches, Jeffrey Sayer and his colleagues write, "seek to provide tools and concepts for allocating and managing land to achieve social, economic, and environmental objectives in areas where agriculture, mining, and other productive land uses compete with environmental and biodiversity goals" (Sayer et al. 2013, 8349).

The landscape approach understands itself as a corrective to earlier forms of top-down planning in environmental conservation that led to exclusion and conflicts with communities on the ground. Thus, it does not advocate the kind of focused, sectoral intervention that high-modernist schemes pursued. "Sectoral approaches, despite still being predominant, have long been recognized as inadequate," Sayer et al. argue (2013, 8349). The landscape approach seeks to reconcile conservation and development by balancing the different stakes involved. This requires compromise and continuous adaptation rather than the vague promise of a future win-win situation for all parties involved.

The landscape approach found entry into mainstream debates. It ties in with the notion of ecosystems championed by the Convention on Biological Diversity (CBD 2019). In fact, CBD's Subsidiary Body on Scientific, Technical, and Technological Advice adopted the ten principles on which the landscape approach relies. These principles include continual learning and adaptive management; a common concern as entry point for interventions; working at multiple scales; taking into account the multiple uses of land and the various stakeholders; a negotiated and transparent logic of aspired change; forms of monitoring that are user-friendly and participatory; and strengthening the resilience and capacity of stakeholders.

All of this fits perfectly with ICIMOD's explicit goal to foster integrated development and conservation for the benefit of mountains and people. Derived from decades of "lessons learned," it resonates with the growing global concern for the future of the planet. The ten principles provide a blueprint for ICIMOD's curational ambitions.

Landscape approaches, including ICIMOD's "Transboundary Landscapes" program, are based on certain assumptions that are seldom discussed because they are simply taken for granted.

The Limi Valley. *Source*: Martin Saxer, 2011.

The first such assumption concerns the meaning of the term "landscape." A landscape can be defined as "an area delineated by an actor for a specific set of objectives" (Sayer et al. 2013, 8350). The important words here are "delineated" and "objectives." The question is: Who draws the line on the map, and who defines the objectives?

In the case at hand, the idea of a transboundary landscape initiative brought ICIMOD's expertise as an intergovernmental organization working across borders together with the landscape approach. KSLCDI served as the pilot project for this larger endeavor. It was a simple and brilliant idea, easy to pitch and promising in terms of funding. Throwing the sacredness of Mount Kailash into the mix only added to the appeal. In other words, KSLCDI did not start from a thorough analysis of the different sociocultural situations and political economies in the Kailash area but from an idea that made sense in the context of the global development industry. In a certain way, it was the promise of a cure at hand that led to the identification of the patient and the ill.

Singling out the KSLCDI project area was a collaborative process that involved partners in Nepal, India, and China; it did not, however, involve those living in the greater Kailash region. Only once drawn on a map and endowed with a name did the Kailash Sacred Landscape come into being. The Kailash Sacred Landscape is thus first and foremost a dreamscape derived from a mainstream idea in the world of global development; it conjures up a geography that hardly correlates with the experiences of those living in and moving through the area. No local toponym describes the delineated Kailash Sacred Landscape. The boundary of the project area (the only uncontested boundary, for that matter) did not exist prior to the project. The project area includes different topographies and ecological zones as well as considerable linguistic, sociocultural, and religious diversity. While some of the places within the Kailash Sacred Landscape do have a shared history of trade and exchange, others do not lie in proximity to any old pathway and had little contact with each other.

Nevertheless, defining the Kailash Sacred Landscape as a target for an intervention created an inside and an outside. Only those living inside the Kailash Sacred Landscape can participate and become local stakeholders. Delineation thereby reinforces the trope of the local, sedentary community and erases practices of mobility. The only stakeholders not expected to be sedentary and local are the project partners. Their stake in the landscape is a direct result of the intervention itself.

The second implicit assumption concerns management. At ICIMOD, as elsewhere in the world of global development, it is taken for granted that more and better management is key to solving problems. The other way around, the lack of management is typically blamed for environmentally destructive practices, such as overharvesting of medicinal plants or rangeland degradation caused by intensive grazing. Where local systems of dealing with scarce resources are already in place—such as rules for access to pastures, water for irrigation, or firewood—they are reified as "traditional management practices." This, however, does not free these systems from calls for better management. Strengthened and formalized training and management guidelines are seen as indispensable.

The notion of management is paramount at ICIMOD. Together with the UN Environment Programme, ICIMOD developed frameworks for "integrated ecosystem management" and "long-term environmental and socio-ecological monitoring," for example. The organization offered training for the project partners of the transboundary landscape initiatives to support their management capacities (ICIMOD 2016e).

Particular emphasis is also given to *local* management. ICIMOD produced a plethora of guidelines to improve the local management of almost every aspect of its work, ranging from transboundary rivers and springsheds to plant collection, waste, and sustainable tourism.

One of these guidelines, the management guidelines for the Api Nampa Conservation Area (ANCA) in Nepal's section of the Kailash Sacred Landscape, was discussed during the review and planning session. Established in 2010 as a community-led conservation area, ANCA is still in its infancy. One major issue is that the Api Nampa region is not just a biodiversity hot spot worthy of protection, but it is also a major *yartsagunbu* area that attracts scores of collectors each year. Yartsagunbu (*Ophiocordyceps sinensis*, caterpillar fungus) brought prosperity to the region; at the same time, it led to tensions over access and entry fees, conflicts in the camps of the collectors, and concerns over the environmental impact of the boom. Early on, ICIMOD identified the issue as a management problem and pushed the ANCA management council, an elected body of representatives from twenty-one villages in the conservation area, to develop a yartsagunbu management plan (Rana and Wallrapp 2015).

While the landscape approach and ICIMOD's transboundary initiatives acknowledge the need to balance sociocultural, economic, and environmental goals, the focus on management highlights how this balance is to be achieved. ICIMOD's Annual Progress Report 2016 for the Kailash Sacred Landscape initiative argues that the landscape approach provides tested solutions and tools to achieve international commitments—"from climate projects that deliver cobenefits for communities, or safeguard ecosystem services through regional commitments to large-scale restoration of degraded lands at scale." The analytical starting point is clearly the need for conservation. The international commitments require local management on the ground. Getting a community to commit to better management thus appears as the logical way forward.

Local, community-based resource management, however, depends on the existence of a "local community." In the local management committees that ICIMOD helps establish and train there is no place—literally or conceptually—for the wayfarers and their businesses, for those who push for roads, buy trucks, and run tent shops, for those thriving on short-lived booms, or those working on construction sites in Tibet over the summer.

To be clear: ICIMOD's efforts to cure mountains and people *necessitate* delineating project areas, defining objectives and developing management guidelines. All of these efforts are important. While there is ample reason to be critical of the global development industry, my goal is not to add to this debate. My aim is to understand the blind spots ICIMOD's work in the Kailash area creates—despite its benevolent, integrated, and assessment-conscious landscape approach.

Training for Stewards

The gospel of management is also the hymn of training. The aspiration to train rural communities to improve management and become responsible stewards of the local environment is visible in ICIMOD's training manuals. These "knowledge products" are meant to be used in workshops in the field. They cover topics ranging from the problem of invasive plant species in the Kailash Sacred Landscape to the management of yartsagunbu collector camps that outline "best practices" for waste disposal and the collection of firewood.

Several of these training manuals were exhibited during the review and planning session. One that caught my eye was aimed at Tibetan yak herders (ICIMOD 2016c). It addresses ecosystems, biodiversity, and livelihoods in the Tibet Autonomous Region of China. It consists of a series of twenty illustrations printed on cardboard and a teacher's handbook. When I first saw the manual, I mistook it for a picture book for children. I quickly learned, however, that "picture series" is a "a participatory, inclusive adult education training method" that "simplifies difficult technical subjects into the language and messages that resonate with the local communities, NGO staff, and other stakeholders in the field" (ICIMOD 2016c, 6). The instructions for teachers give general advice: arrange seats in a semicircle, encourage women to participate, make sure there is enough light to see the pictures. Moreover, six steps for conducting a two-hour training session are outlined.

The stated aim of the training is that "community members and yak herders understand the connection between biodiversity, ecosystems, and yak herding in the Tibet Autonomous Region of China" (ICIMOD 2016c, 7). The manual begins with an introduction to the concept of ecosystems. It then proceeds to ecosystem services and argues that the yak herders' lives depend on what nature gives them—good soil, clean water, food, medicinal plants, as well as the "spiritual, cultural, educational, and recreational services that ecosystems provide when they are kept in a healthy and stable state" (ICIMOD 2016c, 12). Then, the notion of biodiversity is introduced; finally, the linkages between biodiversity and livelihoods are discussed. The message is clear: The loss of biodiversity disrupts ecosystems and their services and thus negatively affects livelihoods. "Do not lose biodiversity or else you will lose your livelihood" is one of the talking points (ICIMOD 2016c, 16).

What strikes me about this training manual is not primarily that amid its pedagogical fervor, it arguably infantilizes the yak herders. I imagine the herders having good fun being shown their world in twenty pictures; simple tools can work well and I have no reason not to trust the trainers, who tell me that they find picture series a useful and productive method. What really strikes me is that in the manual, the landscape is replaced almost entirely with an idealized dreamscape, an imaginary world in which traditional local communities need to be prepared and made resilient for the change to come. From this dreamscape are erased the waves of Chinese interventions in the name of development and security that shaped the history of western Tibet for several generations.

A second, similar "knowledge product" exhibited at the review and planning session was an illustrated brochure for Tibetan yak herders offering transportation services around Mount Kailash (ICIMOD 2016b). The brochure illustrates encounters between Indian pilgrims and yak herders and provides useful phrases in Chinese, Tibetan, and English. The illustrations, professionally drawn in a style marrying Tibetan thangka painting with the art of cartoons, show the typical problems arising in such situations and address them with a pragmatic tool to facilitate communication.

> Don't touch the prayer flags!
> Don't walk in front of the yak!
> Don't walk closely behind the horse!

The brochure, I was assured, was helpful to facilitate communication on the trail. Unlike the training manual, the teachers here are the herders-turned-service-providers. The "knowledge product" takes care of the simple everyday problems they all experience.

In both the community training manual and the illustrated phrase book, ICIMOD's emphasis on capacity building and local management are obvious. To return to the meme on men and fish, this approach invests in teaching a future fisherman the skills and awareness of sustainable fishing. Meanwhile, the Chinese approach is rather to build a fishpond or attract investors with tax cuts and subsidies to do so. While international development agencies based in Europe, the United States, or Australia are satisfied with outcome indicators measuring the number of people trained, a local Chinese party bureaucrat responsible for development will likely not advance his career by pushing such measures. The other way around, a steep rise in the number of private vehicles in Purang County, which a member of the Chinese delegation mentioned to me as anecdotal evidence of increasing prosperity, could hardly become an indicator in an ICIMOD initiative.

Cures for Tibet

On a rhetorical level, Chinese approaches to development have much in common with frameworks such as Theory of Change and Impact Pathways. The Chinese party state's notion of a "scientific outlook on development" (*kexue fazhan guan*), a central concept in former party secretary Hu Jintao's efforts to build a "Harmonious Society," advocates a similarly structured and evidence-based approach as Theory of Change. The Chinese scientific outlook on development also emphasizes sustainability, social welfare, and democracy—although with an explicit reference to Engels's notion of "scientific socialism." Nevertheless, the terms used in Chinese development discourse (at least in their English translations) are remarkably similar to the lingo of global development. But their meanings, and the practical forms they assume in the course of designing and implementing development interventions, diverge considerably. Ideas like evidence, participation, democracy, and welfare have quite distinct connotations in each of these contexts.

In a certain sense, these differences in outlook echo the old debate about idealism and materialism. From the perspective of Marxist materialism, real change cannot happen without transforming the material basis on which a society grows. Frameworks like the Theory of Change or Impact Pathways, on the other hand, typically rely on sociocultural interventions aimed at empowering communities, increasing resilience, or improving institutions. In other words, while the Chinese approach relies on the construction of a garden, assuming that it will provide the necessary conditions in which gardeners can improve, the Western approach seeks to teach the gardeners new skills in the hope that a better garden will result.

Of course, things are more complicated than such a blueprint suggests. The landscape approach tries to correct former conservation efforts that ignored the material basis of local livelihoods, and Marxist materialism is clearly only one of the ideological forces at work in China today. The notions of self-improvement—raising the "quality" of oneself—has become a dominant discourse in an era when selective neoliberalism is layered on top of Marxist and Maoist frameworks (cf. Sigley 2006; Greenhalgh 2011; Hoffman 2006; Hsu 2007).

Nevertheless, much of the skepticism that Indian, Nepali, and Western ICIMOD staff harbor against development in China stems from what is perceived of as crude top-down planning by the party state and a lack of local participation. From the perspective of ICIMOD's staff in Kathmandu, Chinese development has no regard for the failures and lessons learned in many decades of development cooperation around the globe. Global, or maybe rather Western, development often claims if not the moral then at least the professional high ground. From the perspective of ICIMOD staff coming back from brief field visits in Tibet, the Kailash area is undergoing obvious Sinicization and a rapid erasure of everything genuinely Tibetan.

To understand this clash of perceptions and the larger context that ICIMOD's curational efforts encounter in Tibet, we need to take a closer look at the large-scale initiatives and current dynamics in China's western border regions.

In 2000, under the leadership of General Secretary Jiang Zemin and Premier Zhu Rongji, the People's Republic of China (PRC) embarked on the Great Western Development strategy (*xibu dakaifa*), also referred to as the "Go West" or "Open Up the West" program. It targeted more than two-thirds of China's territory, covering six provinces, five autonomous regions (including the Tibet Autonomous Region), and the municipality of Chongqing. The strategy involved infrastructure development, benefits for investors, and environmental conservation efforts. Hundreds of billions of US dollars were channeled to the region to accelerate development and mend the widening gap between China's booming Pacific rim and its vast hinterlands.

The strategy initially focused on developing urban industrial centers and special economic zones in western China, following the model of eastern China's success. Acknowledging that this did little to narrow the gap between rich and poor areas, and in light of rising rural unrest, Jiang Zemin's successor Hu Jintao launched a series of initiatives that directly targeted rural China. The Eleventh Five-Year Plan (2006–2010) stipulated the initiative of building a "New Socialist Countryside." The initiative increased rural investment and abolished agricultural taxes, replacing them with subsidies to address the ills of rural underdevelopment. The initiative was an important part of Hu Jintao's vision to create a "Harmonious Society." It addressed environmental and social issues rather than just economic growth.

One aspect of building a New Socialist Countryside was the construction of Socialist New Villages—an initiative that took very different forms in different places (Ahlers and Schubert 2009; Bray 2013; Ptackova 2012). In some rural regions of central China, the program transformed villages into urban towns with multistory apartment blocks (Ong 2014; Rosenberg 2013). In the grasslands of Qinghai, the initiative was closely related to the resettlement of pastoralists in the name of grassland conservation (Robin 2009; Ptackova 2015, 2018). In the Dulong Valley of western Yunnan, bordering Myanmar, new houses were provided for each and every resident of the valley in return for a minimal amount of labor (Rippa 2020). Building new villages went together with environmental legislation, as it had on the Tibetan Plateau. The Sloping Land Conservation Act outlawed agriculture on the valleys steep gradients, stripping Dulong farmers from their agricultural subsistence (Hathaway 2013, 18). And here, too, subsidies replaced former income from agriculture and pastoralism.[1]

While new houses were provided for free in some places, in other areas people received only minimal subsidies. Instead, they were granted access to special bank loans with no or very low interest rates. In some regions, the program was based on voluntary participation; in other regions, it was pushed through with force or a mixture of incentives and threats. In some cases, the program was welcomed by a majority of residents; in other cases, it was seen as a burden put on the shoulders of the poor. In some areas, houses were designed and built by construction companies while in other areas, local residents would only get construction materials.

The construction of Socialist New Villages was thus not one large intervention but rather the framework in which a plethora of interventions with clearly
curational ambitions took shape on the level of counties or prefectures. These
interventions carried dozens of different names, which makes it impossible to
speak of one coherent government scheme.

In the Tibet Autonomous Region (TAR), the initiative became known as the
Comfortable Housing Project. Announced with relatively little fanfare in 2006,
it only gained traction in the aftermath of the Tibetan protests in March 2008
and the unfolding global financial crises. Tibetan unrest provided the impetus
to counter discontent with accelerated, physical development. The world financial crises led the Chinese government to double down on infrastructure investment as a means to isolate the People's Republic from the global turmoil and
keep gross domestic product (GDP) growth above target in view of ailing manufacturing and export. Infrastructure, already one of the party state's top pri-
orities, became the pervasive and often exclusive answer to all ills.

During my fieldwork in Tibet between 2007 and 2009, I saw the program grow
and enter the lives of more and more people. It started with new houses pop-
ping up along the highway from Lhasa to the airport in Gonkar. The houses, built
or renovated in a short time frame, typically featured a new facade facing the
road. Their backyards remained unpainted and raw. At first, everybody around
me made jokes about them. They seemed like a new Potemkin decor in a well-
rehearsed spectacle. Similarly, Emily Yeh's interlocutors described this approach
as a form of "image engineering" (2013a, 9). However, by the end of my fieldwork in 2009, new rural houses were omnipresent, especially in the Kongpo region of the southeastern TAR. Most of them were equipped with blue corrugated
roofs—the same material that has since flooded the northern valleys of Nepal.[2]

In her book *Taming Tibet* (2013a), Emily Yeh discusses the Comfortable Housing Project and its diverse outcomes. Then TAR party secretary Zhang Qingli
called the program both a "incision point" and a "breakthrough point" for the
New Socialist Countryside initiative in Tibet (Yeh 2013a, 241). The program was
managed by the Comfortable Housing Bureau, a subsidiary of the Finance Ministry, and it became an umbrella under which other, earlier projects were integrated, including pastoral sedentarization, resettlement in the name of poverty
alleviation, and the Prosperous Borders and Wealthy Households Project (*xin-
bian gongcheng*). The latter was meant to enrich border residents, enhance patrio-
tism, and strengthen defense through new roads, communications infrastructure,
towns, and—again—subsidies for the construction of new private houses (Yeh
2013a, 239).

In the TAR, the program raised many issues. Just like in the rest of rural
China, it was implemented with various means of persuasion (Goldstein, Childs,

and Wangdui 2008). In many places, it involved resettling people to major roads. It also included rules directly targeting lifestyles. The program stipulated, for example, that people and livestock be separated in houses and barns, which marked a departure from the traditional practice of using the ground floor of a house for livestock (Yeh 2013a, 240).

Very much in the sense of Marxist materialism, the program aimed at creating material conditions, a physical environment, meant to change people's mindsets. As Yeh (2013a, 242) writes, "Government leaders claim that through participation in the Comfortable Housing Project, rural residents' 'wait, depend, and request' mentality has changed to one that is more proactive and market oriented."

At the end of 2010, the TAR authorities declared the completion of the Comfortable Housing Project. However, in the Kailash area of western Tibet, subsidized construction was only gaining steam around that time. The various programs focusing on infrastructure created the labor market in Purang that has become so crucial for the livelihoods in the Limi Valley. The construction of new houses, together with the conservation initiative to reduce herd sizes on the Tibetan Plateau and the subsidies from the Prosperous Borders and Wealthy Households Project, had already started to transform the sacred landscape around Kailash when the ICIMOD initiative arrived.

During the three-day review and planning meeting in Kathmandu, these Chinese development efforts remained remarkably absent. None of these programs was mentioned in any of the presentations, regardless of the many shared ambitions of improving rural lives and conservation. ICIMOD's curational ambitions and the Chinese state's interventions remained separate—despite the fact that the former was taking place amid the latter. The yak herders to be trained in ecosystem services and tourist communication were also the yak herders provided with subsidies and new houses while facing restrictions regarding access to pastures. The Chinese delegation's appeal to "understand their government," directed at the non-Chinese participants of the ICIMOD meeting, was taken as an excuse for the problems in China rather than as an invitation to engage with the overlapping curational efforts at stake.

Over another cigarette outside the ballroom, one member of the Chinese delegation put things in context. The funds coming in through ICIMOD projects were peanuts compared to the grants Chinese research institutes had become used to. It was sometimes difficult to find willing students in master's programs to carry out research for ICIMOD's Kailash Sacred Landscape initiative. The limited funds, the high expectations, and the work of translation necessary to produce outputs acceptable in ICIMOD's framework were just too much of a hassle.

It is important to note that ICIMOD was not a newcomer in the People's Republic. The organization has a long history of engaging with China. China is

one of the ICIMOD's eight member countries, and its former division of mountain natural resources was headed by Pei Shengji in the 1990s. Pei, the prominent founder of the renowned department of ethnobotany at the Kunming
Institute of Botany, was instrumental in extending ICIMOD's reach to China and
simultaneously tying China (particularly Yunnan Province) into the world of
global environmental conversation (Hathaway 2013, 132). Today, several Chinese
researchers have leading positions at ICIMOD. The organization is keen to foster scientific cooperation and—not least—tap into the flow of generous Chinese
research money.

During my tenure as visiting researcher, a Chinese professor joined ICIMOD
as head of one of the transboundary landscape initiatives. Giving the meme of
fish and men another and altogether literary twist, he brought with him the
promise of funding through a Gansu-based mountain fishery project. The fishery project, combining scientific research with government subsidies and private enterprise, was looking to expand into other highland regions with ample
supplies of cold water. In Tibet and Bhutan, the idea met with Buddhist concerns
about the killing of small animals; in the Hindukush and Pamirs, however, it
could provide an important avenue for employment and livelihoods, he argued.
And, who knows, once successful there, the Tibetans and Bhutanese may still
come around, he added.

Long-Term Goals, Short-Term Efforts

The encounters of ICIMOD's Kailash initiative with Chinese curational interventions in Tibet during the planning session were elusive. On the one hand,
both curational approaches explicitly subscribe to a deductive logic: They start
with a broad ideological aim and jump to interventions imagined to help it gain
gestalt. They converge in most of their overarching goals and are entangled in
practice. On the other hand, the thrust of curational interventions derived from
these two approaches differ considerably and are usually blind toward each other.

This blindness and the resulting evasiveness stem from the partial erasures that
curational interventions entail. In the case of ICIMOD's curational efforts, the
partial erasures include the history of profound changes in livelihood strategies
going on in Humla and Tibet. Neither the importance of trade and foraging, nor
the labor market in Purang, the new roads, the subsidized rice, and the labor of
distribution find entry into the basic analysis of the situation in which ICIMOD
projects try to foster positive change. Despite the emphasis on official transboundary cooperation, the founding of a Humla Chapter of the Nepal China Chamber of
Commerce and Industry was not a topic at ICIMOD; the labor market in Purang

was never part of the discussions I witnessed; and foraging mainly surfaced as a potential threat to the Api Nampa Conservation Area, requiring management plans and training manuals to keep it in check. In other words, neither the legacies and the present of the evolving pathway economy nor, in the case of Upper Humla more than Tibet, the translocal lives of Himalayan families inspired the design and planning of ICIMOD's curational intervention. The trope of the local community with all its sedentarist connotations is too dominant to allow for an honest evaluation of the existing connections and socio-spatial structures at stake. They *need* to be overlooked in order to further the agendas of conservation and heritage, which are meant to help the imagined sedentarist subsistence farmers develop sustainable livelihoods.

In the Chinese agendas for the Kailash region, on the other hand, trade, business, and infrastructure are acknowledged aspects of interventions. This can be seen, for example, in the new trade center built in Purang. The layout of multistory shops and warehouses grouped around a structure reminiscent of a Buddhist stupa hints at the importance of a certain kind of trade (legal, orderly, legible) combined with a certain kind of religious-cultural heritage ("cleansed" and nonpolitical).

The Chinese approach also heeds environmental issues, injecting rangeland management policies into the mix of curational efforts in the Kailash Sacred Landscape. These policies, however, are derived from experiences elsewhere on the Tibetan Plateau. They are not based on local studies of grassland degradation but rather on estimates of the area's carrying capacity copied from studies elsewhere in Tibet. On the sidelines of the Kailash meeting, I learned that the Tibet Academy of Agricultural and Animal Husbandry Sciences (TAAAS) was asked to verify the assumptions on which planning relied only after the policies were already implemented.

Furthermore, the curational efforts by the Chinese authorities imply a partial erasure of the importance of mobility for trade and extensive pastoralism. Rangeland management policies restrict the movement of livestock and prevent access to certain areas traditionally used as pastures; the tightening of customs controls increases the hurdles for goods moving across the border; and a series of restrictions regulate the movement of people. Travel has become more and more difficult, both within Tibet and internationally. The restrictions, however, do not apply to Han Chinese; they only target Tibetans and foreigners. Even ICIMOD's non-Chinese personnel faced difficulties reaching their project sites in the Tibet Autonomous Region. They found themselves limited, with field visits too tightly scheduled and closely monitored. The head of one of the KSLCDI's components, a Bhutanese national, was never granted a visa. Ironically, the border—which was analytically and discursively erased from ICIMOD's transboundary initiatives because of political sensitivities while an evaluation by the German Society for International Cooperation (GIZ) called for more "transboundariness"—continued to haunt the practical work on the ground in every respect.

Curbing free movement for non-Han Chinese, resettling pastoralists in subsidized houses along the roads, and building a new trade center while immobilizing trade goes far beyond the sedentarist metaphysics in which much of global development is rooted. It turns the sedentarist bias into state policies. While these policies are increasingly enforced, they are sweetened by subsidies.

In light of the troubles to implement a certain style of curational intervention close to the international borders at the core of the Kailash Sacred Landscape, it is no surprise that ICIMOD's Indian and Nepali partner institutions chose places at the margins of the delineated project area—in safe distance from international borders—for most of their pilot projects. Here, well-accepted approaches to rural and agricultural development could be followed. Unlike in Purang County, these pilot sites were unencumbered by competing curational interventions.

One such approach is value chain development for local agricultural products. Several value chain projects were part of KSLCDI. One concerned the Indian butter tree: *Diploknema butyracea* or *Bassia butyracea* (*chyura* in India and *chyuri* in Nepal). Chyura butter is extracted from the oily kernels of dried seeds. ICIMOD's project focused on soap and lip balm made from chyura butter. The project sought to add value through local production, technological improvement, organic certification, and marketing under the *Kailash—truly sacred* brand (ICIMOD 2015b). The chyura tree, however, only grows up to an altitude of 1,500 meters above sea level.

Another project was dedicated to the Himalayan nettle (*Girardinia diversifolia*), called *allo* in Nepal. The bark of allo stems yields smooth and silk-like fibers. Here, too, ICIMOD emphasizes value chain development—making yarn and weaving (ICIMOD 2015a). Khar, situated at the southern tip of Api Nampa Conservation Area in Darchula District, was chosen as a pilot site. Other value chain projects targeted Himalayan bamboo and soap nut.

The success of such projects feeds back into the outlook and self-understanding of ICIMOD, and the experience gained is used to design further curational interventions elsewhere. It is in such interventions that ICIMOD's strength lies. Here, the parts fit together: Through value chain development—training, technical assistance, certification, and branding—a commonly available forest resource kickstarts local production and improves the livelihoods of a predominantly sedentary community. Unlike foraging for rare medicinal herbs or maple burls to make *phuru*, these products are part of the sunny side of global markets rather than boom-and-bust-driven, semi-legal frontier economies. Furthermore, value chain development is compatible with the broad ideological aims of ICIMOD. Its staff is familiar and comfortable with the role of providing guidance in such curational efforts.

ICIMOD's projects in Tibet were more difficult to reconcile with such visions. One of these projects supported vegetable farming in greenhouses. Unhappy with the lack of progress, ICIMOD decided not to pursue it any further. No doubt, there would have been good reasons for this decision. Greenhouse vegetable production is predominantly in the hands of Han Chinese migrants flocking into Tibet, attracted by considerable incentives. In Purang County, Tibetans would lease their land to Chinese farmers who would get subsidies for greenhouse construction and typically stay for only a few years. This short-term engagement, a researcher from TAAAS complained to me, often resulted in deteriorating soil quality. The vegetable producers had little interest in long-term productivity. These problematic aspects of greenhouse farming and Han immigration, however, were not discussed when ICIMOD decided to cancel the project. The problem was the lack of properly documented results that could be used to apply for the next grant. In a five-minute break during the review and planning session, a successor project was agreed on: cultivating wild oat species for winter fodder production. However, considering that the project only lasted for another seventeen months, it remained highly doubtful whether a measurable outcome could be achieved.

Around Kailash, in the heartland of KSLCDI, ICIMOD's curational interventions remained epiphenomenal to the larger thrust of Chinese development. The projects that ICIMOD continued to pursue were toilets and waste management on the Kailash circuit—tempering the side effects of Chinese efforts to cure western Tibet's remoteness and underdevelopment with tourism, better roads, and an airport.[3]

Apart from overlapping and competing curational ambitions, there is also a mismatch of temporalities that impedes aspirations to cure mountains and people. Curational interventions usually work on a different temporal scale than the problems they seek to address. Desertification, climate change, or cultural heritage concern the *longue durée* of history. Curational interventions (but not the curational ambitions they rest on) come packaged in the form of projects with a typical life span of three to five years.

This is not only true for the assessment-conscious approach to development and conservation that Nepal has embraced but also for the way things work in China: Over the past couple of generations, citizens of the People's Republic have witnessed a series of sweeping interventions under a gazillion of different names.

The programs and slogans change with each party secretary's quest to establish his own legacy. Collectivization and the Cultural Revolution swept into the remotest corners of the country only to disappear after a decade or two. Since then, the succession of interventions has, if anything, only sped up. Nobody talks about Hu Jintao's "Harmonious Society" any longer. The New Socialist Countryside and the Comfortable Housing Project define all but moments in history. Since Xi Jinping announced his Belt and Road Initiative in 2014, it is all belts and roads now. Whoever will finally succeed Xi will pay rhetorical reference to the Belt and Road Initiative but start building his own legacy under a new tagline.

Citizens in Nepal and China are acutely aware of this temporal disjuncture between long-term curational ambitions and the project nature of curational interventions. The Chinese subsidies for leaving behind agricultural or pastoral incomes, for example, are temporary by default. While they probably will be extended for the foreseeable future, they are meant to run out eventually. Thus, becoming part of a curational intervention is important in the here and now. Not unlike the kind of resource-based frontier capitalism with its booms and busts, curational interventions provide opportunities. Not to hedge one's bets under these circumstances would mean to neglect past experience.

I once got to know two brothers (not in Humla but elsewhere in the Himalayas): One brother had an NGO job in a conservation area; the other was a businessman shipping large quantities of a particular herb from the very same conservation area to Tibet (plus, once in a while, some pangolin scales to raise the profit margin). The brothers were not at odds with each other. The one working in the business of conservation was serious about environmental protection. The one doing business agreed with him. But conservation and trade were the two pillars on which their livelihood depended. Given the ephemeral nature of both conservation projects and trade, they felt that they could not risk giving up one. Booms do bust, and conservation projects eventually end. The only sensible strategy was to diversify their sources of income.

My colleagues at ICIMOD felt this temporal disjuncture between long-term curational ambitions and the limited duration of projects (and their own contracts). Many were concerned that the project nature of development and conservation work only allowed for pilot projects, with no chance to "scale up" interventions to a regional level.

In private, over tea in a humble *dhaba* right outside ICIMOD's impressive campus, my colleagues expressed these doubts without hesitation. Venting about ICIMOD over sweet Nepali tea was like a recreational activity. For my colleagues, more than for me, life at ICIMOD was extremely busy. There was always another deadline for a report coming up, always an evaluation looming with the potential to kill off further funding. Resources were scarce, and my colleagues did whatever was possible within these constraints.

At the same time, the teahouse opposite ICIMOD's entry gate was also a place where we shared our experiences of long days on a trail and told stories of the people we met along the way—it was a place where the landscapes we dedicated our work to met with our own dreamscapes.

9

MAPPING MOUNTAINS

One of the most important technologies in development and conservation is mapping. Those striving for curational interventions have a great interest in the production of cartographic representations. Mapping simplifies complex realities. It highlights certain aspects considered to be important while leaving out others. As a basis for planning and reflection, maps promise to isolate the signal from the noise. They allow the curators to conjure the world they seek to foster. This means that maps necessarily depend on partial erasure to become useful. By doing so, they simultaneously suggest a reality and point to a potential future. When disagreements about these futures arise, the inherent partial erasure of mapping becomes a conflict-laden issue.

Consider the vegetation map that the International Centre for Integrated Mountain Development (ICIMOD) produced for the Kailash Sacred Landscape. The erasure of borders became a bone of contention because it conflicted with a particular Chinese vision of a national future. Of course, drawing any kind of borderline would have been contentious given the unsettled borders in the Lipu Lekh area (Cowan 2015).

But dropping the borderlines altogether was more than a somewhat naive attempt to address these concerns; it was also in line with the landscape approach and its focus on features like vegetation and land use. Following the call for more "transboundariness," the mapping effort sought to transcend territorial concerns by erasing borders and replacing them with a representation of the landscape as such.

The names of the countries involved (India, China, and Nepal) still feature on the map. They are typeset in the blank space outside the Kailash Sacred Landscape—as if state territory would only start beyond the object of curation. Further adding to the confusion is an overview map that locates the project area in the larger context of the Greater Himalayas. This overview map does not features national borders and the familiar shapes of nation-states that help us orient ourselves; it just depicts the somewhat unfamiliar outline of what ICIMOD has identified as the Hindu Kush Himalayas—a shape nobody outside ICIMOD's headquarters is familiar with.

Scales of Anxiety

Conjuring the Kailash Sacred Landscape meant leaving behind the standard scales of the global, the national, and the local. Nevertheless, mapping the Kailash Sacred Landscape was an effort in the making of scale. Scale is "the spatial dimensionality necessary for a particular kind of view . . . It is not just a neutral frame for viewing the world; scale must be brought into being: proposed, practiced, and evaded, as well as taken for granted" (Tsing 2005, 58).

This scale-making project clashed with, and at the same time was also driven by, cartographic anxieties (Krishna 1994; Gregory 1994). When the Chinese delegation at the review and planning session saw the erasure of national borders and the name of "their country" in the blank space outside the Kailash Sacred Landscape, they feared that Chinese authorities would take it as a form of "cartographic aggression" (Blij 2012). ICIMOD, on the other hand, was anxious that the urgent problems at hand could not be solved within the boundaries of nation-states. Ecosystems, wildlife, and also the old cultural and economic ties in the region were not confined by borders. Cartographic anxiety, thus, arises "from the perceived misalignment between a political imagination of separateness and the reality of a cultural, ethnic, and economic continuum on the ground" (Billé 2016, 11).

The notion of anxiety lends itself well to a range of inquiries that go beyond the question of state borders. Anxiety refers not only to fear but also to ambition. Followed by an infinitive, the term "anxious" alludes to potential futures of various kinds. Mining companies, for instance, are anxious *to* claim territories for mineral extraction, just as ICIMOD's cartographic efforts are tied to ecological anxiety and the need for conservation.[1]

Cartographic anxiety, thus, denotes fears and hopes relating to and deriving from maps. Rather than being mere representations of existing geographic realities, maps hold particular visions of potential futures. Some are produced to justify, guide, or prohibit action; others more directly depict curational ambitions for a better future. Even when meant to mitigate cartographic anxiety, maps often help produce it. In this sense, maps relate to time as much as to space.

While maps may seem "a mere instrument of utility, showing us where to go and how to put things in place," they also contain "invisible ingredients" that "render every map a Pandora's box" (Ludden 2003, 1057). This is certainly true for ICIMOD's endeavor to map the Kailash Sacred Landscape. At the same time, however, the strategy was also a form of conscious "counter-mapping" (Pickles 2004, 179–194). ICIMOD's cartographic ambitions added more than simply another layer of interest on top of existing cartographic representations. It turned the delineated space of the initiative's territory into a simple shape. Mimicking what Benedict Anderson describes as the "logoization" of the national map— "instantly recognizable, everywhere visible, the logo-map penetrated deep into the popular imagination" (Anderson 1991, 175, cited in Billé 2014, 168)—ICIMOD's aim was to establish the Kailash Sacred Landscape as a graphic icon in public consciousness.

This effort to bring into being the particular regional scale of the Kailash Sacred Landscape (KSL) and establish it as a recognizable cartographic entity required broad support. In a twist that largely went unnoticed, the quest for a KSL logo-map harnessed the logos of the fourteen partner organizations and sponsors. Adorning the map along its lower edge, the logos were meant to appease the ghosts of cartographic anxiety and appeal to the parties involved that they all shared a common concern for the sacred and precious *landscape* at stake.

Amid the confusion arising from this erasure of nation-states, the simple yet substantial accomplishment of the mapping project was somewhat lost. This accomplishment was directly addressing "transboundariness." The three countries had their own systems to classify vegetation types. Harmonizing these systems was the goal of the mapping project. The task took two years and involved ecologists with ground knowledge as well as cutting-edge remote sensing technology. The cartographers at ICIMOD were proud of the result: Theirs was the first accurate and harmonized transboundary vegetation map of the region. This sense of pride comes across in the press release entitled "Anchoring Transboundary Cooperation" (ICIMOD 2016a). It emphasizes the achievement as the "basis for planning and management" for most of ICIMOD's various curational ambitions, ranging from conservation, tourism, and value chain development to studies of climate change, biomass, and ecosystem services.

ICIMOD's Geospatial Solutions Group is among the largest in the organization. At the time of writing, thirty-nine staff members are listed on the website. The group includes geographic information system (GIS) analysts, remote sensing specialists, and software developers. ICIMOD puts much faith in GIS technology. According to ICIMOD's website, "Technology is starting to fill in the blanks in the scientific record for the Hindu Kush Himalayas, whose size and remoteness has served in the past as a major obstacle to data collection" (ICIMOD 2019b). For the Kailash initiative, ICIMOD set up a dedicated mapping infrastructure: the Kailash Sacred Landscape Information System, or KSLIS. Its explicit goal is to "strengthen the policy formulation process by providing reliable, consistent, and timely data for the remotest part of the Himalayan region" (ICIMOD 2019a).

To overcome remoteness with remote sensing is not an easy task, however. While KSLIS contains plenty of data points in the lower areas around the pilot project sites where value chains are developed, efforts to map Upper Humla have remained sketchy and vague. The base map shows villages far away from where they actually are, and the few data points added by the Geospatial Solutions Group and its contributors are often wrong. The roads on the map bear no relation to reality, and even Nara La, the main pass on the way to Hilsa, is located in the wrong valley. While KSLIS provides an infrastructure to collect and process geographical information, there is clearly still a lot to be done until the tool is able to provide reliable, consistent data and support policymaking.

Herein lies a second form of partial erasure—one that does not stem from a conscious focus or from cartographic anxiety. This kind of erasure is rather the result of being included in the territory of a curational intervention but then left out because of a lack of resources to follow through with the original objectives. Remote sensing does not just "fill the gaps"; it also creates gaps to be filled further down the road.

One of data layers of KSLIS concerns glacial lakes. The topic of glacial lake outburst floods (GLOFs) has been high on the agenda of international development organizations, including ICIMOD. GLOFs are not a new phenomenon in the Himalayas. The flood that washed away more than a third of Walung in the early 1960s was probably a GLOF. However, in the context of climate change, the risk of devastating GLOFs is increasing, experts agree (Ashutosh et al. 2012; Allen et al. 2016; Titzler 2019). The topic has become a prime focus of disaster risk-reduction strategies. For some of the glacial lakes considered to be particularly risky, and where a GLOF would have devastating consequences, monitoring and early-warning systems have been set up.

KSLIS features dozens of glacial lakes in the Kailash Sacred Landscape. One of them lies above Waltse in the Limi Valley. This particular lake is not just a potential future risk; between 2004 and 2011, it burst six times and threatened the village (Hovden 2016, 4). When I first visited Waltse in 2011, the most devastating GLOF had just happened a couple of months ago. The flood cut right through the village. It took two houses and covered a substantial area of agricultural land with debris. The greatest concern for the people of Waltse, however, was their monastery—the social and spiritual heart of the sprawling Waltse community. The Rinchenling Gompa dates back to the eleventh century and the time of the second diffusion of Buddhism in Tibet. It is said to be one of the 108 monasteries established by Rinchen Zangpo, the great translator. Rinchenling Gompa is one of the oldest Tibetan monasteries in Nepal (Church and Wiebenga 2008).

In 2011, the monastery stood precariously close to the unstable riverbank. One corner of the monastery was about ten meters away from the ravine left behind by the GLOF. The flood that occurred almost annually was the most important topic in Waltse. The village assembly was desperately seeking outside help to reinforce the riverbank and assess the situation up at the glacial lake. A fellow anthropologist who had just completed a year of fieldwork was raising awareness (Hovden 2012). She drafted a proposal and started contacting development organizations. Coming back from Limi, I tried to help. I got in touch with some of the organizations I had ties with, among them ICIMOD.

ICIMOD had just published the results of a larger glacial lake study and completed an inventory of glacial lakes in Nepal (Gurung 2010). The specific purpose of this inventory was to "update the glacial lakes mapping of Nepal Himalaya and GLOF records with remote sensing" in order to "standardize the method for prioritizing the critical glacial lakes" (ICIMOD 2011). Although the Kailash Sacred Landscape Conservation and Development Initiative (KSLCDI) had not yet started, I knew that ICIMOD had a great interest in the region. The case of one of the oldest monasteries in Nepal being acutely threatened by a GLOF seemed to tick all the right boxes: precious heritage, the danger of climate change and the need for disaster risk reduction.

Alas, it turned out to be difficult to mobilize support. The case of Waltse strangely fell between the larger concern for GLOFs addressed with remote sensing, on the one hand, and efforts at preserving cultural heritage on the other. Now, with the benefit of hindsight and some more knowledge about the inner workings and the process of establishing development initiatives—the proposal, the carefully selected pilot site—I see that there was not much that the organization was able to do on short notice. Funds and labor were bound to existing projects that depended on milestones completed and outputs produced. The situation in Waltse was not among the deliverables promised.

Eventually, a smaller nongovernmental organization (NGO), The Mountain Institute, submitted an application to the US embassy. Limited funds for gabion wire, transport, and labor were released. To everybody's relieve, no more floods have occurred since 2011. In 2013, a team of geologists arrived to study the glacial lake. They concluded that while a certain risk remained, the retreating glacier would reduce it over time (Kropáček et al. 2014).

In the end, ICIMOD did get involved. In 2018, it offered a reporting grant to Al Jazeera journalist Neelima Vallangi, who published a piece on Waltse and its threatened monastery in the "Climate SOS" section of the network's website (Vallangi 2019).

Ecosystem Services

One standard method to link mapping to planning and concrete action lies in the notion of ecosystem services—the more business-minded and less poetically inclined sibling of the landscape approach. Ecosystem services were a cornerstone of the UN-commissioned Millennium Ecosystem Assessment (MEA), published in 2005. The goal of the MEA was to measure human impact on the environment and its consequences.

The idea behind ecosystem assessment is simple: Ecosystems provide valuable services to humans; destroying them will thus come at a cost. Assessing ecosystem services is a means to put a price tag on their destruction and thereby provide arguments against the notion that conservation always comes at an economic cost. Taking the services that ecosystems deliver into account alters the balance. In addition, as seen in the community training manual for Tibetan yak herders (mentioned in chapter 8), the approach is also used to raise awareness in local communities and foster local environmental stewardship.

The notion of ecosystem services is designed to be comprehensive. Typically, four different ecosystem services are distinguished:

1. Supporting services. Soil formation and nutrient recycling, for example, facilitate the other three categories of services.
2. Provisioning services. Ecosystems yield food, water, energy, and medicinal resources.
3. Regulating services. Examples are climate regulation, waste decomposition, or natural water purification.
4. Cultural services. Ecosystems, broadly understood and aligning with the notion of the "landscape," deliver spiritual, symbolic, and historical value as well as recreational experiences.

In the case of ICIMOD's Kailash Sacred Landscape, being not just a landscape but a sacred geography, cultural ecosystem services play a crucial role. In cooperation with the South Asian Association of Development and Environmental Economics (SANDEE), ICIMOD estimates the value of cultural ecosystem services in the Indian and Nepali pilot sites of the Kailash Sacred Landscape at

US$215 per visit and person, for outside visitors, and US$17 for local residents (ICIMOD 2017b, vii).

However, ICIMOD acknowledges that cultural ecosystems also provide non-monetary value. The organization thus pioneered a comprehensive framework for the assessment of cultural ecosystem services in the greater Himalayas (Pandey, Kotru, and Pradhan 2016). The framework suggests nine indicators, including the presence of beliefs ascribing cultural significance to natural sites, the degrees of prevalence of such sites, the impact of a site's cultural significance on development activities, its influence on community bonding, the presence of pilgrimage and tourism, the presence of local management structures, the influence on a community's perceptions of disasters and climate change, the existence of transboundary linkages, and the health of an ecosystem regulated through belief systems.

While the idea of ecosystem services gained considerable traction in the world of international cooperation and global development, it found relatively little resonance in anthropology and human geography. It comes with a number of implicit assumptions and logical problems that are difficult to reconcile with current debates in these disciplines. The notion of cultural ecosystem services, for instance, subscribes to a utilitarian view of culture that is reminiscent of the functionalist school of thought of the 1950s. Moreover, cultural significance is understood as an inherent property of a particular *site* that can be pinned on a map. The very practices of pilgrimage and worship that endow a sacred place with meaning and power are thereby glossed over. In this way, the notion of cultural ecosystem services reifies culture, meaning, and religion as things natural, beyond change and history.

ICIMOD's comprehensive assessment framework tries to deal with some of these problems. At the same time, it creates new ones. On the one hand, the framework regards a temple or a local deity residing on a mountain as part of the ecosystem that provides services. On the other hand, it locates religious value and symbolic meaning clearly inside humans. The assessment framework takes the practice of worshipping a local deity as an indicator of the services provided by an ecosystem, rather than seeing rituals as a service to deities—keeping them in check and preventing their wrath. The deities themselves become passive features of the very landscape over which they rule.

One of the indicators given in the assessment framework is a particular site's potential to enable community bonding and thereby facilitate conservation: As an example for this indicator, the Yalbang monastery and its current abbot Pema Rigzel Rinpoche are listed. Pema Rigzel Rinpoche has become a revered spiritual leader in Upper Humla. It was his influence that led the monk assembly mentioned in chapter 3 to declare Limi a no-kill zone. Regardless of the side effects of this declaration, Rinpoche clearly has an effect on environmental relations. Reading ICIMOD's framework, however, the abbot seemed to become a *feature* of the monastery (and thus, the ecosystem) that rendered valuable services. The abbot-cum-monastery appeared both as part of the ecosystem and as its custodian.

The framework left me in a state of confusion. I approached my colleague Abhimanyu Pandey, the main author of the assessment framework, whose expertise and engagement I always cherished. I cite our conversation here at length because it shows the work of translation necessary to square an idea born and bred in the arena of global development with the need of international organization for guidelines and with debates in anthropology.

> MARTIN: Is there "cultural value" that is not derived from ecosystem services?
>
> ABHIMANYU: For a cultural site to have value as cultural ecosystem services, that cultural site must include a significant nonhuman, "natural" component. A palace, a temple by itself, will not have cultural ecosystem services. But a temple that has a sacred grove, or a spring, or [whose] surrounding landscape prohibits hunting—for example, Yalbang monastery—will have cultural ecosystem services.
>
> MARTIN: So Yalbang Rinpoche's green, vegetarian Buddhism is part of cultural ecosystem services?
>
> ABHIMANYU: If it has contributed to the reduction of hunting or green felling in the region, then yes.
>
> MARTIN: And if he moves away or dies?
>
> ABHIMANYU: Then the cultural ecosystem service may no longer be there. You have to look at what effects that site has on the natural world at a given time.
>
> MARTIN: But you just argued that a cultural site must include a significant nonhuman, "natural" component. Where is this in the case of green, vegetarian Buddhism?
>
> ABHIMANYU: That's true. This definition of a cultural site—with a significant nonhuman component—is the standard definition of a site that provides ecosystem services. Thus, places like a temple with a sacred grove, an ancient spring well, a sacred mountain, a sacred cave, a beautiful/historic landscape that people wish to maintain for its phenomenological value, etcetera, very well fit into the definition of cultural ecosystem service sites. However, certain cultural sites are such that while they directly do not provide cultural ecosystem services as per this definition, they do have an impact on the surrounding

natural landscape. For example, people say that the second Pema Rigzel Rinpoche of Yalbang has had a positive impact on bringing down hunting. So, under his influence, the Yalbang Gompa comes to contribute to the overall ecosystem services of the landscape.

MARTIN: But then, we have the Yalbang Gompa providing a service to the ecosystem and not the other way around. . . .

ABHIMANYU: You are right! A better example . . . might be a Buddhist "Hidden Valley," where hunting and green felling are prohibited by tradition due to the sacredness of life in that region.

MARTIN: OK, as a basic question, when we say cultural ecosystem services—are we talking about a cultural ecosystem that provides a service, or an ecosystem that provides a cultural service?

ABHIMANYU: Well, that's where in the contemporary cultural ecosystem services discourse there's been a lot of debate. Generally speaking, it goes both ways. Landscape is where culture plays out. Landscape is where ecosystems exist. By definition from the MEA [Millennium Ecosystem Assessment], ecosystems provide cultural services. However, you can see that in light of a more inclusive idea of ecosystems, in the sense of a multifunctional landscape, humans and nonhuman "natural" elements coexist. Therefore, you can't really rule out the "cultural ecosystem," as you put it.

MARTIN: You can't have it both ways, otherwise you end up with a cultural (eco)system that contributes to a cultural (eco)system and the idea of "service" is rendered moot, right?

ABHIMANYU: Well, that perhaps might be actually true in how certain nonmodern societies see themselves in relationship to the nonhuman world. However, in the modern, Western discourse of ecosystem services, there is a much more anthropocentric vision of the world at heart. Therefore, they talk about nature "providing" different kinds of "services" to humans. That's how the four different kinds of ES [ecosystem services] are defined and detailed also within the Millennium Ecosystem Assessment, the founding document for the ecosystem services discourse.

MARTIN: Totally agreed. And herein lies the basic logical conundrum.

ABHIMANYU: Depends on how you define a cultural ecosystem. By that, I understand a socio-ecological system, how a community resides, acts, gets shaped and shapes the natural landscape that it inhabits. I do not see it in terms of just the human realm, as separated from nature.

MARTIN: I fully agree. But your take on things is logically incompatible with the standard definition, I think.

ABHIMANYU: That's true. I try to go as much as possible with the standard definition, but at the same time, looking at how things actually work in the Kailash Sacred Landscape, I feel we need to work with a broader, revised definition of cultural ecosystem services, and also of how the two-way relationship between humans and nature is conceptualized.

Translation is a process, and often an imperfect one. My colleagues at ICIMOD agreed that the assessment framework, in its current form, was only a first step. It clearly needed refinement. The task of assessing the cultural value of a landscape posed a conceptual conundrum that reminds me of the argument made by Latour (1993) that we have never been modern: the framework, and the very idea of ecosystem services, separates culture from nature only to suggest translations meant to re-fuse them again in a different way.

Not everybody at ICIMOD was convinced that such structured assessment frameworks would be capable of doing the necessary work of translation and lead to a better understanding of a landscape. Another approach that was on everyone's lips during my tenure at ICIMOD was called "Landscape *Yatra.*" *Yatra* is the Hindi word for travel or pilgrimage. The notion of "Landscape Yatra" (usually capitalized in ICIMOD documents) means to "travel through a landscape with a multi-disciplinary team, interact with communities to understand their issues to influence practices and policies accordingly" (ICIMOD 2015c).

The G. B. Pant Institute of Himalayan Environment and Development (GBPIHE), one of ICIMOD's partner institutions, writes in its KSLCDI newsletter:

> Yatras, at a much deeper level, function in inner healing through ironing out our own inner conflicts and lead to much greater sensitivity about self . . . This internal motivation serves to commit oneself with greater integrity in thought and action; thus healing the self and developing long lasting motivation to serve the landscape. (GBPIHED 2015, 10)

The same newsletter features an article that lays out its authors' conviction in the power of "Landscape Yatra" (Rawal et al. 2015), portraying the method as a means to "facilitate social interaction [. . .] in a participatory manner" and "understand transitions happening in nature, culture, and society" (GBPIHED 2015, 8).

This is, perhaps, quite similar to what anthropologists call ethnographic fieldwork or participant observation. However, the ambitions behind the method reach further. "The embodied experience of Yatras, if designed appropriately, can support the people within the landscape in rediscovering the values of their own heritage and taking the necessary actions to adapt to the changes following sustainable processes," the authors argue (Rawal et al. 2015, 8).

An ICIMOD delegation presented the idea at the Global Landscapes Forum in Paris in 2015. For this purpose, the method of "Landscape Yatra" received an acronym (LSY) and was repackaged as an innovative tool to produce new kinds of evidence. This was necessary, as the promise of evidence—solid scientific evidence—is a crucial currency on the bazaar of development funding. Neither cultural ecosystems nor yatras to understand and cure can evade the necessity of evidence.

In practice, however, evidence gathered usually remains fragmented. Keeping the fragments in view and knowing about the large gaps in between sometimes seems to require more than human intelligence.

Art and Artificial Intelligence

A few months after the planning and review session, I took part in a workshop that tried to push the mapping of cultural ecosystems services a step forward with the help of artificial intelligence (AI). The three-day event, led by experts from the Basque Centre for Climate Change, sought to provide hands-on training on a cutting-edge software platform for facilitating the geospatial modeling of ecosystem services. The platform is called ARIES, which stands for Artificial Intelligence for Ecosystem Services. The mission was to create an experimental map of the "sacredness" or "cultural value" of each point in the Kailash Sacred Landscape.

After a general introduction and a demo of how ARIES could be used for assessment, the participants of the workshop were given the task to define indicators that could be fed into the model. On the second day, we started weighing these indicators. We sat in groups in front of Excel tables, ranking the variables collected on the first day: peak visibility, number of pilgrims/tourists, availability of lodges, access to site and seasonal accessibility, affordability/cost, permissions/visas required, availability of info-points, communication and hospitality reviews, and potential for wildlife watching.

The exercise was confusing. One workshop participant raised her hand and asked, "From my own perspective or from the locals' perspective?" One of the workshop organizers replied, "Do the ranking with all different stakeholders. Then, we will take the average"—a simple mathematical solution to flatten the topologies involved.

We continued our task but struggled. For pilgrims, peak visibility and availability of lodges may get a weight of 10. The number of tourists? Maybe a 1? Other groups were equally unsure how to proceed, and the organizers found it difficult to get the participants to focus. It was November 9, 2016. The results of the US presidential elections were trickling in. By mid-morning, still night in the United States, the *New York Times* predicted a 95 percent chance for Donald Trump to win. The models that predicted victory for Hillary Clinton failed, and here we sat trying, somewhat clumsily, to come up with a model of the spatial distribution of cultural value in the Kailash Sacred Landscape. What happened meanwhile on the other side of the planet was more than an ironic twist; it was directly relevant for ICIMOD's future. The rise of right-wing nationalism around the globe put a strain on the funding opportunities of development organizations. "America First" was going to make things even harder. ICIMOD's financial situation had already suffered indirectly from the refugee crises in Europe in 2014 and 2015 that channeled project funding toward migration-related issues.

We were still brooding over our Excel sheet when one of the workshop leaders asked whether all groups were done ranking and weighing. Knowing that our results were somewhat random anyway, we stopped and stepped out onto ICIMOD's rooftop. The smog that usually choked the city had almost disappeared. The Himalayas were visible for the first time in weeks.

Over the coffee break, the experts fed our data to ARIES. When we came back, we were curious to see the first AI-supported map of KSL's cultural geography. When the map appeared on screen, we were all a bit disappointed. It showed nothing but a carpet of red covering most of the Kailash Sacred Landscape rather than any kind of readable texture. This, the experts agreed, was not a software issue but a problem of data quality that could not be solved with artificial intelligence. Nevertheless, the consensus was that this first experiment had failed.

The carpet of red indicating the value of cultural ecosystem services could, of course, be read as an affirmation: The Kailash area is *truly* sacred—not in parts, but as a whole. And even if the AI experiment had produced texture showing a spatial differentiation of cultural value and sacredness, what would it have meant? Would ICIMOD have decided to try spreading sacredness more evenly? Or would it have served as a confirmation that the emphasis on well-known sacred sites was worth pursuing further? I don't know.

The ARIES mapping experiment was quickly forgotten. We hardly talked about it again. But the attempt at marrying cultural ecosystem services with geospatial solutions and artificial intelligence rendered something else visible: Mapping the various features and places of an existing ecosystem overlooks, by design, the meshwork of relations between them and the very pathways used for pilgrimage or tourism. While in the case of the vegetation map, technology—namely, remote sensing—was able to fill at least some knowledge gaps, the ARIES experiment only made the gaps more visible. The attempt at re-fusing nature and culture through an AI-based software framework and the notion of "cultural ecosystem services" could not undo the arbitrary separation of nature and culture that made the endeavor necessary in the first place. As a device for translation, it failed.

Art to the rescue. Another map ICIMOD published on the cultural heritage of the Kailash Sacred Landscape was designed by Rohan Chakravarty, a well-known Indian cartoonist and illustrator. Its purpose is to "cartographically represent the uniqueness of the KSL" and represent "the region's fauna, its mountain, pilgrimage sites, cultural sites and various human settlements and communities that are indigenous to the region" (ICIMOD 2016d). Unencumbered by data or precision, the artist was free to conjure a dreamscape more in line with ICIMOD's curational ambitions. The map shows the Kailash area as a forest of pictograms—monasteries and temples, wildlife and people, mountains and lakes. We see pilgrims prostrating in front of Mount Kailash and trekkers with backpacks and walking sticks approaching Milarepa's Rock. A snow leopard, birds and a wild yak are watching from afar. The monasteries of Waltse and Yalbang cover more than half of Upper Humla. A happy herder walks his sheep and goats through a clearing in the southern part of KSL; two Himalayan black bears stride confidently toward the forest.

Still, the partial erasures that come with a certain view of nature and culture are visible here as well. No new roads are shown, but "historical routes" feature prominently. Like the vegetation map, the illustrated map does not show national borders, and the country names also feature outside the boundaries of the Kailash Sacred Landscape. However, given the style of the map, this did not seem to raise any concerns.

A few days after the ARIES workshop, I was leaving for Humla. The day before departure, one of the leaders of KSLCDI approached me with a request: Would I be willing to bring some copies of the maps back to the villages in Upper Humla and distribute them in the monasteries? Of course I was. The mapping department started printing copies of both the vegetation and the illustrated map on their large-format inkjet. I was given a protective tube with a shoulder strap and was kindly asked to return it after my trip.

For three weeks, we carried the long black tube across the mountains and visited the monasteries to find recipients for ICIMOD's gift. I found it difficult to explain the purpose of these cartographic knowledge products. The monks who received the maps, just like everybody else in Upper Humla, were less interested in knowledge products than in actual, substantial assistance. They probably would have rather kept the tube. They saw roads, houses, and subsidies arriving with the People's Republic of China's curational interventions—"gifts" with their own problems (Yeh 2013a), but nevertheless substantial ones. The soft development approach of replacing financial aid with training and knowledge products lacked the most important aspect of how curational interventions foster ties on the ground: an element of alimentation. The cartographic knowledge products I carried through the mountains in a black plastic tube clearly did not do the trick. The dilemma was especially evident in Waltse. Remembering the

Carrying the maps in a black tube through Humla. *Source*: Martin Saxer, 2016.

vain attempts to get ICIMOD support to protect the very monastery now depicted on the illustrated map from the imminent danger of a GLOF, the gift
seemed awkward.

The frontier is a series of ironic twists—something noted by Schmink and
Wood (1992, cited in Tsing 2005, 33). I was left with the feeling that mapping
KSL moved in circles—not around Mount Kailash but around the nexus of ob-
ject, problem, and solution at the heart of ICIMODs curational intervention.

The production of knowledge products also produces ignorance. Shortcutting
object, problem, and solution creates over and over again the very gap that is
sought to be filled. But the (un)making of ignorance is not just a matter of better research and more funding. As Robert Proctor and Londa Schiebinger argue in their book *Agnotology* (2008), the cultural production of ignorance is also
productive. Ignorance can be a selective choice (as in the partial erasure that
mapping requires) or a strategic ploy (as in the decision not to include national
borders). And for those who take ignorance as a primordial state that needs to
be overcome, it is also a resource. It helps "keep the wheels of science turning"
(Proctor and Schiebinger 2008, 5).

ICIMOD, it seemed to me, was like a large container ship. The fervent production of knowledge produced a bow wave that made it difficult to read the rip-
tides and cross seas in the open ocean. While the Kailash Sacred Landscape, as
salvage frontier, came into being through the process of mapping, the frontier

also remained "a zone of unmapping" (Tsing 2005, 28–29). Actively yet not intentionally unmapped, it kept coming back to haunt the various curational ambitions that rubbed shoulders in the KSLCDI. The discursive and cartographic erasure of borders triggered urgent calls for more "transboundariness," a precondition for another round of funding. The erasure of the dynamics of road construction and the boom-and-bust cycles of the resource frontier prevented a deeper engagement with the landscape. The erasure of ambitions and existing translocal relations for the purpose of fostering local communities as stewards of the environment made it difficult for KSLCDI to gain traction outside the pilot project sites.

What KSLCDI created was a stage that demanded collaboration. Collaboration, in turn, required those involved to find translations between the different curational ambitions and their languages. ICIMOD's staff in Kathmandu was busy translating global development trends into projects on the ground; the partner organizations found themselves faced with the challenge of translating their ventures into the logic and lingo of ICIMOD's curational intervention. Anthropologists like me and Abhimanyu struggled to bridge the gaps we saw opening in front of us and make sense of the clash of worlds we witnessed. And my friends in the Himalayas were busy translating their ambitions into a language that would make them able to participate.

TRANSLATING AMBITIONS

In 1935 or 1936, Walter Benjamin walked along the Seine in Paris. In an open-air bookstall, he found a translation of one of Nietzsche's books. He looked for some of the passages he knew and loved but did not find them. Of course, they were there. "But when I looked them in the face, I had the awkward feeling that they no more recognized me than I did them." This, he writes, "was not a deficiency in the translation but something which may even have been its merit: the horizon and the world around the translated text had itself been substituted, had become French" (Benjamin 2002, 249).

I often had the same feeling when I looked at the knowledge products produced by the International Centre for Integrated Mountain Development (ICIMOD). I did not recognize the Himalayan world I had come to know. What I saw was a translated version of it that seemed to breathe the spirit and discourses of the global development industry. I was often confused and sometimes angry. I caught myself thinking that they simply had it all wrong.

Writing this book, however, is a similar act of translation. My efforts to solicit fragments of what I experienced over the past eight years in order to make sense of the world I encountered speaks (critically) to debates in anthropology and Himalayan studies. For some, my rendering of this world may seem as far removed from reality as ICIMOD's knowledge products were for me.

No single narrative can claim a privileged vantage point—not because there are many different ways to see but because the narratives themselves are part of the world they seek to describe. ICIMOD's staff or anthropologists like myself may be outside observers; the stories we tell, however, are not *external* to the worlds from which they emerge. They result from a process of translation; and translation is, in one way or another, a collaborative endeavor.

This is not always visible or known to the narrators, as Anna Tsing (2005) notes. In Kalimantan (Indonesia), Tsing witnessed what she calls a "forest of collaboration": Villages, their leaders, nature lovers and nongovernmental organizations (NGOs) collaborated in their fight against logging and environmental destruction; yet their stories about these collaborations diverged considerably:

> Collaborators may or may not have any understanding of each other's agendas. Such collaborations bring misunderstandings into the core of alliance. In the process, they make wide-ranging links possible: they are the stuff of global ties. They are also the stuff of emergent politics: they make new objects and agents possible. (Tsing 2005, 247).

Using insights from Amerindian perspectivism, Eduardo Viveiros de Castro suggests the notion of "equivocation," to rethink translation and the collaborations it emerged from. An equivocation, Viveiros de Castro writes, "is not an error, a mistake, or a deception. Instead, it is the very foundation of the relation that it implicates, and that is always a relation with an exteriority" (Viveiros de Castro 2004, 11). Equivocations are not neutral; they produce reality. In the words of Walter Benjamin: "the value of bad translation: productive misunderstandings" (Benjamin 2002, 250).

Marisol de la Cadena takes Viveiros de Castro's suggestion to reflect on her own project of working closely with a Peruvian shaman and the earth-beings that make his world. In her reading, equivocation is the "communicative disjuncture" in which collaborators use the same language but do not talk about the same thing (De la Cadena 2015, 27). I experienced such communicative disjuncture at ICIMOD. They were not unproductive but rather generative in particular ways.

In Humla, ICIMOD may not have left the kind of imprint on its imagined Kailash Sacred Landscape that the initiative originally anticipated. Like many other ongoing development projects, it struggled with the problem of translating a curational agenda into experience on the ground. The initiative remained partial, at best. Nevertheless, it played a major role in the lives of many of the people I worked with—if not as a project in itself then as part of the general force that development organizations represent in the Himalayas. Oftentimes, their effects lie less in the outcomes envisioned but rather in the promise of access to powerful networks, prestigious career paths, and potential future funding. Development initiatives offer global ties and opportunities around which ambitions cluster.

I witnessed these subtle but powerful promises at work with many of my acquaintances, friends, and research assistants. In one way or another, development and conservation played a crucial role in their plans for the future. Global development is a presence in the Himalayas, sometimes concrete, often vague, but always there. How to make use of the connections that come with development initiatives is an important skill to learn in this context.

When an opportunity for a grant or a project opened up, I tried to help the people around me by writing recommendation letters or helping them to draft research proposals. Long before my stint as research fellow at ICIMOD, I was thus part of efforts to translate my friends' ambitions into the language of global development. At the same time, their translation efforts were integral to my project of writing this book. Collaboration in translation goes beyond actual cooperation. It is pervasive—meaning it is infused in and constitutes the world in which it takes place.

Consider, for example, the efforts of the Chinese delegation at the review and planning session for the Kailash Sacred Landscape Conservation and Development Initiative (KSLCDI); they wanted to translate their government's concerns for their Indian, Nepali, and Western colleagues. Collaboration not only depended on but was also constituted by this translation effort. Without at least a partial understanding of the Chinese government's own curational ambitions, no activity in Tibet would be possible.

Similarly, ICIMOD's training manuals are an attempt at translation. With the help of picture series and detailed instructions for trainers, the organization tries to translate the idea of ecosystem services for Tibetan herders in the People's Republic of China. Without translation there can be no future collaboration. Translation, here, goes far beyond language and the problem of finding adequate terms in Chinese and Tibetan for universal concepts bred in the global development and conservation industry. What was at stake was a much larger task: to conjure an entire view of the world and translate it into the landscape to be cured. Here, collaboration is translation.

Consider also my own modest contribution to bring ICIMOD's notion of culture and heritage to the cultural heritage sites depicted on ICIMOD's illustrated map of the Kailash area described in chapter 9: distributing copies of the map in the monasteries of Upper Humla, I wandered right into ICIMOD's quest to translate its curational vision and transfuse it to the target that inspired it in the first place.

Furthermore, take Abhimanyu Pandey's work to tame the equivocation of "culture" between the ecosystem services approach, the shifting debates in anthropology, and Buddhist understandings of a sacred landscape. Without at least a provisional translation, no collaboration and no agreement about the value of culture and heritage is possible.

An equivocation, Viveiros de Castro reminds us, is not a failure or an illusion but rather a "tool of objectification." This does not mean, he argues, that we need "to imagine objectification in the post-Enlightenment and moralizing language of reification or fetishization" (Viveiros De Castro 2004, 12). What we find is collaboration in translation, a process that necessarily produces what Anna Tsing (2005) calls "friction."

Equivocation and (mis)translation are constituting parts of collaboration in ICIMOD's work as much as in mine. But collaboration in translation is not unique to curational interventions or academic research. It is at the core of what I call the remoteness-connectivity nexus. The Himalayas have long been a juncture of diverging translocal aspirations, global concerns, and national agendas. Collaborative translation was the bread and butter of erstwhile trans-Himalayan brokerage as much as it features prominently in most of the contemporary stories told in this book. Collaborative translation takes place among actors with different agendas and between evolving expectations, aspirations, and institutions. It drives much of the "event richness" that is a hallmark of seemingly remote areas (Ardener 2012, 531).

Take, for example, the old Himalayan institution of the seasonal entrepôt translated into a new form capable of catering to the needs of the new China trade. Consider the roles of the *goba* and the monastery in the village of Dzang: The expanding place-knot required collaborative translation of these institutions. Similarly, consider the green road guidelines that found entry into Nepal's official policies for rural roads: Building the Limi Road, they needed to be retranslated for the purpose of reviving an old pathway. To achieve this goal, the road construction committee was convinced that an excavator was absolutely necessary. Think of the old salt bags on the shoulders of sheep and goats that required collaborative translation to become containers for subsidized rice coming from the North (the world upside down). Consider Tshewang's efforts to explain the logic of food aid to the people who "stole" the rice he was contracted to bring to Simikot, or Tenzing's ambition for a road to Walung and the letter to Riwu County asking for assistance and declaring the kind of dependence his daughter found difficult to stomach amid the free Tibet rhetoric in Queens, New York.

Within expanding place-knots that make community, along pathways of exchange, and amid curational interventions, the "stories-so-far" (Massey 2005, 130) are infused with collaboration in translation. The notions of remoteness and connectivity echo through these tales at every juncture. Remoteness serves as a positionality for declarations of dependence as much as it helps keep the state at bay; the promise of connectivity drives the expansion of place-knots as much as the frenzied dreams of infrastructural futures in the Himalayas. The making and unmaking of remoteness through connections—total in imaginaries, partial in reality—unfolds in collaborations that require new translations, again and again.

My own project and this book are no exceptions here. My attempt to unmake a certain image of remoteness is equally based on collaboration and translation.

A number of young men from Walung and Humla accompanied me on this journey. Instead of concluding this book with an attempt to pack the many fragments into a comprehensive theoretical framework, I will tell their stories. They, more than anybody, found themselves right in the middle of the various collaborations and equivocations at stake.

Research assistants have a curious absence in much of anthropological writing. On the one hand, they are the very conduits through which most ethnographic endeavors work. As brokers and experts, they facilitate translation—not just between languages but also between ways of seeing the world. On the other hand, they are typically young, smart, and often from elite families. Thus, their lives tend to be seen rather as an exception than as representative for the larger social context waiting to be described. Thus, their role is often diminished (or too rarely elevated to coauthorship).

Dor Bahadur Bista, the eminent Nepali anthropologist and author of *Fatalism and Development* (1991), was the travel companion of Christoph von Fürer-Haimendorf; they visited Walung together in 1958. Both Tenzing, who runs the antique shop at Broadway 888, and Tshewang, the initiator of the Limi Road, worked for anthropologists at stages of their careers. Assisting a researcher is in many ways similar to working for an NGO. Both are ways to extend one's network of relations. In this sense, research assistants and NGO staff do the same as Himalayan traders or trekking guides: They engage in fostering connections. Thus, the smart, young, and polyglot Himalayan men and women who end up dedicating a phase of their lives to helping somebody else's research follow an old and well-established Himalayan pursuit.

Rinzin

On my visits to Humla in 2011 and 2012, Rinzin accompanied me. Rinzin, the son of Tshewang's second wife, was doing a bachelor's degree in forestry at Nepal's Tribhuvan University. He was the first Humli student to become a forester. Rinzin grew up in the Nyin Valley near Simikot. It was through his intimate knowledge and his family's social relations that I found an initial entry into the world of Upper Humla. Rinzin had many ambitions, and helping me with my research provided him with an opportunity to look for potential research topics for his thesis project. At least initially, he also saw me as a potential conduit to find a way into the development and conservation scene, in which he wanted to establish himself.

Like many of my Humli friends, Rinzin dealt with complicated family relations resulting from a polyandric household that split at one point. Questions of labor, responsibility, and the limits of family solidarity were an integral part of his life. Rinzin felt great pressure to succeed in his career. His two brothers—an artist and a musician—were pursuing lives with less of a clear path to a steady income. Rinzin was extremely busy with these manifold responsibilities. At the end of our first trip, Rinzin had to hurry back to his native village to help his family with the harvest. Then, he hastened to Simikot to conduct a training workshop under a short-term contract with an NGO.

After completing his forestry degree, Rinzin obtained a small grant to study the Pallas's cat, which had just been discovered in Nepal. Once he had a foot in the conservation scene, he managed to secure further grants to pursue a six-month training course in the United States, a master's in conservation biology at the University of Göttingen, and a new research project on snow leopard conservation and human-wildlife conflict. He actively and successfully learned the skill of proposal writing. In turn, editing his proposals, I became more familiar with the language and logic of global development. Through his interest in conservation, my interest in curational interventions grew. The idea to join ICIMOD for a fellowship emerged from this collaboration.

While Rinzin was seeking a career in conservation, he was also very critical of the realities he observed. Doing focus group interviews and environmental awareness trainings for NGOs, he witnessed the dynamics of such interventions. NGOs would usually pay participants for their attendance and arrive with the expectation that "locals" would provide a participatory coating to their projects. The "locals," on the other hand, had expectations about what they would receive in return for becoming local "stakeholders." The inherent disconnect in such arrangements bothered Rinzin. His ambition was to do better and combine sound scientific conservation research with the real concerns and problems of life in the Himalayas—problems he was intimately familiar with.

Funding for his own research was limited and did not allow him to pay participants. He found it a struggle to translate his ambitions for a better kind of participatory conservation into these well-established patterns of expectations. To facilitate his snow leopard research among herders in Mustang and Manang, he bought Chinese solar-powered flashlights as presents. These low-cost predator deterrent lights could be used to illuminate the corrals in which animals are kept during the night in order to protect them against snow leopard attacks. Most probably, the snow leopards would soon learn to read the lights and render them worthless, he feared. But as a way to live up to the expectations that prior collaborations in the name of conservation had established, the cheap flashlights would have to do, given his limited funding.

Rinzin's work was an exercise in multiple translations. It required phrasing his ambitions in the language of international development proposals and translating it back into the actual problems that haunted herders; at the same time, he tried to anticipate the future moves of the snow leopards that tied it all together.

I remained on the sidelines. Rinzin no longer needed help with proposals, but I was still writing reference letters and short evaluation reports. Doing so, I tried to translate some of the world I knew through him into an argument for his special role and skills. I emphasized that he had a better shot at bridging the gap between NGO flip charts and the everyday concerns of those meant to become stakeholders in the curational interventions dreamed up in Kathmandu, London, Berlin, or Bern. Conservationists often failed to accomplish such translations. Who better to have a chance to succeed?

Sagar

On a later research trip, Sagar, another young Humli, joined me. Sagar is the younger brother of Mangal, the co-initiator of the Limi Road who turned road contractor and, in 2016, became the first chair of the Humla Chapter of the Nepal China Chamber of Commerce and Industry. Sagar brought much experience with research and development projects to our collaboration. He had worked for the Nepal Trust, a British NGO known and liked in Upper Humla for its hands-on approach. Rather than offering trainings, the Nepal Trust provided villages with solar panels and micro-hydropower plants. When I met Sagar, he was a research assistant in ICIMOD's KSLCDI. He worked on a project in cooperation with the India China Institute at the New School in New York, collecting stories and songs throughout Humla. He also co-organized and guided a "Landscape *Yatra*" to Limi and Mount Kailash.

Like Rinzin, Sagar was involved in many translation endeavors. Coming back from our field trip, he applied for a conference on mountains and sacred landscapes, organized by the India China Institute in New York. Writing the conference abstract required him to leave behind the language of NGOs and applied research in favor of an argument that could stand in the context of an international academic conference. I was better equipped to assist with this task than Rinzin's conservation proposals. Sagar planned to begin a master's program in anthropology in Kathmandu.

If academic research and global development, brimful of potential outside connections, are always already part of the worlds they seek to understand, they nevertheless differ in one crucial aspect: Academic research—more than development, even in its current 2.0 incarnation that favors training over building

Sagar fording a river in Limi. *Source*: Martin Saxer, 2016.

bridges—typically lacks the promise of distribution. Thus, the sole value of academic research in the context of place-knots and pathways is to serve as a conduit for making relations—relations, that ideally go beyond the academic world.

Sagar's academic pursuit was only one of his many ambitions. Even more than Rinzin, he was juggling worlds. Sagar had bought a truck—one of the blue Dong Feng vehicles used in Limi in the first pioneering years. The truck had broken down in Tugling, the camp at the upper tip of the Limi Valley, and the former owners despaired of repairing it. Sagar brought in new mechanics and carried spare parts across the passes. He finally managed to fix the blue Dong Feng and bring it down to Sallikhola, where Tshewang had been guarding his rice four years earlier. In October 2016, Sagar was awaiting the arrival of the official road coming down from Hilsa. He planned to offer transportation services for road construction.

Sagar had also built a guesthouse and restaurant in Sallikhola, where his family owned land. One of his brothers was running the guesthouse together with his wife. Furthermore, Sagar had planted two hundred apple trees near the lodge. Once the road to Tibet was finished, Sallikhola would become an important juncture at the crossroads of the Limi and Hilsa Roads and apples would find a market in China, he reasoned.

But Sagar was thinking even further. Why not start a furniture workshop in the forested Salli Valley? Carpentry and traditional Tibetan painting could be ways to move up the value chain and provide not only steady profits but also new employment opportunities in the region. This, of course, would require sustainable forest management and proper licenses—all possible with dedication, wit, and good relations.

Furthermore, Sagar had just registered a trekking agency with some of his friends. This business, he argued, would not only position him to make use of future developments in the trekking and tourism industry but also allow him to apply for the restricted-area permits that foreigners, regardless of the purpose of their visit, required. With an officially registered trekking company he could handle research trips like mine or field visits by foreign NGO staff. The trekking agency was one more piece in the puzzle of Sagar's overall strategy.

Sagar's many projects did not stand alone. They tied in with his family's endeavors. While his elder brother was extending his construction business, his younger brother tried to get into politics. This would add another dimension to the family's standing in Humla. Sagar and his brothers were not from a rich elite family. However, they were dedicated to making use of the opportunities that presented themselves in the current situation—a situation in which new roads were entangled with local politics and met with old pathway economies amid curational interventions like ICIMOD's. Charming, intelligent, and helpful, Sagar fostered the relations emerging from these dynamics and positioned himself for the future. Hedging his bets in view of the uncertainties and vagaries involved was only prudent.

Phuntsok

It is, of course, no coincidence that Rinzin and Sagar agreed to help me with my research. They had similar skills and similar ambitions and moved within similar circles that made us cross paths. Not all young Humli, however, are as successful as Rinzin and Sagar.

Phuntsok, for example, found it much more difficult to find his way. I met Phuntsok on my first visit to Limi in 2011. He was running the shop in Tugling. The shop was primarily an initiative of Lhundup, his elder brother (and one of the partners in Tshewang's rice contract). The two brothers hailed from a family that belonged to the upper stratum of Waltse. They were from one of the "big houses." Their father was a lama and businessman who traveled frequently between Lhasa, Delhi, and Kathmandu. According to Phuntsok, he was the first businessman from Limi who established this kind of long-distance trade. His main business was in watches bought in India and sold in Purang. Toward the end of his life, he quit the trade and started meditating in Ladakh and Lhasa.

He passed away in Limi when Phuntsok was around six and his elder brother around sixteen.

Just like Rinzin, Phuntsok had to deal with the remains of a polyandric household. After his father's death and while Phuntsok was still a child, the two brothers married a woman from Waltse. She had a child with Lhundup, but the baby died. The union did not last, and Lhundup married a Tibetan woman in Kathmandu. While still providing for his wife in Waltse, the brothers moved outside the fold of Waltse's strict village rules and established their base in Kathmandu. Phuntsok was educated outside Humla and spoke some English, but his role as younger brother in the complex arrangement of family and household made it difficult for him to find his own calling. He had tried many things.

Once, Phuntsok went on a *phuru*-collecting expedition to India with seven or eight partners from Limi. They split into two groups to roam the jungle in search of the precious maple burls. One day, some people approached them, saying they were looking for a fellow hunter who got lost. Phuntsok's group offered them tea. The visitors, however, had been sent by the police. Somebody had tipped them off. Phuntsok and his fellow collectors were escorted to the local police post. On the way, the group sent by the police stopped and took some of the maple burls, hiding them in their own houses. Arriving in the provincial town late at night, the police were all drunk and mistook them for Maoist rebels. Phuntsok translated, trying to "talk nicely," but he was repeatedly beaten. They were threatened with jail and fines; they were told that killing a tree was as severe a crime as killing a human. "But we did not cut trees," Phuntsok argued. In the end, the police demanded a 50,000 Indian rupee "fine" from each of them. Phuntsok managed to negotiate the fine down to 5,000 for the whole group. In the end, even this amount was waived. The police returned the remaining maple burls to them and advised them on which route to take to avoid further scrutiny on the way.

Phuntsok told me this story in the typical style of a heroic odyssey, in which he and his friends finally prevailed against all odds—not least because of his language skills. However, the stress and fear of the expedition left traces. Phuntsok was too fine a character to draw strength from such adventures. He didn't see himself in this type of business, which required taking such high risks. He felt more at ease in Kathmandu. He was a member of the Limi Youth Society that had produced the documentary film about life in Limi, which Phuntsok screened on a solar-powered TV set in the camp in Tugling. He took part in organizing the Limi Youth Society's welfare and community events, many of them related to religious activities in the context of the Karma Kagyu school of Tibetan Buddhism.

The present incarnation of the Limi *trulku*, Senge Tenzin Rinpoche, has close links to the Limi Youth Society. He provided them with space in his private house

Pilgrims and tourists circumambulating the Boudha Stupa in Kathmandu.
Source: Martin Saxer, 2011.

in Kathmandu and later helped fund a new community hall. After the devastating double earthquake of 2015, Rinpoche established the Senge Tenzin Relief Team. Many members of the Limi Youth Society, including Phuntsok, volunteered. This work was extremely important to Phuntsok. In many of our conversations, he kept coming back to the experiences he had gained during the relief effort.

While Phuntsok had little interest nor the necessary relations to engage with the curational ambitions of development and conservation organizations, he was nevertheless part of this curational initiative in the name of relief. And he was also part of the transnational Buddhist community that supported it. Senge Tenzin Rinpoche runs two dharma centers in Taiwan. His many Taiwanese disciples provided funds for the relief effort in Nepal. Taiwan is an important locus in the expanding Limi place-knot. Several Limi monks stay there. The Karma Kagyu monastery in Nayapati near Kathmandu, named Rinchenling Gompa after the monastery in Waltse, started offering Chinese classes for its young student monks.

Notably, the transnational Buddhist community surrounding Senge Tenzin Rinpoche never surfaced in the action plans of ICIMOD's Kailash initiative—despite a shared concern for sacred sites, community, heritage, and conservation. It remained invisible in ICIMOD's cartographic endeavors.

Nyima

My closest collaboration was with Nyima, a fellow anthropologist and, in many ways, a kindred spirit. Nyima grew up in Walung and went to school in Kalimpong, India. He then studied history in Delhi. When we met, he was enrolled in a master's program in social and cultural anthropology at Tribhuvan University in Kathmandu.

In November 2012, Nyima guided me on my first visit to Walung. His mother used to be a Village Development Committee (VDC) chairwoman for some time and was very well known in the region. Nyima's family, however, did not belong to the elite.

His father used to work as a helper for one of the richest Walung families and gradually worked his way up, starting his own business. Nyima's parents were among those who took over a house of one of the rich families who left. They followed their footsteps. His father traded in wristwatches, as many did at the time. Nyima told me how he spent an evening with his father and a few of his acquaintances somewhere in the Terai. His father was explaining geopolitics and the entire world history starting with World War II to them. Nyima remembered him as a cosmopolitan who spent his life between Shigatse and Kolkata, following news and making sense of what he learned.

Through Nyima's translation of the world he grew up in—a world he had left for studies abroad and was now returning to with me—I started understanding the mobility of the Walung community not as out-migration but as an expansion of community. One of his sisters lived in the house in Walung, one was in Taiwan, and one in the United States. Nyima lived with his mother in Kathmandu. Through Nyima and the story of his family, I realized that my image of Walung, derived from long interviews with its former elite, was incomplete at best.

Nyima was not eager to follow the standard Walung trajectory and become a businessman. He also had no plans to move abroad. Nyima once told me that whenever he went to circumambulate the Boudha Stupa (the prime meeting place of Tibetan-speaking communities in Kathmandu), people would approach him and ask, "When are you leaving for the United States? When are you going abroad? When are you bringing back money?"

Nyima, like myself, had more of an analytical interest in trade and mobility. We had read the same books and shared the same interests. Nyima's endeavor to see the world in which he grew up anew, with the eyes of an anthropologist, was at the core of our collaboration. His work of translation—both for me and for himself—profoundly shaped my understanding of pathways and places in knots.

In 2016 and 2017, Nyima and I embarked on a joint project on the recent history of the translocal Walung community. Nyima did interviews in Kathmandu,

Hile, Taplejung, Darjeeling, and Kalimpong; I went to New York and met with Tenzing and the Walung Community of North America. Our collaboration intensified, and so did the work of translation. Translation was thereby not unidirectional. While working with me, Nyima was also trying to explain his academic pursuits to the people around him—an effort at translation in which our collaboration and my presence clearly played a role.

The stories of Rinzin, Sagar, Phuntsok, and Nyima are all about young men from the highlands. This, of course, is no coincidence. It is the result of my own role and position as a male anthropologist and the practicalities tied to it. While gender relations in Tibetan communities are less sensitive than in many Hindu or Muslim contexts, it would still have been considered odd had I chosen to wander about the Himalayas, and share a tent when necessary, with a female research assistant. It was impossible for me to establish the same kind of companionship with women. The stories of the four young men and (by way of collaboration) my overall narrative thus cannot be gender neutral.

Generally, it may be true that mobility, business, and venturing out tend to play a more prominent role in the lives of men than women. However, Himalayan women are neither immobile nor excluded from careers. Women run roadside shops, work on construction sites, forage for medicinal plants, collect firewood—just like men. Women undertake the same odysseys to the United States as their brothers and fathers. Furthermore, NGOs often have a preference for female co-workers. Women, they argue, are more trustworthy and less prone to bending a development initiative's goal to their own ends. Moreover, those on the receiving end of development initiatives, such as the local representatives singled out to be trained and become part of a pilot project, are often predominantly women.

In brief, had this book emerged from different collaborations and a different set of translation efforts, it would not be the same. Other experiences would be woven into it, other equivocations would have come to light, and other conversations would have served as its narrative backbone. However, I would argue that the work of tying places into knots, the ways exchange and ambitions congregate along pathways, and the role curational interventions play in the Himalayas are important in the lives of both women and men.

One way to think about place-knots, pathways, and curation is to take them as broad categories for the heterogeneous elements that aggregate in an evolving assemblage. The notion of assemblage, loaned from Gilles Deleuze and Felix Guattari (1987), has become a veritable conceptual toolbox (Rabinow 2003; Ong and Collier 2005; DeLanda 2006; Bennett 2009). Thinking in assemblages promises an elegant way to understand the manifold relations between materials, discourses,

policies, humans, and nonhumans. The term assemblage found entry into a myriad of analytic endeavors. However, as Tim Ingold (2020) notes, the original term
Deleuze and Guattari used was not assemblage but *agencement* (a result of joining
or fitting), despite the fact that *assemblage* is also a French word. Something got
lost in translation, Ingold argues. An assemblage consists of discrete elements and
shifting relations between them. But in the work of joining or fitting, things do not
remain discrete. They transform and become something else in the process; they
coalesce rather than aggregate.

Collaboration is such an attempt to fit or join things. In the process, entities
that looked discrete a moment ago break open; they become susceptible to the
worlds that translation brings along. In this process, a monastery also becomes
heritage and its abbot also becomes part of an ecosystem; a trail is also a future
road; a Himalayan flower also an endangered species; a simple trek also a Landscape Yatra; an act of Buddhist compassion also a relief effort; an old salt bag
also a container for aid; a fungus also a resource more precious than gold.
Whether we describe this process as equivocation (Viveiros De Castro 2004) or
as friction in the forest of global collaboration (Tsing 2005) is a matter of choice.
What is important is that these transformations are relevant but never total.

Meanwhile, totalizing stories of great transformations abound: from the end
of remoteness through connectivity to the promise of infrastructure, the plight
of migration, and the risk of climate change. These stories ignore the multiplic-
ity of collaborations and thus necessarily remain partial. And yet they are integral to the translations at work.

What we find, then, are twists and turns. What may seem like the last chapter in a story of transformation suddenly appears to be another beginning.

Somewhere in Thailand. *Source*: Martin Saxer, 2018.

NAVIDAD

One evening in Queens, after a long day of work, Pemba told me the story of his odyssey traveling from Nepal to the United States. Pemba was born in a village near Walung. His sister came to the United States about five years ago. In 2015, Pemba decided to follow her footsteps.

Unable to get a visa, he approached two Nepali brothers well known as brokers for such journeys. One of them lived in Thailand, one of them in Mexico. Pemba paid them US$22,000 upfront for their services—all inclusive. He flew to Bangkok to meet one of the two brothers, a very nice guy who since became a friend. The broker took Pemba and three fellow Nepali travelers on a tour around Thailand for six days, visiting temples in the north, beaches in the south. Then, he brought them to the airport and put them on a plane to Moscow.

From Moscow, the group flew via Panama to Trinidad and Tobago. They had an onward ticket to Saint Vincent and the Grenadines, where Nepali citizens were able to get a visa on arrival. The broker had scheduled for a twenty-two-hour stopover in Trinidad. Following his instructions, Pemba and his companions in fate approached the transfer counter and asked for a transfer lounge. They knew well that no such facility existed. Airside, there was neither food nor a place to rest. The four Nepalis were directed to immigration and obtained a two-day transit visa. With this, they were able to leave the airport and stay overnight in a hotel.

But instead of checking into a hotel, they met with a prearranged guide who took them on a small boat across the Caribbean Sea to Venezuela. As instructed, Pemba and his friends disposed of their passports and other documents. They just kept a small daypack, a mobile phone, a minimal amount of cash, and a slip of paper with the telephone numbers of the two broker brothers. In Caracas, they hired a driver and proceeded to the Colombian border. At the border, they showed the police their prearranged fake student IDs, telling them that they were based in Colombia and were just returning from a day trip to catch a glimpse of beautiful Venezuela. For a small fee, the guards let them cross. On the Colombian side of the border, they found a car that brought them to Bogotá.

In Bogotá, they went to a specific hotel and called their broker in Thailand. Through the hotel owner, the broker wired some additional money to pay for accommodation and the next leg of the journey. Another driver, arranged by the hotel, brought them to Medellín, where the same routine started again: a hotel, a phone call to Bangkok, money wired, and onward transport. They drove north toward the "Darian Gap," the stretch of dense and roadless jungle that interrupts the Pan-American Highway at the border to Panama. The region is known as one of the main pathways along which drugs are smuggled to Central America and onward to the United States.

The four Nepalis joined a larger group of migrants, mostly from Bangladesh and Latin America. They crossed the jungle together in three days. For the first two stages they traveled on riverboats. At the end of the second day, they received rubber boots as protection against snake bites. From here on, they had to walk. Without a guide but equipped with instructions, the group hiked for a full day until they arrived at the Panama border. This was hard but not very dangerous, Pemba remarked. His sister had followed the same route three years before, and she had to walk for seven days. Yes, they were a bit afraid to encounter bandits, but they only met people begging for clothes. In the end, they lost the single change of clothes they had carried with them, but nobody was hurt. There was nothing else to lose. They carried no money and no documents. The only thing they had to hold onto were the phone numbers of the brokers and an old mobile phone. They knew that at each step they would receive new instructions and cash.

In Panama, they gave themselves up to the border guards, knowing that if they did not have documents and did not speak Spanish, they would not be deported. Deportation is just too much hassle and too expensive for Panama. Only the Spanish speakers risked being turned back to the jungle.

Pemba and his peers paused a few days in Panama City before proceeding to Costa Rica. In Costa Rica, they stayed with another guide in his rural cabin. Pemba and his friends were cooking a Nepali meal for him, which he found exquisite. The group's host and guide owned a black Ferrari, which he had equipped with curtains in the back. Three of the Nepalis had to squeeze in on the back bench and one rode shotgun. They were speeding like mad until the police stopped them and inquired about the curtains. This, for sure, was an unusual sight on a black Ferrari, but their guide managed to explain away the curtains. He said that the sun was simply too strong these days and he could not afford to be vain. Near the border with Nicaragua, the four companions said goodbye to their guide. He instructed them to cross a short patch of jungle along the border. This was not a problem.

They arrived in Nicaragua just before Christmas and were hosted by a very friendly family. The family invited the four Nepalis to celebrate with them. It was the first Catholic Christmas in their lives, a joyful Navidad full of warm-hearted hospitality. These are beautiful memories, Pemba said.

From Nicaragua to El Salvador, they took as speedboat across the open sea. This was a frightening experience. They all got wet and the phone they carried died. The precious slip of paper with the two phone numbers survived, however. At this point, they were handed over from the Bangkok-based broker to the one in Mexico, who handled the rest of their trip. He was as reliable and nice as his brother.

They reached El Salvador on New Year's Eve and were again hosted by a friendly family with two children who invited them to celebrate the new year. It was a great party with plenty of alcohol. The family also provided them with new clothes from the remaining stock of a shop they had formerly run.

From El Salvador, they walked across the border to Guatemala, where they had to await the arrival of another group of six Nepalis traveling behind them. Together, they were taken across the border to Mexico. A minibus picked them up and brought them to Mexico City. They were driving day and night. Their driver paid small bribes to the police along the way.

From Mexico City, they embarked on the last leg of their journey. At Reynosa, a small boat brought them across the Rio Grande to Texas. There, they looked for police to give themselves up. Pemba spent some time in a detention center and finally was allowed to pay a bond and travel onward to Queens, New York.

Pemba recounted his journey almost as if it were an adventurous vacation trip: certainly expensive, but the service was good and reliable. And he got to know many friendly people along the way. When I met Pemba, he worked two jobs, paid taxes, and was waiting for his case to be decided.

Notes

INTRODUCTION

1. For the sense of vulnerability that comes with the lack of barriers to the outside world, see Brachet and Scheele 2019.

2. In relation to this media attention, it has often been argued that the Tibetans in South Asia are the most successful refugee community in the world. For an overview, see, for example, Frechette 2002.

3. This is the introduction to a collection of articles in volume 27 of *Social Anthropology/Anthropologie Sociale* (2019), shedding light on instances of the return of remoteness in our current era around the globe. The argument here is based on our discussions on the topic.

4. The project was part of the medicinal and aromatic plants program of The Mountain Institute (mountain.org).

1. TYING PLACES INTO KNOTS

1. A *ngagpa* is a nonmonastic practitioner of Dzogchen, a central teaching in the Nyingma School of Tibetan Buddhism and Bon.

2. On this visit to Walung, I was accompanied by team members of my project *Remoteness & Connectivity: Highland Asia in the World*.

3. My attempt to carbon-date a piece of wood from the doorsteps of one of the houses failed, as the method is too imprecise for such recent times.

4. See the Secretariat of the Convention on Biological Diversity (https://www.cbd.int) for more on the Biodiversity Convention and the Nagoya Protocol.

5. This vision also underpins UNESCO's take on intangible cultural heritage; see https://ich.unesco.org.

6. While the importance of income generated outside agriculture is widely acknowledged around the world, the term implicitly takes farming as the center of a rural household. See, for example, Off-Farm Income's website (https://www.offincome.com/).

7. On the role of local mountain deities in the Himalayas and the ritual work required to appease them and harness their protection, see, for example, *The Navel of the Demoness* (Ramble 2008) and the edited volume *Reflections of the Mountain* (Blondeau and Steinkeller 1996).

8. In some contexts, sponsorship relies less on voluntary donations by community members doing business outside the valley than on rotating obligations in the village. This, for example, is the case in the Limi Valley (Hovden 2013), discussed in chapter 2.

9. Between 1990 and 2017, Nepal was organized into districts and VDCs. This administrative structure is now replaced with provinces and rural municipalities (*gaunpalika*).

2. MOVING IN, MOVING UP, MOVING OUT

1. Kyirong and Kuti are the historical shorthands for the two main trade routes between Tibet and Nepal. The Kuti route refers to what is now the Araniko or Friendship Highway, crossing the border at Kodari/Dram. The Kyirong route leads from Rasuwa to Kyirong.

2. These tribute obligations, however, turned out to be excellent trading opportunities. The missions enjoyed diplomatic immunity, which provided cover against Chinese scrutiny and allowed for smuggling, especially opium. These missions continued until 1908 (Uprety 1998, 178–81).

3. Over the course of the twentieth century, Kalimpong became more than just a trading hub. The Kalimpong–Darjeeling area was a cosmopolitan center that attracted intellectuals, political activists, writers, and artists (Goldstein 2007; Shakya 1999; Harris et al. 2016).

4. For a broader discussion of systems of taxation in Nepal, see Regmi 1978.

5. Later, during Tamla's tenure as consul general in Lhasa, he inquired about the fate of the elephant. People told him that they saw it until October or November 1959. Then, it suddenly vanished and was never seen again.

6. This section draws on two dozen biographical interviews that my colleague Nyima Dorjee Bothia carried out among elderly Walungnga from low- and middle-income families.

7. To the best of my knowledge, interest rates were typically not calculated per annum but only came due once the entire amount was repaid. They were not accumulating over time; rather, they were meant to facilitate a particular transaction or endeavor. Thus, they are difficult to compare to bank loans.

8. In 2006, the Dalai Lama called on Tibetans to stop wearing traditional fur-trimmed clothes during festivals. Throughout Tibet, people gathered to burn their fur-trimmed robes. The Chinese authorities regarded this as an act of defiance—regardless of the fact that the Dalai Lama's appeal was very much in conformity with the PRC's wildlife protection laws already in place. In 2007, people in Yushu found themselves in a dilemma, as the government ordered them to wear fur-trimmed robes for the annual horse-racing festival, which had become a tourist attraction. Not dressing traditionally Tibetan meant being fined (French 2007). For a discussion of the cultural politics surrounding these events, see the articles "Blazing Pelts and Burning Passions" (Yeh 2013b) and "Precious Skin" (Yondon 2018).

9. While the heyday of wildlife trade may be over, the business has not come to an end. See, for example, Sonia Awale, "Nepal-China Connectivity Aid Wildlife Smuggling," *The Pangolin Reports*, September 6, 2019, https://www.pangolinreports.com/nepal-china-connectivity/.

INTERLUDE

1. Waltse is more commonly, but maybe less correctly, spelled Halji. While both renderings of the name are in use, Waltse has become the preferred option among Limiwa, at least in Kathmandu.

2. This conflict between getting used to city life while getting an education and continuing a household in Limi is also described by Astrid Hovden (2016, 98). Many families in Limi call their children back after they have spent a number of years in schools outside the community.

3. BINDING RULES

1. See, for example, Fisher (1990) for a discussion of the Solukhumbu District and Lim (2008) for Langtang, both thoroughly reshaped by trekking tourism.

2. According to Hovden (2016, 94), using data from 2011, 381 of 1,070 Limiwa live outside the valley, mainly in Kathmandu, India, and the United States. One complaint that I heard several times was that the Limiwa were "less successful" than people from other Himalayan communities in moving to the United States; within Limi, Til and Dzang seem to be "more successful" than Waltse. In Dzang, ten households have family

members living in the United States (Hovden 2016, 96). As I focused on the Walung community during my research stay in New York, I have not collected any data on Limi.

3. Irrigated, double-cropped fields closer to the village were usually provisioned with manure from the village itself.

4. Such reasoning resonates with the findings of Barbara Aziz (1978) regarding Tibetan communities from Tingri in central Tibet.

5. Astrid Hovden's PhD thesis (2016, 33) provides an overview of the different regulations. Limi is one of the few remaining places in the Tibetan world where the recruitment on monks is based on a levy system. According to Hovden, the household of each monk has to provide for a total of fifteen years of patronage, paying for festivals, meals, and other needs (2016, 285).

6. In Waltse, however, monks are not allowed to spend the winter away from the village. Dzang and Til do not have this rule.

7. In Limi, seeking outside labor has a longer history. It was not uncommon to seek employment during winter in communities further south. However, such arrangements were hardly lucrative and did not offer households a substantial income like the labor market in Purang.

8. The epilogue of Astrid Hovden's dissertation (2016, 316) describes the precursor meeting in Dzang in June 2015 and the attempt to end the monk levy for good. A monastic management committee was formed and handed over the keys of the monastery to the village. Hovden (1996, 93) also describes the difference between taking temporary leave from the village (in Wylie transliteration: *khral dgongs*) and breaking the village obligations and taxes for good (*khral gcog*).

4. THE BUSINESS OF WAYFARING

1. For a visual impression of sheep caravans today, see my blog post on "Salt Traders," *The Other Image*, July 27, 2012, https://www.theotherimage.com/salt-traders/.

2. Around the same time, in 2010, a satellite phone dish was also installed in Waltse.

3. I captured the moment described here in a short video. See "Double Narration," *The Other Image*, January 25, 2014, https://www.theotherimage.com/double-narration/.

4. See the website of Nepal's Department of Roads (https://dor.gov.np).

5. While corridor imaginaries tend to gloss over terrain, they nevertheless change the landscape even before they arrive, turning terrain into territory and highlighting issues of land rights and property. In this sense, the land grabs in Timure and the rising land prices along the road point to a deeper question: How do expected futures of *mobility* change affective and legal relations to *land*?

6. One could argue, following Ingold (2007, 2008), that transport is associated with types of knowledge and skill radically different from wayfaring—less driven by stories and more linear, more "genealogical," as one of the reviewers of this book put it. This may be true at the very beginning of a major infrastructural intervention, but the more it proceeds, the less I see such a difference.

7. Two posts on my blog *The Other Image*, from December 2013 and February 2014, respectively, give an impression of this fragile balance. "Red Carpet" captures the moment the first truck with Chinese goods arrives in Dzang (https://www.theotherimage.com/red-carpet/); "Cold Water" shows the moment the empty truck got stuck in the river on the way back (https://www.theotherimage.com/cold-water/).

5. A QUEST FOR ROADS

1. The Maoist Youth League is an organization of the Communist Party of Nepal (Maoist), which split in 1995 from the Communist Party of Nepal (Unity Center) and

embarked on the ten-year People's War that led to end of the monarchy in 2006. The party further split in 2014. The names and acronyms of the communist parties in Nepal have changed several times since 2011.

2. The Lhasa–Shigatse extension of the Qinghai–Tibet railway opened in 2014.

3. In Limi, land outside the three villages belongs to all residents of the valley. Putting a claim on a piece of land requires building at least a knee-high wall for a future house. Once the road reached Tugling, many families from all three villages rushed to stake their claims in this way.

4. See "The Operator," *The Other Image*, June 26, 2012, https://www.theotherimage .com/the-operator/.

5. The argument that roads can separate rather than connect is convincingly made by Pedersen and Bunkenborg (2012). Looking at Sino-Mongolian border roads and the interaction between local Mongolians and Chinese workers in the oil industry, they show how roads can serve as "technologies of distantiation" (Pedersen and Bunkenborg 2012, 563). In a similar vein, Demenge (2013) shows for Ladakh that new roads to seemingly isolated places do not necessarily increase mobility, echoing an argument by Dalakoglou and Harvey (2012).

6. In autumn 2016, Mangal was working on the Hilsa to Simikot road, upgrading the stretch around Nara La. For a visual impression of the road and construction site, see "Red, Blue, Brown," *The Other Image*, May 10, 2018, https://www.theotherimage.com /red-blue-brown/.

7. In the larger context of rural road construction, these cases of grassroots initiatives may play a minor role. However, beyond resisting such infrastructure developments, co-opting them, or refusing to engage with them—the "impossible public," as Harvey and Knox (2015, 175–184) put it—such grassroots initiatives broaden our understanding of the myriad of ways communities react to infrastructure in the making.

INTERLUDE

1. See my blog post "Moonlight Departure," *The Other Image*, November 14, 2012, https://www.theotherimage.com/moonlight-departure/.

6. THE LABOR OF DISTRIBUTION

1. Farideh Heyet (2002) makes this point for Azerbaijan, Carolin Maertens (2017) for Tajikistan.

2. A pilot project for Chinese food aid to Nepal's northern districts was launched in 2008 and renewed in 2013 (Murton 2017a). After the 2015 earthquakes, Chinese aid gained visibility and became embroiled in competition with India (Seemangal 2015). My impression is that much of the direct Chinese food aid in Humla falls outside official programs and takes the form of small deliveries organized at the county level. Such deliveries often have a transactional nature—little perks in the larger scheme of things.

3. An interesting argument could be made regarding the shift from the erstwhile tax burdens often complained about in the Tibetan world to subsidies as a form of negative tax. In Limi, for example, taxes paid to Tibet stopped after the Chinese takeover, and taxes paid to Nepal were never adjusted for inflation and are now only nominal. While local obligations to sponsor rituals and pay for the monastery remain, no more heavy taxes have to be paid to any overlords (Hovden 2016, 161–81). While this is certainly a relief, it also means that the bonds of dependence—and thus assistance—vanished. In this sense, the race today is to increase the influx of money and forge new bonds with the state and other outside actors such as NGOs and development agencies.

INTERLUDE

1. All the major development agencies are entitled to blue diplomatic number plates in Nepal.

7. CURATION AT LARGE

1. Dor Bahadur Bista is a fascinating figure in Nepali anthropology. He started his career as a research assistant for Christoph von Fürer-Haimendorf and with him visited most of Nepal's northern border areas, including the Walung region and Humla. Dor Bahadur Bista became one of Nepal's most eminent and critical intellectuals. He mysteriously disappeared in 1995, and many legends surround his fate. Kelsang Tseten's 2015 film *Castaway Man* provides an intimate portrait of Bista and his legacy.

2. For a discussion of Scott's argument in relation to Gramsci's notion of social hegemony and the role of hidden transcripts in a Himalayan setting, see Charles Ramble (2013).

3. The research initiative Materiality and Connectivity was a cooperation between Philipp Schorch and me. It consisted of three workshops between 2015 and 2017 (see Highland Asia Research Group, http://highlandasia.net/projects/matcon.html) and led to the edited volume *Exploring Materiality and Connectivity in Anthropology and Beyond* (Schorch, Saxer, and Elders 2020).

8. LANDSCAPES, DREAMSCAPES

1. For a glimpse of Socialist New Villages, see two articles on my blog, *The Other Image*: "Engineering Dulong," May 27, 2015, https://www.theotherimage.com/engineering-dulong/, and "New Socialist Countryside," September 5, 2013, https://www.theotherimage.com/new-socialist-countryside/.

2. The blue roofs are visible from space. On satellite images, they can be seen throughout western China. Comparing images from different years reveals how the wave of blue tin has not stopped at the border. Over the past decade, it penetrated ever deeper into the valleys of northern Nepal. For a visual impression, see "Red, Blue, Brown," *The Other Image*, May 10, 2018, https://www.theotherimage.com/red-blue-brown/.

3. The Ngari Gunsa Airport is 4,274 meters above sea level. Completed in 2010, it serves both military and civil use. Flights from Lhasa have been rather expensive so far, and the airport has had less of an impact on tourism than originally anticipated.

9. MAPPING MOUNTAINS

1. For the role of cartographic anxiety in the Pamirs of Tajikistan, see Saxer 2016a.

References

Acharya, B. N., R. Aryal, B. B. Karmacharya, and Werner Paul Meyer. 2003. "The Green Road Concept in Nepal: Best Practices from the Nepal Himalayas—An Update 2003." Kathmandu: GTZ German Technical Cooperation and SDC Swiss Agency for Development and Cooperation.

Adhikari, J. 2008. *Food Crisis in Karnali: A Historical and Politico-Economic Perspective*. Kathmandu: Martin Chautari.

Ahlers, Anna L., and Gunter Schubert. 2009. "'Building a New Socialist Countryside'— Only a Political Slogan?" *Journal of Current Chinese Affairs* 38:35–62.

Alff, Henryk. 2016. "Flowing Goods, Hardening Borders? China's Commercial Expansion into Kyrgyzstan Re-Examined." *Eurasian Geography and Economics* 57 (3): 433–56.

——. 2017. "Trading on Change: Bazaars and Social Transformation in the Borderlands of Kazakhstan, Kyrgyzstan and Xinjiang." In *The Art of Neighbouring: Managing Relations across China's Borders*, edited by Martin Saxer and Juan Zhang. Amsterdam: Amsterdam University Press.

Allen, S. K., A. Linsbauer, S. S. Randhawa, C. Huggel, P. Rana, and A. Kumari. 2016. "Glacial Lake Outburst Flood Risk in Himachal Pradesh India: An Integrative and Anticipatory Approach Considering Current and Future Threats." *Natural Hazards* 84 (3): 1741–63.

Amnesty International. 2013. *"Changing the Soup but Not the Medicine?" Abolishing Re-Education through Labour in China*. London: Amnesty International Publications. https://www.amnesty.org/download/Documents/12000/asa170422013en.pdf.

——. 2018. "China Families of up to One Million Detained in Mass Re-Education Drive Demand Answers." *Amnesty International*, September 24. https://www.amnesty.org/en/latest/news/2018/09/china-xinjiang-families-of-up-to-one-million-detained-demand-answers/.

Anagnost, Ann. 1997. *National Past-Times: Narrative Representation and Power in Modern China*. Durham, NC: Duke University Press.

Anderson, Benedict. 1991. *Imagined Communities: Reflections on the Origin and Spread of Nationalism*. Rev. ed. London: Verso.

Andrugtsang, Gompo Tashi. 1973. *Four Rivers, Six Ranges: Reminiscences of the Resistance Movement in Tibet*. Dharamsala: Information and Publicity Office of H. H. The Dalai Lama.

Appadurai, Arjun. 1988. "Putting Hierarchy in Its Place." *Cultural Anthropology* 3 (1): 36–49.

——. 1991. "Global Ethnoscapes: Notes and Queries for a Transnational Anthropology." In *Recapturing Anthropology: Working in the Present*, edited by Richard Gabriel Fox, 191–210. Santa Fe: School of American Research Press.

——. 1996. *Modernity at Large: Cultural Dimensions of Globalization*. Minneapolis: University of Minnesota Press.

Ardener, Edwin. 2012. "Remote Areas: Some Theoretical Considerations." *HAU: Journal of Ethnographic Theory* 2 (1): 519–33.

Armbrecht Forbes, Ann. 1999. "The Importance of Being Local: Villagers, NGOs, and the World Bank in the Arun Valley, Nepal." *Identities* 6 (2–3): 319–44.

Ashutosh, Mohanty, Mishra Manoranjan, Mohanty Bijoyini, and A. BalaSuddaresh-waran. 2012. "GLOF Risk Assessment in Hindu Kush-Himalayas (HKH) Region in the Era of Climate Change." Paper presented at Climate Changes and Natural Hazards in Mountain Areas, "Mountainhazards 2011," September 19–21, Dushanbe, Tajikistan. https://www.researchgate.net/publication/329268065.

Aziz, Barbara Nimri. 1978. *Tibetan Frontier Families: Reflections of Three Generations from D'ing-ri*. New Delhi: Vikas Publishing House.

Bauer, Kenneth M. 2004. *High Frontiers: Dolpo and the Changing World of Himalayan Pastoralists*. New York: Columbia University Press.

Benjamin, Walter. 2002. *Selected Writings, 3: 1935–1938*. Cambridge, MA: The Belknap Press of Harvard University Press.

Bennett, Jane. 2009. *Vibrant Matter: A Political Ecology of Things*. Durham, NC: Duke University Press.

Billé, Franck. 2014. "Territorial Phantom Pains (and Other Cartographic Anxieties)." *Environment and Planning D: Society and Space* 32 (1): 163–78.

——. 2016. "Introduction to 'Cartographic Anxieties.'" *Cross-Currents: East Asian History and Culture Review* 21:1–18.

——. 2018. "Skinworlds: Borders, Haptics, Topologies." *Environment and Planning D: Society and Space* 36 (1): 60–77.

Bista, Dor Bahadur. 1967. *People of Nepal*. 3rd Edition. Kathmandu: Ratna Pustak Bhandar, 1976.

——. 1991. *Fatalism and Development: Nepal's Struggle for Modernization*. Calcutta: Orient Blackswan.

Blij, Harm de. 2012. *Why Geography Matters, More than Ever*. Oxford: Oxford University Press.

Blondeau, Anne-Marie, and Ernst Steinkeller. 1996. *Reflections of the Mountain: Essays on the History and Social Meaning of the Mountain Cult in Tibet and the Himalaya*. Vienna: Verlag der Österreichischen Akademie der Wissenschaften.

Brachet, Julien, and Judith Scheele. 2019. "Remoteness Is Power: Disconnection as a Relation in Northern Chad." *Social Anthropology* 27 (2): 156–71.

Brauen, Martin. 1985. "Millenarianism in Tibetan Religion." In *Soundings in Tibetan Civilization*, edited by Barbara Aziz and Matthew Kapstein, 245–56. New Delhi: Manohar.

Bray, David. 2013. "Urban Planning Goes Rural: Conceptualising the 'New Village.'" *China Perspectives* 3:53–62.

Brickell, Katherine, and Ayona Datta. 2011. *Translocal Geographies*. Farnham, UK: Ashgate.

Brindley, Erica. 2003. "Barbarians or Not? Ethnicity and Changing Conceptions of the Ancient Yue (Viet) Peoples, ca. 400–50 BC." *Asia Major* 16 (1): 1–32.

Campbell, Ben. 2010. "Rhetorical routes for development: a road project in Nepal." *Contemporary South Asia* 18 (3): 267–279.

CBD. 2019. "Ecosystem Approach." *Convention on Biological Diversity*. https://www.cbd.int/ecosystem/.

Certeau, Michel de. 1984. *The Practice of Everyday Life*. Berkeley: University of California Press.

Childs, Geoff. 1981. "Polyandry and Population Growth in a Historical Tibetan Society." *History of the Family* 8 (3): 423–44.

——. 1999. "Refuge and Revitalization: Hidden Himalayan Sanctuaries (*Sbas-yul*) and the Preservation of Tibet's Imperial Lineage." *Acta Orientalica* 60:126–58.

Childs, Geoff, and Namgyal Choedup. 2019. *From a Trickle to a Torrent: Education, Migration, and Social Change in a Himalayan Valley of Nepal.* Oakland: University of California Press.

Childs, Geoff, Sienna Craig, Cynthia M. Beall, and Buddha Basnyat. 2014. "Depopulating the Himalayan Highlands: Education and Outmigration from Ethnically Tibetan Communities of Nepal." *Mountain Research and Development* 34 (2): 85–94.

Church, Mimi, and Mariette Wiebenga. 2008. "A Four-Fold Vairocana in the Rinchen Zangpo Tradition at Halji in Nepal." *Asian Art,* October 21. http://www.asianart .com/articles/halji/index.html.

Citrin, David M. 2010. "The Anatomy of Ephemeral Health Care: 'Health Camps' and Short-Term Medical Voluntourism in Remote Nepal." *Studies in Nepali History and Society* 15 (1): 27–72.

Clifford, James. 1988. *The Predicament of Culture: Twentieth-Century Ethnography, Literature, and Art.* Cambridge, MA: Harvard University Press.

——. 1997. *Routes: Travel and Translation in the Late Twentieth Century.* Cambridge, MA: Harvard University Press.

Commonwealth Legal Information Institute. 1973. "Agreement between the Government of India and His Majesty's Government of Nepal regarding the Supply of Iodised Salt." *Indian Treaty Series,* February 2. http://www.commonlii.org/in/other /treaties/INTSer/1973/4.html.

Corn, Joseph J., and Brian Horrigan. 1984. *Yesterday's Tomorrows: Past Visions of the American Future.* New York: Simon & Schuster.

Cowan, Sam. 2013. "All Change at Rasuwa Garhi." *Himalaya* 33 (1–2): 97–102.

——. 2015. "The Indian Checkposts, Lipu Lekh, and Kalapani." *The Record Nepal,* December 14. http://recordnepal.com/wire/indian-checkposts-lipu-lekh-and -kalapani.

Dalakoglou, Dimitris, and Penny Harvey. 2012. "Roads and Anthropology: Ethnographic Perspectives on Space, Time and (Im) mobility." *Mobilities* 7 (4): 459–65.

Das, Sarat Chandra. 1902. *Journey to Lhasa and Central Tibet.* London: John Murray.

Dawson, William Harbutt. 1986. "The Swiss House Industries." *The Economic Journal* 6 (22): 295–307.

Debord, Guy. 1970. *Society of the Spectacle.* Detroit: Black & Red.

De la Cadena, Marisol. 2015. *Earth Beings: Ecologies of Practice across Andean Worlds.* Durham, NC: Duke University Press.

DeLanda, Manuel. 2006. *A New Philosophy of Society: Assemblage Theory And Social Complexity.* London: Continuum.

Deleuze, Gilles, and Felix Guattari. 1987. *A Thousand Plateaus: Capitalism and Schizophrenia.* Minneapolis: University of Minnesota Press.

Demenge, Jonathan P. 2013. "The Road to Lingshed: Manufactured Isolation and Experienced Mobility in Ladakh." *Himalaya* 32 (1): 51–60.

Dewatshang, Kunga Samten. 1997. *Flight at the Cuckoo's Behest: The Life and Times of a Tibetan Freedom Fighter.* New Delhi: Paljor Publications.

Diemberger, Hildegard. 1996. "Political and Religious Aspects of Mountain Cults in the Hidden Valley of Khenbalung: Tradition, Decline and Revitalisation." In *Reflections of the Mountain: Essays on the History and Social Meaning of the Mountain Cult in Tibet and the Himalaya,* edited by Anne-Marie Blondeau and Ernst Steinkeller, 219–32. Wien: Verlag der Österreichischen Akademie der Wissenschaften.

Edelman, Marc. 2005. "Bringing the Moral Economy Back in . . . to the Study of 21st-Century Transnational Peasant Movements." *American Anthropologist* 107 (3): 331–45.

Ehrhard, Franz-Karl. 1997. "A 'Hidden Land' in the Tibetan-Nepalese Borderlands." In *Mandala and Landscape*, edited by Alexander W. Macdonald, 335–64. New Delhi: DK Printworld.

Fairbank, J. K., and S. Y. Teng. 1941. "On the Ch'ing Tributary System." *Harvard Journal of Asiatic Studies* 6 (2): 135–246.

Ferguson, James. 1999. *Expectations of Modernity: Myths and Meanings of Urban Life on the Zambian Copperbelt*. Berkeley: University of California Press.

———. 2006. *Global Shadows: Africa in the Neoliberal World Order*. Durham, NC: Duke University Press.

———. 2015. *Give a Man a Fish: Reflections on the New Politics of Distribution*. Durham, NC: Duke University Press.

Fischer, Andrew M. 2011. "The Great Transformation of Tibet? Rapid Labor Transitions in Times of Rapid Growth in the Tibet Autonomous Region." *Himalaya* 30 (1–2): 63–78.

———. 2015. "Subsidizing Tibet: An Interprovincial Comparison of Western China up to the End of the Hu–Wen Administration." *China Quarterly* 221 (March): 73–99.

Fisher, James F. 1986. *Trans-Himalayan Traders: Economy, Society and Culture in Northwest Nepal*. Berkeley: University of California Press.

———. 1990. *Sherpas: Reflections on Change in Himalayan Nepal*. Berkeley: University of California Press.

Fiskesjö, Magnus. 1999. "On the 'Raw' and the 'Cooked' Barbarians of Imperial China." *Inner Asia* 1 (2): 139–68.

Frechette, Ann. 2002. *Tibetans in Nepal: The Dynamics of International Assistance among a Community in Exile*. Oxford: Berghahn.

Freitag, Ulrike, and Achim von Oppen. 2010. *Translocality*. Leiden: Brill.

French, Howard. 2007. "At a Festival for Tibetans, Quiet Resistance Reigns." *New York Times*, August 14. https://www.nytimes.com/2007/08/14/world/asia/14iht-tibet.1.7111545.html.

Fürer-Haimendorf, Christoph von. 1975. *Himalayan Traders: Life in Highland Nepal*. London: J. Murray.

———. 1981. "Introduction." In *Asian Highland Societies in Anthropological Perspective*, edited by Christoph von Fürer-Haimendorf. New Delhi: Sterling Publishers.

GBPIHED, G. B. Pant Institute of Himalayan Environment and Development. 2015. "SANGJU—Sacred Attempt for Natural Growth and Joyful Union." *KSLSCI-Newsletter (India)* 2 (1).

Giri, Anil. 2017. "Nepal to Create World's Highest Free WiFi Service at Everest Base Camp." *Hindustan Times*, February 8. https://www.hindustantimes.com/world-news/nepal-to-create-world-s-highest-free-wifi-service-at-everest-base-camp/story-2Csge4BK2aObTGQp4t0lYK.html.

Global Times. 2017. "Tibet Creates Nation's First Border Subsidy System to Manage Border." *Global Times*, October 9.

Goldstein, Melvyn C. 1975. "A Report on Limi Panchayat, Humla District, Karnali Zone." *Contributions to Nepalese Studies* 2 (2): 89–101.

———. 1976. "Fraternal Polyandry and Fertility in a High Himalayan Valley in Northwest Nepal." *Human Ecology* 4 (3): 223–33.

———. 1981. "High-Altitude Tibetan Populations in the Remote Himalaya: Social Transformation and Its Demographic, Economic, and Ecological Consequences." *Mountain Research and Development* 1 (1): 5–18.

———. 2007. *A History of Modern Tibet, Volume 2: The Calm before the Storm, 1951–1955*. Berkeley: University of California Press.

Goldstein, Melvyn C., Geoff Childs, and Puchung Wangdui. 2008. "'Going for Income' in Village Tibet: A Longitudinal Analysis of Change and Adaptation, 1997–2007." *Asian Survey* 48 (3): 514–34.

Goldstein, Melvyn C., and Donald A. Messerschmidt. 1980. "The Significance of Latitudinality in Himalayan Mountain Ecosystems." *Human Ecology* 8 (2): 117–34.

Government of Nepal. 2009. *Nepal Disaster Report 2009*. Kathmandu: Ministry of Home Affairs.

——. 2011. "Memorandum of Understanding between Government of the Republic of India and Government of Nepal regarding Indian Grant Assistance for the Goitre Control Programme in Nepal."

Green, Sarah. 2014. "Anthropological Knots: Conditions of Possibilities and Interventions." *HAU: Journal of Ethnographic Theory* 4 (3): 1–21.

Greenhalgh, Susan. 2011. "Governing Chinese Life: From Sovereignty to Biopolitical Governance." In *Governance of Life in Chinese Moral Experience: The Quest for an Adequate Life*, edited by Everett Zhang, Arthur Kleinman, and Weiming Tu, 146–62. London: Routledge.

Gregory, Derek. 1994. *Geographical Imaginations*. Cambridge, MA: Blackwell.

Greiner, Clemens, and Patrick Sakdapolrak. 2013. "Translocality: Concepts, Applications and Emerging Research Perspectives." *Geography Compass* 7 (5): 373–84.

Grocke, Michelle U., and Kimber Haddix Mckay. 2016. "Like Mother, Like Child? Understanding Transitions in Diet, Health, and Nutrition in Humla." *Studies in Nepali History and Society* 21 (2): 305–31.

Gupta, Akhil, and James Ferguson. 1992. "Beyond 'Culture': Space, Identity, and the Politics of Difference." *Cultural Anthropology* 7 (1): 6–23.

Gurung, Nira. 2010. "ICIMOD Shares Results of Glacial Lakes Studies." Press release, International Centre for Integrated Mountain Development, February 22.

Haddix McKay, Kimber, and Jit Bahadur Gurung. 1999. "'Excess Women': Non-Marriage and Reproduction in Two Ethnic Tibetan Communities of Humla, Nepal." *Himalayan Research Bulletin* 19 (1): 56–62.

Hamashita, Takeshi, Linda Grove, and Mark Selden. 2008. *China, East Asia and the Global Economy: Regional and Historical Perspectives*. London: Routledge.

Hannerz, Ulf. 1986. "Theory in Anthropology: Small Is Beautiful? The Problem of Complex Cultures." *Comparative Studies in Society and History* 28 (2): 362–67.

——. 1996. *Transnational Connections: Culture, People, Places*. London: Routledge.

Hardin, Garret. 1968. "The Tragedy of the Commons." *Science* 162:1243–48.

Harms, Erik, Shafqat Hussein, Sasha Newell, Louisa Schein, Sara Shneiderman, Terence S. Turner, and Juan Zhang. 2014. "Remote and Edgy: New Takes on Old Anthropological Themes." *HAU: Journal of Ethnographic Theory* 4 (1): 361–81.

Harris, Tina. 2008. "Silk Roads and Wool Routes: Contemporary Geographies of Trade between Lhasa and Kalimpong." *India Review* 7 (3): 200–22.

——. 2013. *Geographical Diversions: The Geography of Tibetan Trade*. Athens: University of Georgia Press.

Harris, Tina, Amy Holmes-Tagchungdarpa, Jayeeta Sharma, and Markus Viehbeck. 2016. "Global Encounters, Local Places: Connected Histories of Darjeeling, Kalimpong, and the Himalayas—An Introduction." *Transcultural Studies* 2016 (1): 43–53.

Harvey, David. 1989. *The Condition of Postmodernity: An Enquiry into the Origins of Cultural Change*. Cambridge, MA: Blackwell.

Harvey, Penny, and Hannah Knox. 2015. *On Roads: An Anthropology of Infrastructure and Expertise*. Ithaca, NY: Cornell University Press.

Hathaway, Michael J. 2013. *Environmental Winds: Making the Global in Southwest China*. Berkeley: University of California Press.

Hetherington, Kevin. 1997. "In Place of Geometry: The Materiality of Place." *Sociological Review* 45 (S1): 183–99.

Heyat, Farideh. 2002. "Women and the Culture of Entrepreneurship in Soviet and Post-Soviet Azerbaijan." In *Markets and Moralities: Ethnographies of Postsocialism*, edited by Ruth Mandel and Caroline Humphrey, 19–31. Oxford: Berg.

Höfer, András. 1979. *The Caste Hierarchy and the State in Nepal: A Study of the Muluki Ain of 1854* (Khumbu Himal: Ergebnisse des Forschungsunternehmens Nepal Himalaya, Band 13/2). Innsbruck: Universitätsverlag Wagner.

Hoffman, Lisa. 2006. "Autonomous Choices and Patriotic Professionalism: On Governmentality in Late Socialist China." *Economy and Society* 35 (4): 550–70.

Holmberg, David, Kathryn March, and Suryaman Tamang. 1999. "Local Production/Local Knowledge: Forced Labor from Below." *Studies in Nepali History and Society* 4 (1): 5–64.

Hooker, Sir Joseph Dalton. 1854. *Himalayan Journals: Or, Notes of a Naturalist in Bengal, the Sikkim and Nepal Himalayas, the Khasia Mountains, Etc.* Kolkatta: Calcutta Trigonometrical Survey.

Hopkins, Benjamin D. 2008. *The Making of Modern Afghanistan.* New York: Palgrave Macmillan.

Hovden, Astrid. 2012. "Glacial Lake Outburst Flood in Halji, Limi VDC, 30 June 2011." *Asian Art*, July 16. http://www.asianart.com/articles/halji2/index.html.

——. 2013. "Who Were the Sponsors? Reflections on Recruitment and Ritual Economy in Three Himalayan Village Monasteries." In *Tibetans Who Escaped the Historian's Net: Studies in the Social History of Tibetan Societies*, edited by Charles Ramble, Peter Schwieger, and Alice Travers, 209–28. Kathmandu: Vajra Books.

——. 2016. "Between Village and Monastery: A Historical Ethnography of a Tibetan Buddhist Community in North-Western Nepal." PhD thesis, University of Oslo, Faculty of Humanities.

Hsu, Carolyn L. 2007. *Creating Market Socialism: How Ordinary People Are Shaping Class and Status in China.* Durham, NC: Duke University Press.

ICIMOD. 2011. "Glacial Lakes of Nepal 2011." *Regional Database System.* International Centre for Integrated Mountain Development. http://rds.icimod.org/Home/DataDetail?metadataId=20831.

——. 2015a. *Promotion of the Allo (Himalayan Nettle) Value Chain in Nepal.* Kathmandu: International Centre for Integrated Mountain Development.

——. 2015b. *Promotion of the Chyura Soap and Lip Balm Value Chain in India.* Kathmandu: International Centre for Integrated Mountain Development.

——. 2015c. *Transboundary Landscape Cooperation Needs Good Communication and Coordination.* Kathmandu: International Centre for Integrated Mountain Development. http://lib.icimod.org/record/31170.

——. 2016a. "Anchoring Transboundary Cooperation: Vegetation and Land Use Type Map of Kailash Sacred Landscape." *Kailash Sacred Landscape Initiative.* Kathmandu: International Centre for Integrated Mountain Development.

——. 2016b. "Communication Booklet for Yak and Horse Transportation Team in the Kailash Sacred Landscape." *Kailash Sacred Landscape Initiative.* Kathmandu: International Centre for Integrated Mountain Development.

——. 2016c. "Community Training Manual." *Kailash Sacred Landscape Initiative.* Kathmandu: International Centre for Integrated Mountain Development. http://lib.icimod.org/record/32184/files/icimodEconomicManual1-16.pdf.

——. 2016d. "The Kailash Sacred Landscape Illustrated Map." *Kailash Sacred Landscape Initiative.* Kathmandu: International Centre for Integrated Mountain Development. http://lib.icimod.org/record/33725/files/KSL-Map.pdf.

——. 2016e. "Training Workshop on Planning Management for Ecosystem Services." *Hindu Kush Pamir Landscape*. Kathmandu: International Centre for Integrated Mountain Development.

——. 2017a. "De-populating Villages in the Kailash Sacred Landscape, India: Rethinking Policy Interventions." *Kailash Sacred Landscape Initiative*. Kathmandu: International Centre for Integrated Mountain Development. http://lib.icimod.org/record /32595/files/icimodSPM017.pdf.

——. 2017b. "Kailash Sacred Landscape Conservation and Development Initiative (2012–2017): Annual Progress Report 2016." *Kailash Sacred Landscape Initiative*. Kathmandu: International Centre for Integrated Mountain Development. http:// lib.icimod.org/record/32592/files/icimodKSLCDI-AR016.pdf.

——. 2019a. "Kailash Sacred Landscape Information System (KSLIS)." *Kailash Sacred Landscape Initiative*. Kathmandu: International Centre for Integrated Mountain Development.

——. 2019b. "Remote Sensing and GIS." *Mountain Topics*. Kathmandu: International Centre for Integrated Mountain Development.

Ingold, Tim. 1980. *Hunters, Pastoralists and Ranchers: Reindeer Economies and Their Transformations*. Cambridge: University Press Cambridge.

——. 1993. "The Temporality of the Landscape." *World Archaeology* 25 (2): 152–74.

——. 2007. *Lines: A Brief History*. London: Routledge.

——. 2008. "Against Space: Place, Movement, Knowledge." In *Boundless Worlds: An Anthropological Approach to Movement*, edited by Peter W. Kirby, 29–43. Oxford: Berghahn.

——. 2010. "Bringing Things Back to Life: Creative Entanglements in a World of Materials." Working Paper. National Centre or Research Methods (NCRM), Realities/ Morgan Centre, University of Manchester.

——. 2020. "In the Gathering Shadows of Material Things." In *Materiality and Connectivity in Anthropology and Beyond*, edited by Philipp Schorch, Martin Saxer, and Marlen Elders, 17–33. London: UCL Press.

Ives, Jack D., and Bruno Messerli. 1989. *The Himalayan Dilemma: Reconciling Development and Conservation*. London: Routledge.

Jayshi, Damakant, and Suhasini Haidar. 2014. "Modi Offers $1-bn Package to Nepal." *The Hindu*, August 3.

Kansakar, Vidya Bir Singh. 2001. "Nepal-India Open Border Prospects, Problems and Challenges". Papers presented in a series of seminars organized by the Institute of Foreign Affairs and FES in Nepalgunj, Birgunj, Biratnagar and Kathmandu, 2001. https://integrety.wordpress.com/2011/04/04/nepal-india-open-border-prospects -problems-and-challenges/

Karkee, Rajendra, and Jude Comfort. 2016. "NGOs, Foreign Aid, and Development in Nepal." *Frontiers in Public Health* 4 (177): 1–5.

Karmakar, M. G., and C. S. Pandav. 1985. *Iodine Deficiency Disorders in Nepal: Monitoring and Quality Control of Iodated Salt—A Report*. New Delhi: All India Institute of Medical Sciences.

Kilpatrick, Kate. 2011. "Improving Food Security for Vulnerable Communities in Nepal." *Oxfam Case Study*. https://policy-practice.oxfam.org/resources/improving -food-security-for-vulnerable-communities-in-nepal-132377/

Kitchin, Rob, and Martin Dodge. 2007. "Rethinking Maps." *Progress in Human Geography* 31 (3): 331–44.

Klatzel, Frances. 2000. *Green Roads: Building Environmentally Friendly, Low Maintenance Rural Roads through Local Participation*. Deutsche Gesellschaft für Technische Zusammenarbeit (GTZ) Food for Work, Nepal. http://lib.icimod.org/record/10516 /files/355.pdf.

Kolås, Ashild. 2008. *Tourism and Tibetan Culture in Transition: A Place Called Shangrila*. London: Routledge.

Krishna, Sankaran. 1994. "Cartographic Anxiety: Mapping the Body Politic in India." *Alternatives: Global, Local, Political* 19 (4): 507–21.

Kropáček, Jan, Niklas Neckel, Bernd Tyrna, N. Holzer, Astrid Hovden, Noel Gourmelen, Christoph Schneider, Manfred Buchroithner, and Volker Hochschild. 2014. "Periodic Glacial Lake Outburst Floods Threatening the Oldest Buddhist Monastery in North-West Nepal." *Natural Hazards and Earth System Sciences Discussions* 2 (11): 6937–71.

Lama, Sonam. 2013. "Road from Nowhere to Nowhere." *Nepali Times*, July 5–11, #663. http://archive.nepalitimes.com/article/nation/Nation-road-from-nowhere-to -nowhere,549.

Lama, Tsewang. 2002. *Kailash Mandala: A Pilgrim's Trekking Guide*. Simikot: Humla Conservation and Development Association.

Larsen, Jonas, John Urry, and Kay Axhausen. 2006. *Mobilities, Networks, Geographies*. Hampshire, UK: Ashgate.

Laszczkowski, Mateusz, and Madeleine Reeves. 2015. "Introduction: Affective States: Entanglements, Suspensions, Suspicions." *Social Analysis* 59 (4): 1–14.

Latour, Bruno. 1993. *We Have Never Been Modern*. New York: Harvester Wheatsheaf.

——. 2005. *Reassembling the Social: An Introduction to Actor-Network-Theory*. Oxford: Oxford University Press.

Levine, Nancy E. 1988. *The Dynamics of Polyandry Kinship: Domesticity and Population on the Tibetan Border*. Chicago: University of Chicago Press.

Levine, Nancy E., and Joan B. Silk. 1997. "Why Polyandry Fails: Sources of Instability in Polyandrous Marriages." *Current Anthropology* 38 (3): 375–98.

Lim, Francis Khek Gee. 2008. *Imagining the Good Life: Negotiating Culture and Development in Nepal Himalaya*. Leiden: Brill.

Ludden, David. 2003. "Presidential Address: Maps in the Mind and the Mobility of Asia." *Journal of Asian Studies* 62 (4): 1057–78.

Lydon, Ghislaine. 2009. *On Trans-Saharan Trails: Islamic Law, Trade Networks, and Cross-Cultural Exchange in Nineteenth-Century Western Africa*. Cambridge: Cambridge University Press.

Madhu, K. C., Sussana Phoboo, and Pramod Kumar Jha. 2010. "Ecological Study of *Paris polyphylla* SM." *Ecoprint* 17:87–93.

Maertens, Carolin. 2017. "'No Debt, No Business': The Personalisation of Market Exchange in Gorno-Badakhshan, Tajikistan." In *Approaching Ritual Economy: Socio-Cosmic Fields in Globalised Contexts*, edited by Roland Hardenberg, 159–92. Tübingen: RessourcenKulturen.

Malkki, Liisa. 1992. "National Geographic: The Rooting of Peoples and the Territorialization of National Identity among Scholars and Refugees." *Cultural Anthropology* 7 (1): 24–44.

Marsden, Magnus. 2016. *Trading Worlds: Afghan Merchants across Modern Frontiers*. London: Hurst.

Marx, Karl. (1857–1858) 1983. "Einleitung [zu den 'Grundrissen der Kritik der politischen Ökonomie']." In *Karl Marx-Friedrich Engels. Werke Band 42*. Berlin: Dietz.

Massey, Doreen. 1994. *Space, Place and Gender*. Minneapolis: University of Minnesota Press.

——. 2005. *For Space*. London: Sage.

Mauss, Marcel. 1923. "Essai sur le don: forme et raison de l'échange dans les sociétés archaïques [The gift: forms and functions of exchange in archaic societies]." *L'Année Sociologique* 1:30–186.

McGranahan, Carole. 2006. "Tibet's Cold War: The CIA and the Chushi Gangdrug Resistance, 1956–1974." *Journal of Cold War Studies* 8 (3): 102–30.

——. 2010. *Arrested Histories: Tibet, the CIA, and Memories of a Forgotten War*. Durham, NC: Duke University Press.

Michaud, Jean. 2010. "Zomia and Beyond (Editorial)." *Journal of Global History* 5 (2): 187–214.

Mitchell, Katharyne. 1997. "Different Diasporas and the Hype of Hybridity." *Environment and Planning D: Society and Space* 15 (5): 533–53.

Munkelt, Marga, Markus Schmitz, Mark Stein, and Silke Stroh. 2013. *Postcolonial Translocations: Cultural Representations and Critical Spatial Thinking*. Leiden: Brill.

Murton, Galen. 2016. "Making Mountain Places into State Spaces: Infrastructure, Consumption, and Territorial Practice in a Himalayan Borderland." *Annals of the American Association of Geographers* 4452 (October): 1–10.

——. 2017a. "Bordering Spaces, Practising Borders: Fences, Roads and Reorientations across a Nepal–China Borderland." *South Asia: Journal of South Asia Studies* 40 (2): 239–55.

——. 2017b. "The Pragmatism of Sino–Nepali Humanitarianism." *East Asia Forum*, May. https://www.eastasiaforum.org/2017/05/20/the-pragmatism-of-sino-nepali -humanitarianism/.

——. 2018. "Nobody Stops and Stays Anymore: Motor Roads, Uneven Mobilities, and Conceptualizing Borderland Modernity in Highland Nepal." *Routledge Handbook of Asian Borderlands*, edited by Alexander Horstmann, Martin Saxer, and Alessandro Rippa, 315–24. London: Routledge.

Murton, Galen, Austin Lord, and Robert Beazley. 2016. "'A Handshake across the Himalayas': Chinese Investment Hydropower, Development, and State Formation in Nepal." *Eurasian Geography and Economics* 57 (3): 403–32.

Navaro-Yashin, Yael. 2012. *The Make-Believe Space: Affective Geography in a Postwar Polity*. Durham, NC: Duke University Press.

NeKSAP, Nepal Khadya Surakshya Anugaman Pranali (Nepal Food Security Monitoring System). 2009. *The Cost of Coping: A Collision of Crises and the Impact of Sustained Food Security Deterioration in Nepal*. Kathmandu: World Food Programme.

Nyíri, Pál. 2006. *Scenic Spots: Chinese Tourism, the State, and Cultural Authority*. Seattle: University of Washington Press.

Oakes, Tim. 1998. *Tourism and Modernity in China*. London: Routledge.

Oakes, Tim, and Louisa Schein. 2006. *Translocal China: Linkages, Identities, and the Reimagining of Space*. London: Routledge.

OGBIR, Office of the Geographer Bureau of Intelligence and Research. 1965. "China–Nepal Boundary." *International Boundary Study* 50 (May 30).

Omura, Keiichi, Grant Jun Otsuki, Shiho Satsuka, and Atsuro Morita. 2019. *The World Multiple: The Quotidian Politics of Knowing and Generating Entangled Worlds*. London: Routledge.

Ong, Aihwa, and Stephen J. Collier. 2005. *Global Assemblages: Technology, Politics, and Ethics as Anthropological Problems*. Malden, MA: Blackwell.

Ong, Lynette H. 2014. "State-Led Urbanization in China: Skyscrapers, Land Revenue and Concentrated Villages." *China Quarterly* 217:165–71.

Pandey, Abhimanyu, Rajan Kotru, and Nawraj Pradhan. 2016. *A Framework for the Assessment of Cultural Ecosystem Services of Sacred Natural Sites in the Hindu Kush Himalayas*. Kathmandu: International Centre for Integrated Mountain Development.

Pedersen, Morten Axel, and Mikkel Bunkenborg. 2012. "Roads That Separate: Sino-Mongolian Relations in the Inner Asian Desert." *Mobilities* 7 (4): 555–69.

Penfield, Amy. 2019. "The Wild Inside Out: Fluid Infrastructure in an Amazonian Mining Region." *Social Anthropology* 27 (2): 221–35.

Pickles, John. 2004. *A History of Spaces: Cartographic Reason, Map Making and the Geo-Coded World.* London: Routledge.

Pokharel, Bharat K., Peter Branney, Mike Nurse, and Yam B. Malla. 2007. "Community Forestry: Conserving Forests, Sustaining Livelihoods and Strengthening Democracy." *Journal of Forest and Livelihood* 6 (2): 8–19.

Porst, Luise, and Patrick Sakdapolrak. 2017. "How Scale Matters in Translocality: Uses and Potentials of Scale in Translocal Research." *Erdkunde* 71 (2): 111–26.

Pratt, Mary Louise. 1991. "Arts of the Contact Zone." *Profession* 1991:33–40.

Proctor, Robert N., and Londa Schiebinger. 2008. *Agnotology: The Making and Unmaking of Ignorance.* Stanford, CA: Stanford University Press.

Ptackova, Jarmila. 2012. "Implementation of Resettlement Programmes Amongst Pastoralist Communities in Eastern Tibet." In *Pastoral Practices in High Asia: Agency of 'Development' Effected by Modernisation, Resettlement and Transformation,* edited by Hermann Kreutzmann, 217–34. Amsterdam: Springer.

——. 2015. "Hor—A Sedentarisation Success for Tibetan Pastoralists in Qinghai?" *Nomadic Peoples* 19 (2): 69–88.

——. 2018. "Orchestrated Environmental Migration in Western China." In *Routledge Handbook of Environmental Policy in China,* edited by Eva Sternfeld, 223–36. London: Routledge.

Pyakurel, Uddhab P. 2017. "Nepal–China Border Management and the Future of People to People Relations." Working Paper, Center for Studies on South Asia and the Middle East, Graduate Institute of International Politics, National Chung Hsing University, Taiwan. https://cssametw.wordpress.com/2017/01/21/research-analysisnepal-china-border-management-and-the-future-of-people-to-people-relations/.

Rabinow, Paul. 2003. "Midst Anthropology's Problems." In *Anthropos Today: Reflections on Modern Equipment,* 13–30. Princeton, NJ: Princeton University Press.

Ramble, Charles. 2008. *The Navel of the Demoness.* Oxford: Oxford University Press.

——. 2013. "Hidden Himalayan Transcripts: Strategies of Social Opposition in Mustang (Nepal), 19th–20th Centuries." In *Tibetans Who Escaped the Historian's Net: Studies in the Social History of Tibetan Societies,* edited by Charles Ramble, Peter Schwieger, and Alice Travers, 231–51. Kathmandu: Vajra Books.

Rana, Pradyunmna J.B., and Corinna Wallrapp. 2015. "Towards Improved Management of Yarsagumba in Api Nampa Conservation Area." *Kailash Sacred Landscape Initiative.* Kathmandu: International Centre for Integrated Mountain Development.

Rankin, Katharine N., Tulasi S. Sigdel, Lagan Rai, Shyam Kunwar, and Pushpa Hamal. 2017. "Political Economies and Political Rationalities of Road Building in Nepal." *Studies in Nepali History and Society* 22 (1): 43–84.

Ratanapruck, Prista. 2007. "Kinship and Religious Practices as Institutionalization of Trade Networks: Manangi Trade Communities in South and Southeast Asia." *Journal of the Economic and Social History of the Orient* 50 (2/3): 325–46.

Rauber, Hanna. 1980. "The Humli-Khyampas of Far Western Nepal: A Study in Ethnogenesis." *Contributions to Nepalese Studies* 8 (1): 57–79.

——. 1981. "Humli-Khyampas and the Indian Salt Trade: Changing Economy of Nomadic Traders in Far Western Nepal." In *The Other Nomads: Peripatetics in Cross Cultural Perspective,* edited by Aparna Rao, 141–76. London: Academic Press.

——. 1987. "Stages of Women's Life among Tibetan Nomadic Traders: The Humli-Khyampa of Far Western Nepal." *Ethnos* 52 (1–2): 200–28.

Rawal, Ranbeer S., Rajeev L. Semwal, Ajay Rastogi, and Pitamber P. Dhyani. 2015. "Landscape Yatra: Connecting with Nature to Bring in Transformation." *SANGJU—*

Sacred Attempt for Natural Growth and Joyful Union. KSLSCI-Newsletter (India) 2 (1): 8–10.

Regmi, M. C. 1978. *Land Tenure and Taxation in Nepal.* Kathmandu: Ratna Pustak Bhandar.

Rippa, Alessandro. 2020. *Where China Ends: Trade, Infrastructure Development and Control in the Borderlands of Xinjiang and Yunnan.* Amsterdam: Amsterdam University Press.

Robin, Françoise. 2009. "The 'Socialist New Villages' in the Tibetan Autonomous Region." *China Perspectives* 3:56–64.

Rose, Leo E. 1971. *Nepal: Strategy for Survival.* Berkeley: University of California Press.

Rosenberg, Lior. 2013. "Urbanising the Rural: Local Strategies for Creating 'New Style' Rural Communities in China." *China Perspectives* 3:63–71.

Saxer, Martin. 2011. "Herbs and Traders in Transit: Border Regimes and Trans-Himalayan Trade in Tibetan Medicinal Plants." *Asian Medicine* 5 (2009): 317–39.

——. 2012. "The Moral Economy of Cultural Identity: Tibet, Cultural Survival, and the Safeguarding of Cultural Heritage." *Civilisations* 61 (1): 65–81.

——. 2013a. *Manufacturing Tibetan Medicine: The Creation of an Industry and the Moral Economy of Tibetanness.* Oxford: Berghahn.

——. 2013b. "Between China and Nepal: Trans-Himalayan Trade and the Second Life of Development in Upper Humla." *Cross-Currents: East Asian History and Culture Review* 8 (September): 31–52.

——. 2014. "Re-Fusing Ethnicity and Religion: An Experiment on Tibetan Grounds." *Journal of Current Chinese Affairs* 43 (2): 181–204.

——. 2016a. "A Spectacle of Maps: Cartographic Hopes and Anxieties in the Pamirs." *Cross-Currents: East Asian History and Culture Review* 21 (December): 111–36.

——. 2016b. "Pathways: A Concept, Field Site and Methodological Approach to Study Remoteness and Connectivity." *Himalaya* 36 (2): 104–19.

——. 2017. "New Roads, Old Trades: Neighbouring China in Nepal." In *The Art of Neighbouring: Making Relations across China's Borders*, edited by Martin Saxer and Juan Zhang, 73–92. Amsterdam: Amsterdam University Press.

——. 2019. "Provisions for Remoteness. Cutting Connections and Forging Ties in the Tajik Pamirs." *Social Anthropology/Anthropologie Sociale* 27 (2): 187–203.

Saxer, Martin, and Ruben Andersson. 2019. "The Return of Remoteness: Insecurity, Isolation and Connectivity in the New World Disorder." *Social Anthropology/Anthropologie Sociale* 27 (2): 140–55.

Saxer, Martin, and Philipp Schorch. 2020. "Materiality and Connectivity." In *Materiality and Connectivity in Anthropology and Beyond*, edited by Philipp Schorch, Martin Saxer, and Marlen Elders, 1–14. London: UCL Press.

Sayer, Jeffrey, Terry Sunderland, Jaboury Ghazoul, Jean-Laurent Pfund, Douglas Sheil, Erik Meijaard, Michelle Venter et al. 2013. "Ten Principles for a Landscape Approach to Reconciling Agriculture, Conservation, and Other Competing Land Uses." *Proceedings of the National Academy of Sciences* 110 (21): 8349–56.

Scheele, Judith. 2012. *Smugglers and Saints of the Sahara: Regional Connectivity in the Twentieth Century.* Cambridge: Cambridge University Press.

Schein, Louisa. 1997. "Gender and Internal Orientalism in China." *Modern China* 23 (1): 69–98.

——. 1999. "Performing Modernity." *Cultural Anthropology* 14 (3): 361–95.

Schendel, Willem van. 2002. "Geographies of Knowing, Geographies of Ignorance: Jumping Scale in Southeast Asia." *Environment and Planning D: Society and Space* 20 (6): 647–68.

Schmink, Marianne, and Charles H. Wood. 1992. *Contested Frontiers in Amazonia.* New York: Columbia University Press.

Schorch, Philipp, Martin Saxer, and Marlen Elders. 2020. *Exploring Materiality and Connectivity in Anthropology and Beyond.* London: UCL Press.

Scott, James C. 1976. *The Moral Economy of the Peasant: Rebellion and Subsistence in Southeast Asia.* New Haven, CT: Yale University Press.

——. 1985. *Weapons of the Weak: Everyday Forms of Peasant Resistance.* New Haven, CT: Yale University Press.

——. 1990. *Domination and the Arts of Resistance: Hidden Transcripts.* New Haven, CT: Yale University Press.

——. 1998. *Seeing Like a State: How Certain Schemes to Improve the Human Condition Have Failed.* New Haven, CT: Yale University Press.

——. 2002. "The Invention of the Passport: Surveillance, Citizenship, and the State." *Journal of Modern History* 74 (1): 142–44.

——. 2009. *The Art of Not Being Governed: An Anarchist History of Upland Southeast Asia.* New Haven, CT: Yale University Press.

Seemangal, Robin. 2015. "Disaster Diplomacy: After Nepal Earthquake, China and India Race to Give Aid." *Observer,* May 1. https://observer.com/2015/05/in-nepal -china-and-india-engage-in-disaster-diplomacy/.

Shakya, Tsering. 1999. *The Dragon in the Land of Snows: A History of Modern Tibet since 1947.* London: Pimlico.

Sheller, Mimi, and John Urry. 2006. "The New Mobilities Paradigm." *Environment and Planning A* 38 (2): 207–26.

Sheppard, Eric. 2002. "The Spaces and Times of Globalization: Place, Scale, Networks, and Positionality." *Economic Geography* 78 (3): 307–30.

Sherpa, Tsering Gyaltsen. 2017. "Wireless Broadband—My View." Cambium Network. https://www.cambiumnetworks.com/wp-content/uploads/2017/09/SP_everest _05312017.pdf

Shin, Leo K. 2006. *The Making of the Chinese State: Ethnicity and Expansion on the Ming Borderlands.* Cambridge: Cambridge University Press.

Shneiderman, Sara B. 2013. "Himalayan Border Citizens: Sovereignty and Mobility in the Nepal–Tibetan Autonomous Region (TAR) of China Border Zone." *Political Geography* 30: 1–12.

——. 2015. *Rituals of Ethnicity: Thangmi Identities between Nepal and India.* Philadelphia: University of Pennsylvania Press.

Shrestha, Chandra, Tshewang Lama, Werner Paul Meyer, and Guy Schneider. 2010. *Trans-Himalayan Heritage Routes Pilot Project in Kailash Sacred Landscape (KSL)/ Nepal: Inception Phase Report.* Kathmandu: International Centre for Integrated Mountain Development (ICIMOD).

Sigley, Gary. 2006. "Chinese Governmentalities: Government, Governance and the Socialist Market Economy." *Economy and Society* 35 (4): 487–508.

Siva, Nayanah. 2010. "A Sprinkle of Salt Needed for Nepal's Hidden Hunger." *Lancet* 376 (9742): 673–74.

Spengen, Wim van. 2000. *Tibetan Border Worlds: A Geohistorical Analysis of Trade and Traders.* New York: Kegan Paul International.

Sprigg, Richard Keith. 1995. "1826: The End of an Era in the Social and Political History of Sikkim." *Bulletin of Tibetology* 31:88–92.

Starkey, Paul, Ansu Tumbahangfe, and Shuva Sharma. 2013. *Building Roads and Improving Livelihoods in Nepal: External Review of the District Roads Support Programme (DRSP), Final Report.* Kathmandu: Swiss Agency for Development and Cooperation (SDC).

Steenberg, Rune. 2014. "Crossing at Irkeshtam: Networks of Trade and Kinship across the Southern Sino-Kyrgyz Border." In *Tracing Connections: Explorations of Spaces and Places in Asian Contexts*, edited by Henryk Alff and Andreas Benz, 53–70. Berlin: Wissenschaftlicher Verlag Berlin.

——. 2018. "Accumulating Trust: Uyghur Traders in the Sino Kyrgyz Border Trade after 1991." In *Routledge Handbook of Asian Borderlands*, edited by Alexander Horstmann, Martin Saxer, and Alessandro Rippa, 294–303. London: Routledge.

Steenberg, Rune, and Alessandro Rippa. 2019. "Development for All? State Schemes, Security, and Marginalization in Kashgar, Xinjiang." *Critical Asian Studies* 51 (2): 274–95.

Steinmann, Brigitte. 1988. Les marches tibétaines du Népal: État, chefferie et société traditionnels à travers le récit d'un notable népalais [The Tibetan frontiers of Nepal: state, chiefdom, and traditional society according to the story of a notable Nepali]. Paris: Editions L'Harmattan.

——. 1991. "The Political and Diplomatic Role of a Tibetan Village Chieftain (*go-ba*) on the Nepalese Frontier." In *Wiener Studien zur Tibetologie und Buddhismuskunde 26: Tibetan History and Language*, edited by Ernst Steinkellner, 467–86. Vienna: Arbeitskreis für Tibetische und Buddhistische Studien, Universität Wien.

Stoler, Ann Laura. 2004. "Affective States." In *A Companion to the Anthropology of Politics*, edited by David Nugent and Joan Vincent, 4–20. Malden, MA: Blackwell.

Subba, J. R. 2008. *History, Culture and Customs Of Sikkim*. New Delhi: Gyan Publishing.

Tagliacozzo, Eric, and Wen-chin Chang. 2011. *Chinese Circulations: Capital, Commodities and Networks in Southeast Asia*. Durham, NC: Duke University Press.

Takahashi, Dean. 2017. "You Can Now Get Wi-Fi Connectivity on Mount Everest." *VentureBeat*, June 3. https://venturebeat.com/2017/06/03/you-can-now-get-a-wi-fi-connection-on-mount-everest/.

Thapa, Krishna. 2016. "Timure Locals Protest over Land Acquisition." *Kathmandu Post*, April 20. https://kathmandupost.com/money/2016/04/30/timure-locals-protest-over-land-acquisition.

Thongchai, Winichakul. 1994. *Siam Mapped: A History of the Geo-Body of a Nation*. Honolulu: Hawaii University Press.

Thrift, Nigel. 2008. *Non-Representational Theory: Space | Politics | Affect*. London: Routledge.

Titzler, Arley. 2019. "GLOF Risk Perception in Nepal Himalaya." *GlacierHub*, January 30. https://glacierhub.org/2019/01/30/glof-risk-perception-in-nepal/.

Tsing, Anna Lowenhaupt. 1993. *In the Realm of the Diamond Queen: Marginality in an Out-of-the-Way Place*. Princeton, NJ: Princeton University Press.

——. 1994. "From the Margins." *Cultural Anthropology* 9 (3): 279–97.

——. 2005. *Friction: An Ethnography of Global Connection*. Princeton, NJ: Princeton University Press.

Uprety, Prem R. 1998. *Nepal-Tibet Relations, 1850–1930: Years of Hopes, Challenges, and Frustrations*. Kathmandu: Ratna Pustak Bhandar.

Urry, John. 2000. *Sociology beyond Societies: Mobilities for the Twenty-First Century*. London: Routledge.

——. 2007. *Mobilities*. Cambridge: Polity Press.

Vallangi, Neelima. 2019. "Climate Change Threatens 1,000-Year-Old Monastery in Remote Nepal." *Al Jazeera*, January 24. https://www.aljazeera.com/indepth/features/climate-change-threatens-1000-year-monastery-remote-nepal-190124000208470.html.

Viveiros De Castro, Eduardo. 2004. "Perspectival Anthropology and the Method of Controlled Equivocation." *Tipití* 2 (21): 3–22.

Wang, Maya. 2018. *Eradicating Ideological Viruses: China's Campaign of Repression against Xinjiang's Muslims*. New York: Human Rights Watch. https://www.hrw.org/sites/default/files/report_pdf/china0918_web.pdf.

Werbner, Pnina. 2007. "Global Pathways: Working Class Cosmopolitans and the Creation of Transnational Ethnic Worlds." *Social Anthropology* 7 (1): 17–35.

WFP, World Food Programme. 2010. *Nepal Food Security Bulletin*. Nepal: World Food Programme. https://un.info.np/Net/NeoDocs/View/5317.

White, Sidney D. 2010. "The Political Economy of Ethnicity in Yunnan's Lijiang Basin." *Asia Pacific Journal of Anthropology* 11 (2): 142–58.

Wilkinson, Freddie. 2019. "Meet the Sherpa Bringing Wi-Fi to Everest." *National Geographic*, May 22. https://www.nationalgeographic.com/adventure/article/mount-everest-link-internet-wifi-perpetual-planet.

Winkler, Daniel. 2017. "The Wild Life of Yartsa Gunbu (*Ophiocordyceps sinensis*) on the Tibetan Plateau." *Fungi* 10 (1): 53–64.

Wolf, Eric R. 1955. "Types of Latin American Peasantry: A Preliminary Discussion." *American Anthropologist* 57 (3): 452–71.

——. 1957. "Closed Corporate Peasant Communities in Mesoamerica and Central Java." *Southwestern Journal of Anthropology* 13 (1): 1–18.

——. 1982. *Europe and the People without History*. Berkeley: University of California Press.

——. 1986. "The Vicissitudes of the Closed Corporate Peasant Community." *American Ethnologist* 13 (2): 325–29.

Yeh, Emily T. 2013a. *Taming Tibet: Landscape Transformation and the Gift of Chinese Development*. Ithaca, NY: Cornell University Press.

——. 2013b. "Blazing Pelts and Burning Passions: Nationalism, Cultural Politics and Spectacular Decommodification in Tibet." *Journal of Asian Studies*. 72 (2): 319–44.

Yeh, Emily T., Kevin J. O'Brien, and Jingzhong Ye. 2013. "Rural Politics in Contemporary China." *Journal of Peasant Studies* 40 (6): 915–28.

Yondon, Lobsang. 2018. "Precious Skin: The Rise and Fall of the Otter Fur Trade in Tibet." *Inner Asia* 20 (2): 177–98.

Zatsepine, Victor. 2008. "The Amur: As River, as Border." In *The Chinese State at the Borders*, edited by Diana Lary, 151–61. Vancouver: UBC Press.

Zhang, Juan, and Martin Saxer. 2017. "Neighbouring in the Borderworlds along China's Frontiers (Introduction)." In *The Art of Neighbouring: Making Relations across China's Borders*, edited by Martin Saxer and Juan Zhang, 11–29. Amsterdam: Amsterdam University Press.

Index

References to illustrations and maps are indicated by italicized page numbers.

Hovden, Astrid, 67, 200n2 (Interlude), 201n5 (Ch. 3), 201n8
Hu Jintao, 153, 155, 161
Humla. *See* Lower Humla; Upper Humla
Humli-Khyampas (itinerant group of caravan traders), 80–81
Humli traders, 93, 103
hutong (narrow alleyways in Chinese cities), 141

ICIMOD. *See* International Centre for Integrated Mountain Development
ignorance, 177
image engineering, 156
India: caste structure used in Nepal, 137; food aid from, 202n2 (Ch. 6); foreign direct investment in Nepal, 90; iodized salt provided to Nepal, 64, 122; Tibetan Children's Villages, 55–56; Tibetan refugees in, 48–49; trade with, 49, 87. *See also* Kailash Sacred Landscape Conservation and Development Initiative; *specific locations by name*
India China Institute (New School), 185
Indian butter tree (Chyura butter), 160
Indian Kailash pilgrims, 105, 109, 153
indigenous knowledge, 29
inequality: Chinese rural development and, 155; distribution and, 117; in Walung, 44, 47–48
Ingold, Tim, 17, 32, 33, 36, 79–80, 82, 192, 201n6 (Ch. 4)
International Centre for Integrated Mountain Development (ICIMOD), 19–20, 147–63; assumptions of, 136–37; author working at, 16, 130, 135–36, 145, 184; best practices for waste disposal and firewood collection, 152; blind spots in work of, 136–37, 151, 170–71, 175, 177; "Climate SOS" section of website, 169; communicative disjuncture of, 180; Geospatial Solutions Group, 132, 166–67; glacial lake study and website report, 168; greenhouse vegetable farming in Tibet, 161; "Green Road" approach of, 100–101, 182; knowledge products (training manuals) of, 151–53, 159, 169, 179, 181; landscape approach, 19, 136, 148–51, 164; member countries of, 135, 157–58; NGO-mindset of, 138; outside observer role of staff, 179–80; participatory approach of, 138–39; pilot projects situated to avoid Chinese borders, 160; press release "Anchoring Transboundary Cooperation," 166; project nature of work as concern, 162, 178; role of, 135–36, 160, 166; scaling up of interventions,

unlikelihood of, 162; soft development approach, 166; staffing of, 136; students to hire, difficulty in finding, 157; training of stewards of the environment, 151–53, 169; Transboundary Landscapes initiative, 136–37, 148–51, 164; value assessment of cultural ecosystem services by, 19, 169–70, 175; value chain development of, 160–61. *See also* curation; ecosystem services; Kailash Sacred Landscape Conservation and Development Initiative; mapping and Kailash Sacred Landscape
International Union for Conservation of Nature's Red List of Threatened Species, 103
iodized salt, 64, 81, 119, 122, 135, 142
isolation, 10, 15, 26–27, 85, 145
isomorphism of place and culture, 15, 27

Jackson Heights, New York, 9
Jiang Zemin, 154
jobs and labor, out-migration for, 2, 28, 30. *See also* construction work in Purang

Kagbeni (village in Mustang), 91
Kailash Sacred Landscape Conservation and Development Initiative (KSLCDI), 19, 135–46; Annual Progress Report (2016), 151; assumptions of, 150, 158–59; blind spots in work of, 151, 158, 189; Chinese delegation's political concerns, 132–33, 158, 164–66, 176, 178, 181; choice of projects to complement Chinese development goals, 161, 203n3 (Ch. 8); communication strategies, suggestions for, 134; conference (Kathmandu, 2016), *130*, 131–34, 157, 165, 181; dreamscape of Kailash Sacred Landscape, 150; guidelines for Api Nampa Conservation Area (ANCA), 150–51, 159; as ICIMOD pilot project, 149; ICIMOD vs. Chinese ambitions in, 147, 153, 154, 157–61; invasive plant species, 152; lack of transboundariness and transboundary cooperation, 132, 158, 164, 166; "Landscape *Yatra*" and, 173; lessons learned, 160; local management and capacity building initiatives of, 150, 151, 153; logo of, 133; member countries of Nepal, India, and China, 131, 149, 165; operating in context of pathways and place-knots, 145–46; pastoralism's erasure by Chinese policies, 159–60; Purang labor market not discussed, 158–59; purpose of, 131; residents of region not participants in, 149, 178; Sagar as research assistant in, 185; stakeholders in, 132, 150; Theory of Change and Impact Pathways as focus, 132, 153;

festival), place-binding of, 23–24, 33–37, *35*; role of place in community of traders, vii; stewardship of the environment by local community, 65; "the translocal," use of term, 28, 30; transport and logistics as business of outsiders, 126–27; trope of local community, 27–28, 30, 32, 74, 159; Upper Humla's scattered community, 74–75; Walung not consistent with idea of local community, 30. *See also* place-knots; remoteness
logistics, 18, 119, 126–27
Lower Humla, 94, 106, 115

Mahendra (king of Nepal), 46
Malkki, Liisa, 15, 27–28
Malla currency, 38–39
Malla kings, 38
Manangi traders, 26
Maoist Youth League and conflict (1996–2006), 93, 122, 201–2n1
mapping and Kailash Sacred Landscape (KSL), 19, 144, 164–78; artificial intelligence's role, 19, 174–78; Chakravarty's map to show uniqueness of KSL, 176; cultural ecosystem services and, 19, 169–70, 173, 175; curational interventions and, 177; distribution of maps to monasteries, 176–77, *177*, 181; ecosystem assessment, purpose of, 169; ecosystem services and, 169–74; glacial lake mapping, 167–68; graphic icon for Kailash Sacred Landscape, 166; ICIMOD's dedicated mapping group of Kailash Sacred Landscape Information System (KSLIS), 167; "Landscape *Yatra*," 173; logoization of national maps, 166; meaning of "cartographic anxieties," 165–69; misalignment with nonboundary-based reality on the ground, 165; partial erasure due to lack of resources, 167; remote sensing for data collection and mapping, 167–68; transboundariness and harmonization in, 166; transboundariness as precondition for funding, 178
maps: of Himalayan roads in Nepal, *89*; of Nepal, *6*; of Upper Humla, *58*; of Walung area, *22*
marginality, 10–12, 18
marriage, 56. *See also* polyandry
Marsden, Magnus, 26
Marx, Karl, 119–20, 123, 127; Marxist materialism, 154, 157
Massey, Doreen, 17, 28, 32
Mauss, Marcel, 120
medicinal herbs industry and trade, 7, 12–13, 18, 50, 68–69, 84, 102, 106–8, 115, 160

micro-hydropower plants, 185
migration. *See* education, out-migration for; mobility
Millennium Ecosystem Assessment (MEA), 169, 172
Mitchell, Katharyne, 28
mobility: as livelihood strategy, 2, 14–15, 28, 30; permanent departure abroad of villagers, 74; place-knots as lens on, 16; seasonal migration from Walung, 23, 44–45, 57; sedentarist bias and, 15–16, 18, 125–27, 159; sense of place and, 28; social mobility linked to physical mobility, 16; of Walungnga, 1, 13, 16, 30–32, 43–45. *See also* education, out-migration for; place-knots
monasteries: dismantling rules in Dzang, 16; monks from households of more than one son, 67, 72; *phutuk* (annual monastery festival) in Walung, 23–24, 33–37, *35*; preference for substantial assistance over soft development, 176; rules of, 16, 56, 67, 72–74, 201nn5–6 (Ch. 3)
The Moral Economy of the Peasant (Scott), 137
mountaineering industry, 12, 59
Mountain Institute (NGO), 13, 168, 199n4
Mount Everest: base camp, 9; mountaineering and trekking tourism, 59
Mount Kailash, 149. *See also* Kailash Sacred Landscape Conservation and Development Initiative
"moving out" vs. out-migration, 16
Mughal empire, 85
mules and mule transport, 18, 81–82, 103–5, 115–16, 118
Muluki Ain (Hindu civil code, 1854), 10
Murton, Galen, 91–92
Mustang, Nepal, 30, 44, 46, 88, 91–92, 105, 110, 184
Myanmar, 50, 84, 135, 155

Nagoya Protocol, 15, 29
Nara Pass (between Upper Humla and Tibetan Plateau), 82, 87, 94–95, 167
National Food Corporation, 122
National Geographic, 9
national imaginaries, 11
natural resources, 12, 68. *See also* extractive schemes; medicinal herbs industry and trade
neoliberalism, 154
Nepal: border protocol with China (1963), 62; China treaty (1956), 45; community forestry, 65; constitution (1962), 46; Department of Local Infrastructure Development and Agricultural Roads (DoLIDAR), 94;